WHAT PEOPLE ARE SAYING

"Immigration law is one of the most demanding practice areas in the profession. When I began working with Allison, my firm was generating $1.4 million – and losing money. Within a year, revenue grew 36% and profit increased ninefold. In three years, we scaled past $4 million, built a true executive team, and paid out over $250,000 in bonuses – while dramatically increasing profitability and improving my family's quality of life.

Crushing Chaos delivers the leadership, sales strategy, and financial discipline required to turn growth into freedom."

Candace Vanderwall, Esq.
CEO & Founding Attorney, Vanderwall Immigration, Beaverton, Oregon

"I've long been a skeptic of the coaching industry, particularly when it comes to lawyers. Allison Williams is a rare exception. She brings integrity, clarity, and deep respect for how lawyers actually practice. *Crushing Chaos* helps attorneys build firms that reflect their values–whether that means scaling thoughtfully or designing a practice that truly supports the life they want to lead."

Carolyn Elefant, Esq.
Founder, MyShingle.com
Author, Solo by Choice: How to Start Your Own Law Firm,
and Be the Lawyer You Always Wanted to Be

"Most law firm owners don't struggle because they lack intelligence or drive – they struggle because chaos quietly erodes performance. In *Crushing Chaos*, Allison Williams does what very few advisors can: she connects leadership psychology, operational discipline, and revenue strategy into one cohesive system.

As someone who has spent decades assessing high performers and building elite teams inside seven- and eight-figure law firms, I can tell you this – talent alone doesn't scale a firm. Structure does. Accountability does. Clarity does. This book delivers all three. It's a must-read!"

Jay Henderson,
Performance and Leadership Expert, Real Talent Hiring

"I met Allison at a legal conference and soon after started working with Law Firm Mentor. Allison helped me rebuild my firm from barely $1 million with five attorneys to well into seven figures with only two – and nearly five times the profit. I've been a client for years, and I am always expanding, growing and learning more about myself and my business. In the year when I faced a major health crisis, I dramatically reduced my workload and hired, causing significant growth – even as I was unavailable to it. The systems worked! *Crushing Chaos* reflects the exact principles that made that possible.

This book captures the mindset shifts and operational discipline required to build a firm that scales sustainably. If you want a business that produces freedom, not just revenue, this is the playbook."

AllynMarie Smedley, Esq.
Founder & CEO, Smedley Law Group, P.C., Woodbury, NJ

CRUSHING CHAOS

The Law Firm Owner's Guide to More Money, More Free Time, and Less Stress

ALLISON C. WILLIAMS

Crushing Chaos: The Law Firm Owner's Guide to More Money, More Free Time, and Less Stress
Published by Allison Speaks, LLC
Parsippany, New Jersey, U.S.A.

Library of Congress Control Number: 2026902727

Paperback ISBN: 979-8-9935669-0-0
Hardcover ISBN: 979-8-9935669-1-7
Ebook ISBN: 979-8-9935669-2-4

BUSINESS & ECONOMICS / Small Business
BUSINESS & ECONOMICS / Leadership
BUSINESS & ECONOMICS / Management

Book Design by Michelle M. White
Cover illustration licensed from Stock.adobe.com, image by Photobank AI.

AI & Case Study Disclaimer:

This book was written by the author and reflects her original thinking, experience, and intellectual property. Certain tools, including artificial intelligence-assisted research and drafting technologies, may have been used in a limited capacity to support organization, clarity, or editing. All final content, conclusions, frameworks, and interpretations are the author's own.

Additionally, this book contains case studies, examples, and narratives drawn from the author's professional experience coaching law firm owners. To protect client confidentiality and privacy, names, locations, practice details, timelines, and identifying characteristics have been altered or combined. In some instances, multiple client experiences have been coalesced into composite representations.

Any resemblance to actual persons or firms, living or deceased, is coincidental and unintentional.

This book is for educational and informational purposes only and does not constitute legal, financial, or professional advice.

This book is published by Allison Speaks, LLC.

*"You do not rise to the level of your goals.
You fall to the level of your systems."*
– James Clear

This book is dedicated to my parents –
my father, Dr. Marion Williams, who transitioned
from this life on November 14, 2023,
and my mother, Mrs. Claudia Williams,
who joined her forever-love on February 19, 2025,
during the writing of this book.
They taught me discipline, faith, resilience,
and the courage to believe that I could
become more than my circumstances.

Further, this book is dedicated to my cousin-aunt
Brenda Law Williams, who is the personification of
unconditional love, who is the sweetest connection I have
to both of my parents – both my father's niece/sister,
and my mother's dearest friend.
I love you more than words can say.

And last but never least, to my forever-love,
Shirone Robinson, who teaches me the meaning of love
every day of our lives, through patience, presence,
and the quiet power of being seen

TABLE OF

PART I: THE JOURNEY

PART II: THE PROBLEM

PART III: THE SOLUTION

CONTENTS

PART IV: THE PILLARS

PART V: THE RESULTS

EPILOGUE

ACKNOWLEDGMENTS

To the extraordinary team at Law Firm Mentor, LLC–especially Wolfgang Tsoutsouris and Deb Bilbao, who have worked alongside me since the earliest days of LFM. Your brilliance amplifies this work and has meaningfully impacted countless law firm owners over the years.

To my Chief Operations Officer at Law Firm Mentor, Lee Ann Enquist–the glue that holds our mighty team together. You are the embodiment of crushing chaos, and I am endlessly grateful that you chose to bring your clarity, discipline, and leadership to LFM.

To Tony Le, our Lead Growth Strategist, who connects with lawyers across the country every day–whether guiding them into deeper work with LFM or simply opening their eyes to what is possible. Your consistency and care make a difference far beyond what you may ever see.

To the leadership team of Williams Law Group (WLG)–my first business and namesake–without whom I could not lead both companies as I do. Your steadiness and commitment allow me to think bigger and lead boldly.

And at the heart of both businesses, Jasmine Harvey, Chief Human Resources Officer at Williams Law Group and a foundational force behind Law Firm Mentor. Your genius, loyalty, and devotion are matched only by your tenacity, courage, and profound ability to crush chaos in law and in life. I owe much of who I am and what I have built to your unwavering support and encouragement over the past decade.

The reason I have been able to crush chaos in business—and in life—is because of the remarkable humans with whom I have chosen to surround myself. It is my honor to lead you, and to grow alongside you and our clients, as we #NeverStopGrowing.

ABOUT THE AUTHOR

Allison C. Williams is an award-winning attorney, entrepreneur, business strategist, and international speaker known for helping law firm owners build profitable, systematized companies that support their lives rather than consume them.

She is the Founder and CEO of Law Firm Mentor, a national coaching and consulting company that helps solo and small law firm owners scale revenue, build leadership capacity, and crush operational chaos. She is also the Founder and Managing Partner of Williams Law Group, a New Jersey-based family law firm she built from $0.00 into a multi–seven-figure enterprise in just 3.5 years. Law Firm Mentor followed a similar trajectory, scaling from $0.00 to multiple seven figures in under three years.

Before becoming a business authority, Allison established herself as a trailblazer in family and child welfare law. She is widely recognized as an innovator in private-practice child abuse and neglect defense and became the first African American attorney certified as a Matrimonial Law Attorney in the State of New Jersey. She was also the first attorney in New Jersey to be certified by the National Board of Trial Advocacy as a Family Law Trial Attorney, a distinction reflecting her deep trial expertise and command of complex, high-stakes litigation.

As a nationally respected authority in child welfare law, Allison built a statewide practice handling some of the most complex and emotionally charged cases in the legal system, including allegations of child sexual abuse, abusive head trauma (formerly known as Shaken Baby Syndrome), termination of parental rights, and other serious maltreatment claims. Her work has been cited by media outlets and practitioners alike, and she has appeared on national television, including The Katie Couric Show, to address the devastating impact of false allegations of child abuse. She also appeared in the 2014 documentary *The Syndrome, examining the science and controversy surrounding abusive head trauma.*

Allison's leadership extends beyond the courtroom. She has delivered continuing legal education programs and keynote presentations across the United States and internationally, including appearances at major conferences such as ABA TechShow, LegalWeek, and Clio Cloud Conference. Her speaking career now spans business leadership, systems thinking, and organizational growth, with a particular focus on helping professionals lead with clarity rather than chaos.

Her work has earned numerous accolades, including being named a Stevie Award Silver Finalist, NJBIZ Top 50 Women in Business, Top 25 Leading Women Entrepreneurs and Business Owners, and recognition by Law Firm 500 as one of the fastest-growing law firms in America. She has been consistently selected as a Super Lawyer and among the Top 100 Super Lawyers in New Jersey by her peers.

Allison is also the author of Tiger Tactics: CEO Edition, and the founder of Allison Speaks, her international speaking platform dedicated to helping leaders reclaim agency, build systems that scale, and create lives of purpose, power, and peace.

Her guiding philosophy and the foundation of her work is simple: #NeverStopGrowing.

PROLOGUE

MORE THAN MY DEMOGRAPHICS

I belong to a lot of categories that the world says make me "less than."

I am a woman in a world that places a higher value on men. I am Black in a world that places a higher value on whiteness. Until 2024, I was very overweight in a culture that prizes thinness. I grew up in the South in a nation that romanticizes the North as somehow superior.

But my demographics are not my story.

My story is one of transformation. I am a matrimonial and child welfare lawyer turned serial entrepreneur with a suite of seven-figure companies and an eight-figure net worth. I found love in my forties. I discovered power in my imperfections.

Along the way, I have battled and overcome depression, alcoholism, obesity, and the relentless compulsion to be more, do more, and have more SOLELY to prove myself worthy. For years, my existence was rooted in chaos—externally in the pressure of running businesses, and internally in the storm of never feeling it was enough, that *I was enough.*

And then I decided to engineer my destiny. Not through perfection, but through systems. Not by erasing my flaws, but by leading through them. Not by surrendering to chaos, but by confronting it, mastering it, and ultimately crushing it.

That is what led me here—to #CrushingChaos.

You may identify with some of these attributes. You may identify with none. It doesn't matter. What matters is this: if you desire to build a law firm that runs without you instead of one that runs you into the ground, this book is for you.

This book is not just about strategies for marketing, sales, finance, people, leadership, and systems. It is about transforming the way you think, the way you lead, and the way you show up for your business and your life.

If I can rise above the labels, the limits, and the lies of chaos, so can you.

This is your invitation to crush chaos in business and make more money by manufacturing from the ground up a law firm, and dare I say a future that actually serves you.

PART I

THE JOURNEY

CHAPTER 1

UNRAVELING CHAOS
MY PERSONAL JOURNEY

Chaos in life is like a storm–sudden, overwhelming, and consuming. It often takes something drastic to make you see it clearly, and for me, it was nearly losing my life on a dark highway. I had been racing to the brink for years, convinced that working harder was the only way to prove my worth and ensure success. But chaos has a way of catching up with you, no matter how fast you try to outrun it.

This book is about crushing chaos, but before we get into how to do that, you need to understand where I came from. I didn't start my firm knowing the systems and strategies that I teach today. I had to learn them the hard way, through trial, error, and nearly fatal mistakes. This is my story of creating chaos and, eventually, learning to crush it.

A RELENTLESS START

When I started my law firm, I was on fire. I had the clients, the reputation, and the drive. I wanted to make my mark in family law, particularly in child abuse and neglect cases. These were emotionally intense cases, and I threw myself into them with fervor. Every case felt like a personal crusade, and every win validated the sacrifices I was making.

I was not your average lawyer. I was the first Black attorney and the youngest ever certified matrimonial law attorney in New Jersey. I was also the first Black attorney in the state to become a Fellow of the American Academy of Matrimonial Lawyers and the first attorney to achieve certification by the National Board of Trial Advocacy as a family law trial attorney. My credentials weren't just important to me–they were part of my identity. My achievements set me apart and fueled my belief that I could conquer anything.

My career began in matrimonial law, where I quickly established a reputation for excellence. But my passion led me into the emotionally charged field of child abuse and neglect law. This was a shift that allowed me to make a meaningful impact on families and the child welfare system. I regularly taught lawyers and judges about child welfare law and spoke at international conferences on the topic. My work earned national recognition, including an appearance on the Katie Couric show to address issues of child maltreatment. I even contributed to a book that detailed the travesties of the child welfare system, further cementing my role as a thought leader in the field.

With all these accolades, I assumed I could figure out how to run a law firm just as I had mastered everything else. My big ego whispered that I was exceptional, that building a business would be another notch on my belt. But running a business is an entirely different beast. The truth is, starting and managing my firm was the hardest thing I'd ever done. The challenges were relentless, and the chaos was unlike anything I'd encountered in my professional life. This shit damn near killed me.

I had 43 clients when I started my firm, and I was the only one managing them. I was running from courthouse to courthouse, sometimes covering cases in two or three different counties in a single day. My mornings began before dawn, my nights ended after midnight, and weekends were consumed by administrative work or drafting motions. I was living in constant motion, mistaking busyness for progress.

The cracks started to show in subtle ways—missed social events, forgotten meals, and the gnawing feeling that no matter how hard I worked, it was never enough. But I ignored those cracks, convincing myself that this was the cost of building something great. I was proving I could do it all. Or so I thought.

At the time, I believed that overworking myself was proof of my dedication. I thought my long hours and constant exhaustion were the marks of someone truly committed to success. My friends and family saw a different picture: someone who was always exhausted, irritable, and absent. My phone was constantly ringing, my calendar was overflowing, and my office was in a perpetual state of disarray. I thought I could push through the chaos, but in reality, I was just digging myself deeper into it.

THE BREAKING POINT

One Thursday night, everything came crashing down. I had worked a grueling day—court hearings in the morning, client meetings in the afternoon, and paperwork that stretched into the evening hours. I hadn't eaten a proper meal, barely drank any water, and was running purely on adrenaline and sheer willpower. By the time I left the office, the hallways were empty, and the parking lot was silent. The world had gone to bed, but I was just leaving work. For once, I had a rare opportunity to leave earlier than usual—by "early," I mean around 10:30 p.m.—and I clung to the idea of getting some much-needed sleep.

For the first time in months, I allowed myself to imagine what rest would feel like. I'd promised myself that I would finally take a real Friday morning off, with no hearings, no client calls, and no emergencies pulling me back into the chaos. The thought of lying in bed, just for a few extra hours, became my singular focus. *Get to the bed,* I told myself, gripping the steering wheel as I sped onto the dark, quiet highway.

The road stretched ahead of me in long, empty ribbons, illuminated only by my headlights. My body was exhausted, but my mind wouldn't stop racing. I replayed the events of the day—every mistake I might have made, every email I hadn't responded to, every client who might be waiting for something I'd forgotten. Despite my exhaustion, my brain kept churning through the endless to-do list that had become my life.

I don't remember the exact moment I fell asleep behind the wheel. I don't remember the weight of my eyelids finally closing or the car veering off course. All I remember is the violent jolt that woke me. My car was just inches from slamming into a guardrail, the metallic barrier flashing in my peripheral vision as I jerked the wheel and swerved back onto the road. The tires screamed against the pavement, the steering wheel vibrated in my hands, and my heart pounded so loudly it drowned out every other sound.

For a moment, everything stopped—the car, the noise, my breath. I sat frozen in the driver's seat, gripping the steering wheel as though it were the only thing anchoring me to reality. The highway was eerily silent, and the guardrail stood stoic, a reminder of how close I had come to disaster. My mind struggled to process what had just happened. One second I was driving home, and the next I was staring at the edge of death.

THE WAKE-UP CALL

That night was my wake-up call. I had spent years trying to outrun the chaos I had created, thinking that if I worked hard enough, I could outwork the inefficiencies, the disorganization, and the endless demands. But chaos isn't something you can outwork. It's something you have to confront.

In the days that followed, I began to see the cost of chaos with painful clarity. I wasn't just exhausted–I was a danger to myself and others. My finances, which I thought were solid, were riddled with inconsistencies because I didn't have a proper system for billing or tracking expenses. My relationships were fraying under the weight of my absence. My health was deteriorating, and my passion for the work that had once driven me was turning into resentment. Chaos wasn't just inconvenient; it was consuming everything.

But perhaps the hardest truth to face was that I had created this chaos. It wasn't the clients, the courts, or the cases–it was me. My inability to set boundaries, delegate tasks, and organize my firm had turned my dream into a nightmare. I prided myself on being the smartest person in the room, on being someone who could figure out anything if I just worked hard enough. The fact that I was failing–at something I had built with my own hands–was the worst part.

Failing as a lawyer was one thing, but failing as a business owner was a blow to my very identity. I had spent my entire career building a reputation as someone who achieved the unachievable. I had walked into courtrooms and won impossible cases. I had trained other lawyers and judges in child welfare law. I had spoken at international conferences and appeared on national television. But none of that mattered when it came to running a business. This wasn't a courtroom, and my trial skills couldn't save me here.

The realization was humiliating. I had built a career on being exceptional, on being the person other lawyers admired and looked up to. But behind the scenes, I was struggling to keep my head above water. The chaos I was drowning in was a mess of my own making, and admitting that was both demoralizing and deeply frustrating. I wasn't just failing my clients or my family–I was failing myself. And for someone with an ego as big as mine, that failure cut to the core.

The emotional toll was crushing. I started to question everything–my abilities, my decisions, even my worth. How could someone as accomplished as me be so bad at running a business? I had spent years building my reputation, only to realize that I had built my firm on a foundation of chaos. It was a harsh but necessary truth. The realization became the foundation for what would later evolve into Law Firm Mentor, the coaching company I founded to help other law firm owners escape the same cycle. What began as a personal reckoning turned into my passion to guide others to reclaim control of their firms and their lives.

TAKING INVENTORY

The first step in my journey to crushing chaos was taking inventory of what was really going on in my firm. I knew that things were a mess, but I had no idea how bad it truly was until I forced myself to lay it all out in black and white. I started by writing down everything I did in a day, from responding to emails to filing motions to answering client calls. I listed every single task, no matter how small or mundane, to get a clear picture of where my time was going.

The list was staggering. There were administrative tasks, like updating client files, scheduling appointments, and preparing invoices. There were legal tasks, like drafting pleadings, researching case law, and attending hearings. There were marketing tasks, like writing blog posts, meeting with referral partners, and managing my firm's social media presence. And then there were the "firefighting" tasks—putting out client emergencies, fixing staff mistakes, and dealing with unexpected issues that popped up throughout the day.

By the time I finished the list, it was painfully clear that I was doing the work of at least three people. Worse, much of it was work I didn't need to be doing. Did I really need to be the one answering every client email or scheduling every court date? Was it a good use of my time to spend hours formatting documents or chasing down unpaid invoices? The answer was obvious, but it was also hard to accept. I had convinced myself that I was indispensable, that my firm couldn't function without me personally handling everything. But the truth was, I wasn't indispensable–I was overwhelmed, and my refusal to delegate was suffocating my practice.

THE LACK OF SYSTEMS

Taking inventory forced me to confront another harsh reality: my systems–or, more accurately, my lack of systems–were a huge part of the problem. My client intake process was inconsistent at best. Sometimes I remembered to send out welcome packets and collect all the necessary documents upfront; other times, I pieced things together haphazardly as the case went on. My billing was sporadic, with invoices sent out whenever I happened to remember them, leading to delayed payments and unpredictable cash flow. My case management relied more on my memory than on any organized system, which meant that important details sometimes slipped through the cracks.

I realized that I was the bottleneck for everything. Every decision, every task, and every client issue had to go through me, and it was choking my firm's potential. If a client called with a question, my staff would transfer the call to me instead of answering it themselves. If a document needed to be filed, my paralegal would wait for me to review and approve it before sending it off. Even small tasks, like ordering office supplies or fixing the printer, somehow ended up on my plate. My need to control everything wasn't just inefficient–it was unsustainable.

CLARITY AS THE FIRST STEP

Despite the discomfort, taking inventory was the first real step toward reclaiming my firm and my life. It forced me to confront the truth about where I was and to acknowledge that my current approach wasn't working. But it also gave me hope. For the first time, I could see a way forward. I could see the areas where small changes could make a big difference, and I could start to imagine what my firm might look like if it were truly organized and efficient.

Taking inventory was a humbling experience, but it was also an empowering one. It reminded me that chaos isn't inevitable—it's a choice. And just as I had chosen to live with it, I could choose to change it. That realization was the beginning of my journey to crush chaos and build a firm that worked for me, not against me.

WHY THIS BOOK MATTERS

The lessons I learned during this journey are the foundation of this book. I didn't just figure out how to manage a law firm—I figured out how to crush chaos. Over time, I developed these systems, strategies, and mindset shifts into the backbone of the work we now do at **Law Firm Mentor**. At LFM we help other law firm owners build the same clarity and control I fought hard to create, to transform my firm from a chaotic, overwhelming mess into a well-oiled machine. And I want to share those lessons with you.

This book is for every law firm owner who feels like they're drowning in chaos. It's for the lawyer who's working 80-hour weeks and still can't get ahead. It's for the attorney who's afraid to take a vacation because their firm might fall apart without them. It's for the parent who misses their child's milestones because they're stuck in the office catching up on paperwork. And it's for anyone who's ready to stop running on the hamster wheel and start building a practice that works *for* them, not against them.

Chaos isn't an inevitable part of success. It's a problem that can be solved. It's the byproduct of unstructured growth, reactive leadership, and misaligned priorities. But as overwhelming as chaos feels, it doesn't have to define your firm—or your life. The tools, systems, and strategies you'll learn in this book are designed to help you crush chaos at its source, creating a firm that's efficient, sustainable, and scalable.

This isn't just a book about managing your law firm; it's a book about reclaiming your life. It's about finding the balance between growth and stability, between ambition and self-care, and between serving your clients and serving yourself. It's about building a firm that reflects your values and supports your goals, so you can enjoy the career–and the life–you've worked so hard to create.

If you've ever felt like the chaos in your firm is too big to tackle, I want you to know that there's hope. I've been where you are. I've faced the late nights, the missed opportunities, and the overwhelming sense that I was failing at everything that mattered. And I've come out the other side. The journey isn't easy, but it's worth it. And this book is here to guide you every step of the way.

PART II

THE PROBLEM

CHAPTER 2

FROM CONFUSION TO CLARITY
DEFINING, DIAGNOSING, AND RECOGNIZING CHAOS

Chaos in a law firm often feels like an unavoidable storm–cases stack up, deadlines loom, and clients demand more than your team can handle. Imagine this: a paralegal calls in sick on the morning of a critical filing deadline, leaving a mountain of documents unorganized and a frenzied attorney scrambling to complete the job alone. The phone rings incessantly, clients demand updates, and the clock ticks closer to the court's closing time. By the end of the day, you're exhausted, frustrated, and wondering how you can keep this pace without something breaking.

Or picture this: a solo attorney suddenly lands a high-profile client. At first, it feels like a golden opportunity, but the influx of work quickly spirals into chaos. Without a system to handle the additional workload, deadlines start slipping. The client grows impatient, asking for constant updates, while other cases languish, creating a ripple effect of dissatisfied clients. Instead of feeling victorious, the attorney is trapped in a cycle of stress and late nights.

Then there's the firm that grows too fast without the infrastructure to support it. New associates join, eager to make their mark, but they lack clear training or role definitions. Everyone works hard, but the lack of coordination turns the office into a whirlwind of miscommunication and missed opportunities. Tensions rise as the staff feels overworked and unsupported, and before long, people start leaving. The owner, now juggling client work, employee grievances, and a chaotic environment, finds themselves stuck in survival mode.

DEFINING CHAOS

Chaos is the predictable disorganization that arises when a law firm operates without clear systems, defined priorities, or aligned leadership. The intersection of unstructured growth, emotional overload, and unexamined systems – a solvable, repeating condition that reveals exactly where clarity is needed.

Chaos is more than a buzzword–it's a reality that affects countless law firm owners. For many, chaos manifests as financial instability, physical exhaustion, or both. The constant pressure to manage client demands, staff issues, and operational inefficiencies leaves little room for strategic growth or personal well-being. For a law firm owner, chaos isn't just inconvenient; it's devastating. It depletes resources, erodes health, and undermines the very purpose of running a business–to create financial stability and a fulfilling career.

Chaos is also deceptive. On the surface, it might look like growth: more clients, more cases, and more revenue. But beneath this façade lies a foundation cracking under the weight of mismanagement and overwork. Law firm owners often mistake being busy for being successful, failing to see how chaos erodes their ability to lead effectively and profitably. Understanding chaos and its impacts is the first step toward conquering it.

For many law firm owners, chaos like this is simply the cost of doing business. It feels inevitable, woven into the fabric of running a firm. But the truth is, chaos doesn't have to be your norm. It's a symptom, not a condition. And like any symptom, it can be diagnosed and treated.

DIAGNOSING CHAOS

Diagnosing chaos is the first step in creating a law firm that operates smoothly, grows sustainably, and delivers consistent results. It begins with observing its symptoms. By addressing the root causes of disarray, you can reclaim control and build a practice that not only functions but thrives. In this chapter, I will guide you through recognizing the signs of chaos, understanding its triggers, and mapping out its impact. By the end, you'll have a clearer understanding of what's broken in your firm and where to focus your efforts to regain control.

Step 1: Recognizing the Warning Signs

These warning signs serve as red flags, pointing to systemic issues in your law firm that require immediate attention. Recognizing these indicators is the first step toward understanding the chaos in your practice and addressing it before it spirals further out of control.

Constantly Putting Out Fires

If your day feels like an endless stream of urgent interruptions—last-minute crises, missed filings, or frantic client emergencies—you're operating in a reactive mode. This constant firefighting is more than just an inconvenience; it's a sign that your firm lacks the systems necessary to prevent problems before they arise. Without proactive measures, small issues escalate into significant crises that consume your time, energy, and focus.

- **Reactive Problem Solving:** Without standard operating procedures (SOPs), tasks that should be routine become chaotic. For instance, a missing document or an overlooked deadline might seem like a one-off problem, but in a firm without clear processes, these incidents multiply. Every time you drop everything to address a crisis, it takes you away from higher-value work like strategic planning or client relationship-building.

- **Unclear Delegation**: When team members don't have defined responsibilities, every question or problem ends up on your desk. This lack of delegation not only overloads you but also prevents your staff from developing problem-solving skills. For example, if your paralegal isn't empowered to troubleshoot minor client issues, they'll consistently escalate them to you, perpetuating a cycle of dependency.
- **Procrastination Amplification**: In a chaotic environment, even small tasks are delayed until they snowball into emergencies. An overdue client callback or a filing that's left for the last minute turns into an unnecessary scramble that could have been avoided with better planning and time management.

The problem with constantly putting out fires isn't just the immediate stress–it's the unsustainable nature of operating in survival mode. A firm stuck in this cycle has no room to grow, as all resources are consumed by the chaos of the present rather than the opportunities of the future.

High Staff Turnover

A revolving door of employees is more than an HR inconvenience; it's a symptom of deeper dysfunction in your firm. High turnover doesn't happen in isolation–it's often the result of systemic issues like role ambiguity, workplace stress, and a toxic or disconnected culture.

- **Role Ambiguity**: Employees without clear job descriptions or expectations often feel unproductive and undervalued. Imagine hiring a legal assistant who ends up juggling administrative work, case management, and client communications with no real direction. They quickly burn out, frustrated by the lack of clarity in their responsibilities.
- **Workplace Stress**: Disorganization creates constant pressure on employees, leading to dissatisfaction and burnout. When a paralegal has to spend hours chasing down case files because

your firm doesn't have a centralized system, it drains their productivity and morale. Employees who feel unsupported or overwhelmed are far more likely to seek opportunities elsewhere.

- **Cultural Disconnect**: A chaotic workplace fosters resentment between team members. Missed deadlines, dropped tasks, and unclear expectations often lead to finger-pointing and strained relationships. When the culture becomes toxic, your most talented employees won't stick around—they'll move to a more stable environment where they can thrive.

Each departure costs your firm in multiple ways: the time and expense of recruiting and training replacements, the loss of institutional knowledge, and the increased workload on remaining staff. Worse, if the cycle isn't broken, turnover becomes a self-perpetuating problem as existing staff members grow increasingly dissatisfied with the chaos.

Missed Deadlines and Overwhelmed Calendars

Deadlines are the backbone of any law firm, and missing them is a surefire sign of underlying dysfunction. When deadlines are consistently missed, it doesn't just signal poor time management—it points to deeper issues like overloaded caseloads, inefficient processes, and a reactive approach to scheduling.

- **Overloaded Caseloads**: Taking on more cases than your team can realistically handle is a common cause of missed deadlines. While it's tempting to say "yes" to every client, an overloaded calendar leads to prioritization issues and work falling through the cracks. For instance, a lawyer juggling 30 active cases may forget a critical filing deadline, damaging the client's trust and the firm's reputation.
- **Inefficient Processes**: Without standardized workflows, even routine tasks become time-consuming. Filing a motion

or drafting a contract might take twice as long as necessary because team members don't have clear instructions or templates to follow. This inefficiency drains valuable time that could be spent on higher-priority tasks.

- **Reactive Scheduling**: A firm that operates without planning for deadlines is always in catch-up mode. Instead of allocating time proactively, you're left scrambling to complete tasks at the last minute. This reactive approach not only increases stress but also raises the risk of mistakes and missed opportunities.

Missed deadlines can hurt your reputation. They also increase the likelihood of malpractice claims and client dissatisfaction. A firm that can't manage its time effectively can't hope to grow sustainably or deliver consistent results.

Client Complaints or Grievances

Chaos within your firm doesn't stay contained—it inevitably spills over to your clients. Complaints and grievances are often the most visible symptom of internal dysfunction, stemming from communication breakdowns, unmet expectations, and a lack of transparency.

- **Communication Breakdowns**: Clients expect regular updates on their cases, but disorganized firms often struggle to maintain consistent communication. For example, a client might call repeatedly for an update, only to receive conflicting information from different team members. This inconsistency erodes trust and leaves clients feeling undervalued.
- **Unmet Expectations**: Chaos leads to missed deadlines, incomplete filings, or inconsistent service, all of which frustrate clients. Even minor errors, like sending an email to the wrong address or forgetting to confirm a court date, can compound into a larger perception of incompetence.
- **Lack of Transparency**: Clients who don't understand your process are more likely to interpret delays or mistakes as

negligence. For instance, if a client isn't informed about the typical timeline for a court decision, they might assume your firm is at fault for delays entirely outside your control.

Every grievance serves as a reminder that your internal chaos is visible to the outside world. High volumes of client complaints don't just harm your reputation–they increase the risk of bar grievances, malpractice claims, and negative reviews that deter future clients.

Step 2: Identifying the Chaos Triggers

Recognizing symptoms is essential, but it's only the beginning. To truly diagnose chaos, you need to understand its underlying causes. These triggers often reflect behaviors, systems, or a lack thereof that create disorder in your firm. Identifying these triggers allows you to address the root problems, not just the surface symptoms, and paves the way for meaningful, lasting improvements.

Reactive Leadership

When your leadership style focuses on solving today's problems instead of preventing tomorrow's, you're in a reactive mode. While addressing immediate issues is sometimes necessary, a pattern of reactive leadership creates long-term instability that ripples throughout your firm.

Reactive leaders are often caught in a cycle of crisis management. Each day brings a new emergency that demands their attention, whether it's resolving a client complaint, handling a filing error, or addressing an internal staff conflict. Because they're constantly firefighting, they have no time to plan proactively, delegate effectively, or invest in high-value activities like business development or systems creation.

Consider a firm owner who spends the first two hours of every morning responding to emails flagged as "urgent." By the time they finish, their day's carefully planned tasks are already derailed. A pressing client call interrupts their mid-morning work, and before they can regroup, another team member asks for clarification on a project. At the end of the day, the owner is exhausted, with little to show for their effort beyond a series of temporary fixes.

Example: A midsize corporate law firm came to Law Firm Mentor with similar struggles under a reactive leader. The managing partner insisted on personally approving all outgoing client communications and resolving all client complaints. While their intentions were good, their inability to delegate left other team members feeling disempowered and uncertain. Over time, client satisfaction dropped, and employee turnover increased. The firm implemented our guidance to develop clear communication protocols and empower senior staff to handle routine decisions so the managing partner could focus on strategic growth, it transformed the firm's culture and profitability.

Ad Hoc Processes

Without consistent workflows, every task becomes a new challenge, leading to inefficiency and frustration. Ad hoc processes turn routine operations into sources of chaos, as staff members struggle to reinvent the wheel for every client intake, case management procedure, or billing cycle.

Ad hoc systems can also make your firm dependent on specific individuals rather than repeatable processes. For instance, a paralegal who has worked with you for years might "just know" how to handle client intakes or filings, but when they leave, the knowledge goes with them. This gap forces the team to scramble, recreating processes on the fly and risking mistakes in the meantime.

Consider a firm where client onboarding lacks structure. Some clients fill out forms incompletely; others provide critical information verbally during phone calls that aren't documented. As a result, case details are scattered across emails, handwritten notes, and team members' memories. When a team member is out sick, a case stalls because no one else knows the client's needs or the next steps.

> **Example:** A boutique family law firm faced inefficiencies because its client intake process varied depending on which paralegal handled it. Some clients provided documents upfront, while others were contacted multiple times for missing information. By implementing a standardized intake workflow, including a checklist and automation for document collection, the firm reduced onboarding time by 30%, improved client satisfaction, and freed staff to focus on casework.

Overdependence on the Owner

If your firm revolves around you, you've created a bottleneck. When every decision, no matter how minor, must go through the owner, the firm's growth stalls, and the pressure on the owner becomes unbearable. This overdependence not only limits scalability but also prevents the team from reaching its full potential.

Owners often fall into this trap because they believe no one else can handle tasks as well as they can. While this mindset might stem from perfectionism or a desire to maintain quality, it ultimately backfires. The team becomes passive, waiting for direction rather than taking initiative. Meanwhile, the owner becomes overburdened, juggling client work, administrative tasks, and strategic decisions.

Imagine a solo practitioner who grows their practice but refuses to delegate client communications. Every email, status update, and consultation must be handled personally, even as their caseload expands. As the workload grows, clients wait longer for responses, and deadlines creep closer before being addressed. The result is a firm that's stuck in place, unable to scale or deliver consistent service.

> **Example:** A small immigration law firm struggled with overdependence on its founding attorney. Team members were hesitant to make even routine decisions without approval, and clients grew frustrated by delays. By hiring a senior

paralegal and empowering them to manage client communications and routine filings, the owner freed themselves to focus on business growth and high-stakes cases. Over time, the team became more confident, and the firm's efficiency skyrocketed.

The Chain Reaction of Chaos Triggers

These chaos triggers—reactive leadership, ad hoc processes, and overdependence on the owner—rarely operate in isolation. They feed into one another, creating a vicious cycle of dysfunction. Reactive leadership exacerbates ad hoc processes, as there's never time to establish proper workflows. Ad hoc processes, in turn, make the firm more reliant on the owner to troubleshoot issues. And overdependence on the owner fuels reactive leadership, as the owner becomes consumed by daily crises instead of focusing on long-term solutions.

Breaking this cycle requires addressing each trigger holistically. By fostering proactive leadership, standardizing processes, and empowering your team, you can lay the foundation for a more stable and scalable law firm. These changes won't happen overnight, but they're essential for turning chaos into clarity.

Step 3: Mapping the Chaos

To turn confusion into clarity, you need a roadmap—a structured way to analyze your firm and identify the root causes of dysfunction. Mapping chaos requires stepping back and evaluating your operations through four critical lenses: client experience, team dynamics, systems and tools, and key performance indicators (KPIs). By thoroughly examining each area, you can pinpoint specific weaknesses and chart a clear path toward stability and growth.

Client Experience

Your clients are the lifeblood of your firm, and their experience is often the most visible indicator of your internal operations. If clients frequently express frustration, confusion, or dissatisfaction, it's a sign that chaos behind the scenes is spilling over into their cases. Mapping the client experience involves stepping into their shoes to understand where friction occurs and identifying opportunities to provide consistent, high-quality service.

- **Communication Gaps:** Disorganized communication systems can frustrate clients and leave them feeling neglected. For example, a client might contact your firm for an update, only to be transferred multiple times or given conflicting information. These inconsistencies erode trust and lead to unnecessary follow-ups.
- **Unclear Expectations:** Chaos in your firm often results in a lack of clarity about timelines and outcomes. If a client expects their case to resolve within three months but receives little guidance on the process, they're likely to grow frustrated when delays occur.
- **Service Inconsistencies:** Without standardized workflows, the level of care clients receive can vary significantly depending on which team member handles their case. This variability creates confusion and makes it difficult to maintain a strong reputation.

Example: A small personal injury law firm noticed that clients frequently complained about delayed updates on their cases. After mapping the client journey, they identified that attorneys were too busy to provide regular updates and that paralegals lacked the authority to communicate key details. By implementing a client portal for real-time updates and assigning paralegals to manage routine communications, the firm dramatically improved client satisfaction and reduced complaints.

Team Dynamics

Your team is the engine that drives your firm, and dysfunction within the team is a major contributor to chaos. Mapping team dynamics means assessing role clarity, collaboration, and alignment between employees' skills and responsibilities. When team members are empowered and supported, they can operate efficiently and contribute to the firm's overall success.

- **Role Clarity**: Confusion about responsibilities often leads to inefficiencies and missed tasks. For example, if two paralegals are unsure who should prepare a specific filing, it may be delayed or forgotten entirely. Clear job descriptions and workflows help eliminate this confusion.
- **Collaboration Issues**: Teams that operate in silos or struggle to communicate effectively are less efficient. Misaligned priorities or poor communication channels can lead to duplicated efforts, dropped tasks, and internal tension.
- **Skill Gaps**: Employees who are assigned tasks outside their expertise may feel overwhelmed, while those whose skills are underutilized may become disengaged. Both scenarios hinder productivity and morale.

Example: A midsize estate planning firm conducted a team audit and discovered that attorneys were spending significant time on administrative tasks instead of high-value legal work. By hiring a dedicated office manager and delegating non-billable tasks, the firm improved efficiency, allowing attorneys to focus on their caseloads and increasing overall profitability.

Systems and Tools

The systems and tools you use to run your firm are the backbone of your operations. If these tools are outdated, underutilized, or nonexistent, chaos is inevitable. Mapping your systems involves identifying opportunities for standardization, automation, and better integration of technology to streamline workflows and improve efficiency.

- **Workflow Standardization:** Without documented processes, employees are left to figure out tasks on their own, leading to inconsistencies and delays. For example, if there's no standardized process for client intake, some clients may wait weeks to receive a follow-up, while others are contacted immediately.
- **Technology Utilization:** Many firms invest in tools like case management software but fail to implement them effectively. If team members don't know how to use these tools or rely on manual processes instead, the potential benefits are lost.
- **Data Accessibility:** Chaos thrives when employees can't access the information they need. A lack of centralized systems forces team members to waste time searching through emails, folders, or physical files to find critical details.

Example: A criminal defense firm struggled with managing deadlines due to reliance on manual calendars. After mapping their systems, they adopted case management software with automated deadline tracking and task assignments. This change reduced missed deadlines by 90% and freed up administrative staff to focus on other priorities.

Key Performance Indicators

KPIs are the metrics that measure the health of your firm, providing data-driven insights into its performance. Mapping chaos through KPIs involves tracking relevant metrics and using them to identify bottlenecks, inefficiencies, and opportunities for improvement.

- **Revenue Metrics:** Tracking monthly revenue, collections rates, and average case value helps you understand the financial health of your firm. A sudden drop in collections, for instance, might signal inefficiencies in your billing processes.
- **Operational Metrics:** Metrics like task completion rates, case timelines, and employee productivity provide insights into

how efficiently your firm operates. A consistently growing backlog of tasks might indicate poor workflow management or insufficient staffing.

- **Client Satisfaction Metrics:** Regularly collecting feedback through surveys or reviews helps you gauge how well your firm meets client expectations. A high volume of negative feedback points to areas that need immediate attention.

Example: A business litigation firm created a KPI dashboard to track key metrics like billable hours, case resolution times, and client satisfaction scores. By analyzing these metrics, they identified that delays in document preparation were a major bottleneck. After addressing this issue by hiring additional support staff, they reduced case timelines and improved client satisfaction scores by 20%.

BRINGING IT ALL TOGETHER

Mapping chaos requires examining your firm through these four critical lenses—client experience, team dynamics, systems and tools, and KPIs. This process helps you identify friction points, uncover inefficiencies, and prioritize areas for improvement. By taking a holistic approach, you can create a roadmap for turning confusion into clarity and chaos into streamlined success.

THE IMPACT AND SIGNIFICANCE OF CHAOS

Once you begin mapping chaos across your firm and see the patterns emerge, you'll also realize the extent of the consequences. Chaos often compounds, spreading from disarray to inefficiencies with real financial and emotional cost. Understanding the impact and significance of chaos means recognizing that it's a firm-wide performance issue. Lost time or money is a serious consequence, but chaos also steals your energy, your happiness, and your clarity.

The Financial Impact of Chaos

Financial chaos in a law firm is often insidious. It starts small—an unpaid invoice here, an untracked expense there. But over time, the lack of financial systems snowballs into a crisis. Without a clear handle on cash flow, many law firm owners find themselves broke despite their hard work. They may be generating substantial revenue, but inefficiencies, missed billing opportunities, and poorly managed expenses erode their profits.

For instance, a firm might consistently underbill for time spent on cases due to a lack of time-tracking systems. Or a solo practitioner might take on too many low-value cases, thinking that more clients mean more revenue, without realizing the hidden costs of overwork and inefficiency. These financial missteps aren't just frustrating—they're unsustainable. A law firm owner who doesn't address financial chaos risks burnout, poor reputation, and eventually, business failure.

Financial chaos also limits growth opportunities. A firm struggling to pay its bills can't afford to invest in necessary improvements, like hiring additional staff, upgrading technology, or expanding marketing efforts. This creates a vicious cycle: the firm remains stuck in survival mode, with no clear path to sustainable profitability. Addressing financial chaos isn't just about avoiding bankruptcy—it's about unlocking the resources needed to scale and thrive.

What makes financial chaos particularly dangerous is its invisibility in the early stages. Many law firm owners don't realize they are operating on the brink of financial collapse because their revenue numbers appear healthy. It's only when a crisis hits—such as a missed payroll or an unexpected expense—that the depth of the problem becomes clear. Building financial systems, such as accurate bookkeeping, regular cash flow analysis, and profit margin tracking, is essential to breaking free from this cycle and creating a truly profitable practice.

The Physical and Emotional Toll of Chaos

The physical and emotional toll of chaos is just as severe as its financial impact. Many law firm owners pour endless hours into their practice, convinced that hard work alone will solve their problems. They skip vacations, miss family milestones, and sacrifice their health in the name of success. But chaos thrives in this environment, feeding on the lack of balance and strategic planning.

Overworking doesn't just lead to exhaustion–it has real, tangible consequences. Chronic stress weakens the immune system, disrupts sleep, and increases the risk of conditions like heart disease, anxiety, and ulcers. For a law firm owner, these health issues aren't just personal; they affect the entire business. An overworked and unwell leader can't effectively manage a team or serve clients, creating a vicious cycle of declining performance and increasing stress.

The emotional toll is equally debilitating. Constantly putting out fires leaves law firm owners feeling like failures, even when they're objectively successful. They experience guilt over neglecting their families, frustration at their inability to fix recurring problems, and a sense of hopelessness about the future. This emotional burden compounds over time, making it harder to take the proactive steps needed to address the chaos.

Beyond burnout, chaos creates isolation. Law firm owners often feel they can't share their struggles with peers or employees for fear of appearing weak or incompetent. This isolation amplifies stress, creating a mental health burden that's difficult to manage alone. Addressing the emotional toll of chaos requires not just better systems but also the willingness to seek support, whether from mentors, coaches, or mental health professionals.

CASE STUDY

REBECCA, A FAMILY LAW ATTORNEY IN TEXAS

Rebecca, a 42-year-old family law attorney in Texas, started her solo practice six years ago with high hopes. She wanted to create a firm that offered compassionate legal services to families in crisis while providing her with financial stability and professional autonomy. But the reality of running a law firm quickly overwhelmed her.

The Financial Chaos

Despite generating $600,000 in annual revenue, Rebecca's profit margins were razor-thin at just 5%. She hadn't implemented consistent billing practices, often forgetting to invoice clients for smaller tasks like phone calls and document reviews. She also spent significant time on low-paying cases, believing she couldn't afford to turn away work. As a result, Rebecca often found herself struggling to cover payroll and office expenses, let alone save for the future.

Her financial challenges came to a head when her paralegal resigned unexpectedly. Lacking savings or credit reserves to hire a replacement quickly, Rebecca took on the additional administrative workload herself. This decision further strained her finances and time, pushing her deeper into chaos.

The Physical and Emotional Burnout

Rebecca's workweek averaged 80 hours. She hadn't taken a vacation since starting her firm, reasoning that time away would only worsen her financial situation. Her mornings started with frantic client calls, her afternoons were spent in court, and her evenings were consumed by administrative tasks she couldn't afford to delegate. Over time, the stress began to manifest physically. Rebecca experienced frequent headaches, digestive issues, and chronic fatigue, but she dismissed these symptoms as minor inconveniences.

Her mental health was also deteriorating. Rebecca often felt trapped, questioning whether she had made a mistake starting her practice. She resented her clients and even her staff for what she perceived as their endless demands. The guilt she felt for missing family gatherings and neglecting her own well-being only deepened her frustration.

The Breaking Point

One Friday afternoon, after a particularly grueling week involving two contested custody cases, Rebecca found herself in the emergency room with severe abdominal pain. Doctors diagnosed her with a stress-induced ulcer, warning her that continuing her current lifestyle could lead to more serious health complications. For Rebecca, this was a wake-up call. She realized that her financial instability and overwork were not sustainable, and she needed to make significant changes to regain control of her life and practice.

Turning the Corner

Rebecca sought help from Law Firm Mentor. We provided her with a business coach who specialized in law firm operations. They worked together to overhaul her billing practices, introduce automated invoicing, and develop a pricing strategy that prioritized high-value cases. Rebecca also hired a part-time assistant to handle administrative tasks, funded by her improved cash flow.

The transition wasn't easy. Rebecca initially struggled to let go of low-paying cases and faced pushback from long-term clients when she raised her rates. However, within a year, her revenue increased to $750,000, with a profit margin of 28%. She also reduced her workload to 50 hours per week, allowing her to take her first vacation in six years and prioritize her health.

Rebecca's story highlights the devastating impact of chaos—and the transformative power of addressing it head-on. By recognizing the signs of financial and emotional instability and taking proactive steps to change her approach, she turned her struggling practice into a thriving business that aligned with her values and goals.

THE CLARITY AHEAD

Understanding chaos is a critical step in systematizing your law firm. It requires a willingness to look beyond the surface-level symptoms–like missed deadlines and client complaints–and dig into the underlying causes and consequences of dysfunction. This process isn't always comfortable; it often reveals areas where leadership, processes, or systems have fallen short. However, this step is essential if you want to transform your firm from a reactive, chaotic environment into a proactive, thriving business.

The first step in this journey is recognizing the warning signs. Whether it's the constant fires that consume your day, high staff turnover, missed deadlines, or client grievances, these red flags point to deeper issues. They remind you that chaos doesn't have to be a permanent feature of your business–it's simply a symptom of something that can be diagnosed and fixed. By addressing these warning signs, you're not just alleviating immediate stress; you're creating the space to build a firm that operates with intention.

From there, you must identify the triggers fueling the chaos. Reactive leadership, ad hoc processes, and overdependence on the owner are common culprits, each contributing to a cycle of inefficiency and frustration. Addressing these triggers means stepping into a new role as a proactive leader–one who creates standardized workflows, empowers their team, and establishes a firm-wide culture of clarity and accountability. This shift allows you to regain control and foster a more resilient organization.

Recognizing impacts reinforces why mapping the symptoms and causes of chaos isn't optional. Chaos carries consequences that ripple through every aspect of your firm. It drains time and energy, weakens morale, quietly erodes profitability, and carries over to both your clients and your team. The longer chaos persists, the more it undermines confidence in your leadership and in the firm's ability to deliver.

Mapping chaos provides the roadmap for transformation. By analyzing your firm through the lenses of client experience, team dynamics, systems and tools, and key performance indicators, you can uncover the specific friction points holding your business back. This process gives you the clarity to prioritize improvements that will have the greatest impact, whether that's standardizing client onboarding, addressing communication breakdowns, or leveraging technology to streamline operations.

Ultimately, understanding chaos isn't just about solving problems—it's about creating opportunities. Every inefficiency you eliminate, every system you build, and every decision you delegate brings you closer to a firm that serves not only your clients but also your vision for success. A well-systematized law firm doesn't just run more smoothly; it enables growth, supports your team, and enhances the quality of service you deliver to clients. It's the foundation upon which you can build a legacy.

With clarity, you can move forward with confidence. The time and energy you once spent fighting fires can now be redirected toward strategic growth and innovation. You can take on more cases without sacrificing quality, attract and retain top talent, and deliver a consistent, exceptional client experience. By systematizing your law firm, you're not just addressing the chaos—you're creating a business that thrives under pressure and adapts to change.

Now that you have the groundwork for the transformation, remember that clarity isn't a one-time achievement; it's an ongoing process. By continuously diagnosing and addressing chaos, you can ensure your firm remains efficient, sustainable, and aligned with your long-term goals.

CHAPTER 3

CHARTING THE COURSE
NAVIGATING THROUGH CHAOS

Chaos in a law firm often feels like a storm you can't escape. The phone doesn't stop ringing, deadlines pile up, and every time you think you've fixed one problem, another appears. Many attorneys are so deep in the chaos that they can't see a way out. They rationalize their struggles, telling themselves, *This is just how it is to own a law firm.* But there's a breaking point for everyone–a moment when you realize the cost of chaos is too high. That's when the journey to navigate through it begins.

The first step in charting a course through chaos is getting sick of it. For many attorneys, it takes a significant event–a missed deadline, a client complaint, or a sleepless night worrying about finances–to make them stop and admit, *I can't keep living like this.* This moment of reckoning, while painful, is also the turning point. It's the catalyst that drives lawyers to come up for air long enough to seek help, even if they're unsure what kind of help they need.

CASE STUDY

REACHING THE BREAKING POINT

For Sarah, a 39-year-old personal injury attorney in Georgia, the breaking point came after an embarrassing mistake. She'd forgotten to file a crucial motion in a client's case, resulting in a delay that infuriated the client and tarnished her reputation. Sarah had always prided herself on being a high-achiever, but the chaos in her firm had reached unmanageable levels. Her desk was a mountain of paperwork, her email inbox was overflowing, and she couldn't remember the last time she'd spent a weekend without working.

One night, after hours of futilely trying to organize her files, Sarah opened her laptop and searched for a Facebook group she'd heard about from a colleague: one where lawyers shared advice and vented about the struggles of running a practice. She hesitated before typing, "Does anyone else feel completely overwhelmed by running their firm? How do you manage all of this without losing your mind?"

The responses came flooding in. Attorneys from all over the country chimed in, sharing tips about time management apps, delegation strategies, and even just words of encouragement. For the first time, Sarah realized she wasn't alone. Chaos wasn't just her burden–it was a common struggle for many lawyers. This small act of vulnerability marked the beginning of Sarah's journey to navigate through the storm.

Breaking points like Sarah's often serve as a wake-up call. They force lawyers to confront the reality of their situation and acknowledge that their current approach isn't working. It's a humbling moment, but also an empowering one. For the first time, they see that change is possible–that the chaos doesn't have to define their practice.

THE ROLE OF ASKING FOR HELP

For many lawyers, asking for help is one of the hardest steps to take. The profession teaches self-reliance and often glorifies the idea of the lone attorney fighting battles in the courtroom. Admitting that you're struggling can feel like an admission of failure. But as Sarah discovered, seeking advice doesn't make you weak–it makes you resourceful.

Lawyers often start by reaching out in small, informal ways. They might ask a colleague in their office suite how they handle client intake or send a quick email to a law school friend asking about billing software. These initial conversations may not provide all the answers, but they plant a seed: the realization that there are solutions out there, and that other attorneys have faced–and overcome–similar challenges.

Another powerful aspect of seeking help is the sense of connection it fosters. For many lawyers, the isolation of running a practice can be as stressful as the chaos itself. Engaging with peers–whether in person or online–reminds them that they're part of a larger community. This sense of solidarity can be incredibly motivating, inspiring lawyers to keep pushing forward even when progress feels slow.

SOCIAL MEDIA AND PEER SUPPORT

Social media, especially groups for lawyers, has become a vital tool in this process. In these spaces, attorneys share recommendations for tools, discuss their struggles, and commiserate over the universal challenges of the profession. The advice might be as simple as, "Try using this app to track your time" or "Automate your email follow-ups." These tips often seem minor, but they can create a domino effect, leading to incremental improvements that inspire further action.

For example, another lawyer in Sarah's group recommended using an app to automate client follow-up emails. Sarah hesitated at first, worried it might seem impersonal. But after trying it for a month, she realized the tool not only saved her time but also improved her client relationships. Clients appreciated the regular updates, and Sarah felt a small but significant weight lifted from her shoulders.

What makes these groups so effective is their accessibility. Lawyers can seek advice anonymously or engage in discussions at their own pace. This low-pressure environment is especially appealing for attorneys who feel too overwhelmed to seek formal help. The informal nature of these interactions helps build confidence, showing lawyers that they can take control of their situation one step at a time.

SMALL CHANGES, BIG IMPACT

When attorneys begin to make small changes, they often experience an immediate sense of relief. For Sarah, the first change was implementing a free task management tool recommended by one of the lawyers in her Facebook group. She used it to create a simple to-do list for the week ahead, prioritizing the most urgent tasks. The tool didn't solve all her problems, but it gave her a sense of control she hadn't felt in years.

Small victories like these encourage lawyers to keep going. Sarah's next step was asking a neighboring attorney how they handled billing. She learned about a cloud-based billing system that simplified invoicing and reduced her monthly billing cycle by several hours. Implementing the system wasn't easy—she had to learn the software, train her assistant, and endure a few hiccups along the way. But the time saved was worth it, and Sarah found herself with a few extra hours each week to focus on her caseload.

These incremental improvements add up over time. For many lawyers, the realization that small changes can lead to big impacts is empowering. It shifts their mindset from one of helplessness to one of agency. Chaos starts to feel less like an inevitable burden and more like a challenge they can manage.

THE LIMITS OF PEER SOLUTIONS

While small changes can make a noticeable difference, they often reveal the limits of DIY solutions. For Sarah, streamlining her to-do list and improving her billing process reduced her stress—but it didn't address the underlying chaos in her firm. She still struggled with delegating tasks, managing her team, and creating a long-term plan for growth. The improvements she'd made were helpful, but they weren't enough to fully eliminate the chaos.

This is the point where many lawyers realize they need more than advice from colleagues or tips from social media. They need structured, professional help to address the root causes of their struggles. The realization often comes gradually, as they notice that the same issues keep cropping up despite their efforts to fix them. For Sarah, it was the nagging feeling that she was still one emergency away from everything falling apart.

Even so, these early steps are invaluable. They create a sense of momentum and show lawyers that change is possible. They also help lawyers overcome the fear of asking for help, laying the groundwork for seeking more comprehensive solutions.

THE BRIDGE TO PROFESSIONAL HELP

Although this chapter focuses on the lower-level help lawyers often seek initially, it's important to recognize its role as a bridge. These early steps—asking for advice, implementing small changes, and seeing incremental improvements—help lawyers build the confidence to seek more comprehensive solutions. They create momentum, showing that chaos isn't an unsolvable problem and that every step forward makes a difference.

The process also helps lawyers overcome the stigma of asking for help. By engaging with peers, they learn that seeking support isn't a sign of weakness—it's a strategy for success. This shift in mindset is crucial for the next stage of the journey: seeking professional business coaching that can transform their practice on a deeper level.

CONCLUSION

Navigating through chaos begins with a simple act: reaching out for help. For lawyers like Sarah, this often starts with small, informal conversations or experimenting with tools and strategies shared by peers. These early efforts may not solve every problem, but they demonstrate that change is possible. By taking these initial steps, lawyers begin to chart a course out of chaos, laying the groundwork for more significant transformations in the chapters to come.

PART III
THE SOLUTION

CHAPTER 4

STRATEGIES TO CONQUER CHAOS
THE G.Y.S.T. FRAMEWORK

Chaos isn't a one-time event–it's a persistent byproduct of growth. Conquering chaos requires more than systems and tools; it demands a fundamental shift in mindset. The G.Y.S.T. principle–*Get Your Shit Together*–was developed through our coaching work at Law Firm Mentor, and distills years of experience into transformative and repeatable steps. It is a call to action for law firm owners who are ready to take responsibility for the chaos they've created and strategically commit to overcoming it. In this chapter, we'll demonstrate the Framework and explore how the right mindset fuels sustainable growth and offers strategies to help you conquer chaos, step by step.

THE MINDSET SHIFTS OF G.Y.S.T.: BREAKING THROUGH LIMITING BELIEFS

Conquering chaos begins in the mind. Many law firm owners operate under false beliefs that keep them trapped in cycles of overwhelm and inefficiency. The G.Y.S.T. principle challenges these misconceptions and offers a new way of thinking–one that prioritizes systems, scalability, and balance. Let's examine three pervasive myths that hold law firm owners back and how reframing these beliefs can unlock new possibilities for growth.

1. "Chaos is a Necessary Part of the Process"

Many law firm owners resign themselves to chaos, believing it's an unavoidable part of running a business. They assume that as long as their firm is growing, there will always be stress, disorganization, and long hours. This belief becomes a self-fulfilling prophecy: instead of building systems to streamline operations, they continue to operate reactively, perpetuating the chaos they dread.

But chaos isn't a prerequisite for growth. In fact, it's the result of a lack of systems. Systems create ease, efficiency, and consistency, allowing you to scale your business without sacrificing your sanity. The key to conquering chaos isn't to accept it–it's to eliminate it by designing processes that prevent disorder before it starts.

Example: A small criminal defense firm was drowning in client intake chaos. Each new client required hours of back-and-forth communication, duplicative paperwork, and untracked deadlines. The firm owner believed this disorganization was just the price of success, but his managing partner convinced him to contact Law Firm Mentor for advice. After reviewing the firm's circumstances, we helped the owner to implement a streamlined client intake system–including automated scheduling, templated forms, and a case management platform–that cut intake time in half and eliminated missed follow-ups. Not only did this improve the client experience, but it also freed the owner to focus on higher-value work.

Takeaway: Chaos thrives in the absence of systems. By identifying pain points and designing workflows to address them, you can create a firm that grows smoothly and predictably, without the constant stress of firefighting.

2. "Time and Money are Necessary Trades"

A pervasive myth in the legal industry is that you must trade time for money–or money for time. Many attorneys believe they can make a lot of money, but only if they work grueling hours, sacrifice their personal lives, and accept constant exhaustion. Conversely, others think work-life balance is possible, but only if they settle for a smaller paycheck and limited growth. Both beliefs are false.

The truth is, you don't have to choose between financial success and personal fulfillment. The key is leveraging systems, delegation, and technology to increase efficiency and profitability while reducing your workload. A well-run firm doesn't rely on the owner to do everything; it relies on a team and processes to maximize output.

> **Example:** A family law attorney was billing 60 hours a week and earning a high income but felt trapped in a lifestyle that left no time for family or hobbies. Believing they had to either work less and earn less or continue the grind, they were stuck in an endless cycle of burnout. By hiring a COO to oversee operations, delegating routine work to associates, and automating document drafting with practice management software, the attorney reduced their workload by 30% while maintaining their income. Over time, the firm's efficiency improvements allowed them to scale, making more money with less effort.

Takeaway: The trade-off between time and money is a false dichotomy. By focusing on efficiency and scalability, you can build a firm that generates significant income without sacrificing your well-being.

3. "More People, More Problems"

Hiring is one of the biggest pain points for many law firm owners. There's a widespread belief that hiring only leads to headaches: you can't find good people, employees are a drain on resources, and managing a team is a nightmare. This belief causes many owners to avoid hiring altogether, bottlenecking their firm's growth and forcing them to do work that could easily be delegated.

The reality is that the *right* people, running the *right* systems, are the key to sustainable growth. When you invest in hiring strategically, onboarding effectively, and building a positive team culture, employees become an asset rather than a liability. And for those who struggle with people management, outsourcing or hiring skilled managers can make team leadership a non-issue.

Example: A personal injury firm was hesitant to expand its team, fearing the time and effort it would take to train new employees. The owner felt burned out by previous bad hires and didn't believe they could find quality staff. By partnering with a recruiting agency to source candidates and implementing a comprehensive onboarding program, the firm hired two associates and a paralegal who quickly became productive. Delegating routine tasks allowed the owner to focus on client acquisition, and the firm's revenue increased by 40% in the first year.

Takeaway: Hiring isn't the problem; poorly planned hiring is. By building a structured recruitment, onboarding, and management process, you can turn employees into a source of strength and scalability rather than stress.

THE MINDSET SHIFT

These three misconceptions–chaos as a necessary evil, time and money as opposing forces, and hiring as a headache–are deeply ingrained in the mindset of many law firm owners. But holding onto these beliefs only perpetuates the very problems they fear.

Conquering chaos starts with rejecting these limiting ideas and embracing a new perspective. Systems create stability. Efficiency enables balance. And people, when empowered and supported, drive growth. By adopting the G.Y.S.T. mindset, you're not just addressing chaos–you're transforming the way you think about your firm and its potential.

STRATEGIC ACCOUNTABILITY: OWN THE CHAOS

Once you've embraced the G.Y.S.T. mindset, the next step is accountability. Accountability isn't just about monitoring your progress; it's about setting clear intentions and following through with deliberate action. Chaos thrives in ambiguity, so clarity and accountability are its antidotes. By taking ownership of your role in both the problem and the solution, you can create the structure needed to conquer chaos.

1. Define Your Priorities

Not all chaos is created equal. Some issues demand immediate attention, while others are distractions that drain your focus. Getting your shit together requires identifying the most pressing challenges and channeling your energy into resolving them systematically. Ask yourself: Which areas of chaos are costing me the most time, money, or energy? Which ones, if resolved, would have the greatest positive impact on my firm?

Example: Emma, a Personal Injury Attorney

Emma owns a small personal injury firm that's grown steadily over the past three years. She came to Law Firm Mentor once she recognized that growth had brought chaos: case deadlines were frequently missed, communication with clients was inconsistent, and her staff felt overworked and unsupported. Emma knew something needed to change, but the sheer volume of issues felt overwhelming. Where would she even start?

Our coaching staff encouraged Emma to take a step back and evaluate her firm's challenges. She realized that missed deadlines were the root cause of many client complaints and team frustrations. She decided to prioritize this issue, knowing that resolving it would have a cascading positive effect on other areas of chaos.

To tackle the problem, we helped Emma implement a project management system that tracks every case deadline and assigns specific tasks to team members. She scheduled a weekly review meeting where the team discusses upcoming deadlines and addresses potential bottlenecks. Within three months, the firm saw a dramatic reduction in missed deadlines, and both client satisfaction and team morale improve.

Takeaway: By focusing your energy on a single, high-impact issue, you can regain control and create momentum for additional improvements.

2. Build a Support System

Accountability is easier when you're not tackling chaos alone. Whether it's a business coach, a peer group, or a trusted mentor, having someone to hold you accountable ensures you stay on track. Share your goals, report your progress, and seek feedback to avoid falling back into old habits.

> **Example:** Robert, a Criminal Defense Attorney
> Robert has been running his criminal defense practice for ten years. Recently, he's found himself stretched thin, juggling client meetings, court appearances, and administrative tasks. Despite his long hours, his firm's growth has plateaued, and he's frustrated by the lack of progress. Robert knows he needs to delegate more, but he struggles to let go of control.
>
> After discussing his challenges with a trusted colleague, Robert decides to hire a business coach and contacts Law Firm Mentor to help him create a plan for delegation. The

coach helps Robert identify tasks he can offload to his paralegal and administrative assistant, such as scheduling, drafting routine documents, and handling client intake. To ensure accountability, Robert commits to weekly check-ins with his coach to review his delegation progress.

The first few weeks are challenging–Robert frequently catches himself micromanaging tasks he's delegated. However, his coach reminds him to trust the process and focus on building his team's confidence. By the end of three months, Robert's team is operating more independently, and he has freed up 15 hours a week to focus on business development and high-stakes cases.

Takeaway: With the support of a coaching firm like LFM, you can transform your firm's efficiency and reclaims your time.

3. Follow Through with Intentional Action

Setting priorities and building a support system are critical steps, but they're only effective if paired with consistent, intentional action. Accountability requires discipline and a commitment to follow through, even when progress feels slow or challenges arise.

Example: Chandler, a Family Law Attorney

Chandler owns a boutique family law firm known for its compassionate approach to clients. However, behind the scenes, her practice is chaotic: client files are disorganized, billing is inconsistent, and team communication often breaks down. Chandler knows these issues are limiting her firm's growth, but she has avoided addressing them because they feel overwhelming.

After attending a Law Firm Mentor workshop on law firm operations, Chandler sets a goal to systematize her firm's processes, starting with client onboarding. She announces this goal to her team and commits to weekly progress updates. Chandler assigns specific tasks to team members, such as creating an onboarding checklist, drafting templated welcome emails, and training staff on the new system.

The process isn't without setbacks– Chandler's team resists some of the changes, and she encounters technical challenges with implementing a new client management platform. However, she stays committed, addressing obstacles as they arise and celebrating small wins along the way. Within six months, her firm has a fully operational onboarding system that improves the client experience and streamlines internal workflows.

Takeaway: Intentional action and accountability for follow-through will help you prepare for future challenges and needed improvements.

The Power of Strategic Accountability

Accountability isn't just about checking boxes or meeting deadlines–it's about owning your role in creating and conquering chaos. Emma's focus on priorities, Robert's reliance on a support system, and Chandler's commitment to intentional action all demonstrate the transformative power of accountability. By taking deliberate steps to address chaos and enlisting the right support, you can create a law firm that operates with clarity, efficiency, and purpose.

THE FOUR COMPONENTS OF THE G.Y.S.T. FRAMEWORK

Conquering chaos isn't just about mindset; it's about action. The G.Y.S.T. Framework focuses on four strategic components that help you tackle chaos systematically and continuously as you grow and scale your law firm. These four components are clarity; delegation; resilience; and continuous improvement. Let's take a look at each of these in more detail.

1. Clarity

Clarity is the foundation of any effort to conquer chaos. Without it, you can't identify the problems that need solving or the goals you want to achieve. Clarity starts with understanding your firm's vision and priorities, but it also extends to your team, processes, and metrics. A firm that lacks clarity operates reactively, constantly putting out fires without any sense of direction. By contrast, a clear vision, defined processes, and measurable metrics provide a roadmap for sustainable growth.

- **Vision**: What kind of law firm are you building? How do you want it to operate in five, ten, or twenty years? A clear vision helps you stay focused on what matters and avoid getting distracted by short-term chaos.
- **Processes**: Do your workflows reflect your goals? If you want to serve high-value clients, do you have systems in place to deliver exceptional service consistently?
- **Metrics**: Are you tracking the right data to evaluate your progress? Without metrics, it's impossible to measure the impact of your efforts or identify areas for improvement.

Example: Amanda's Family Law Firm

Amanda, a 38-year-old family law attorney, had always envisioned her firm as a boutique practice providing highly personalized service to clients navigating difficult divorces. Her life goal was to achieve financial independence by age 50, allowing her to retire early and travel the world. When Amanda opened her practice six years ago, she was doing everything herself–managing client intake, drafting pleadings, and even answering phones. Her hard work paid off, and her firm's revenue grew to $850,000 annually, but chaos quickly followed. Amanda's profit margins had dropped to 8% due to inefficiencies, and she was working 70 hours a week with no time for her two young children.

Amanda realized that the firm's lack of clarity was holding her back. She had no clear vision for what her practice should look like in 10 years, and her processes were cobbled together in a way that didn't reflect her long-term goals. Client complaints about delayed responses and billing errors were piling up, and she knew she couldn't sustain her current pace.

Step 1: Clarifying the Vision

Amanda worked with a business coach to redefine her vision. She wanted her firm to become the go-to boutique family law firm in her city, known for personalized service and efficient case resolution. Her financial goal was to reach $1.5 million in annual revenue within three years, with a 40% profit margin. Equally important, she wanted to reduce her workweek to 40 hours so she could spend more time with her family.

Step 2: Streamlining Processes

Amanda mapped out every client touchpoint, from initial inquiries to case closure. She identified bottlenecks–like inconsistent client onboarding–and created standardized workflows for each stage of the client journey. For example, she introduced an intake checklist to ensure all necessary information was collected upfront and implemented practice management software to streamline case tracking and billing.

Step 3: Tracking Metrics

To measure progress, Amanda established key performance indicators (KPIs) tied to her vision. She began tracking client satisfaction scores, case resolution times, and revenue per case. These metrics gave her real-time insights into her firm's performance and helped her identify areas for further improvement.

Challenges Along the Way

The transition wasn't without hurdles. Amanda's staff initially resisted the new workflows, arguing that they were unnecessary and time-consuming. She addressed these concerns by explaining how the changes aligned with the firm's vision and providing hands-on training. Another challenge was the upfront cost of implementing practice management software, which required a $10,000 investment. However, Amanda viewed this as a long-term investment in her firm's efficiency and profitability.

Results After One Year

After one year of focusing on clarity, Amanda's firm transformed. Revenue increased to $1.2 million, and profit margins rose to 31%. Client satisfaction scores improved by 25%, thanks to consistent communication and faster case resolutions. Most importantly, Amanda reduced her workweek to 45 hours, giving her more time with her children while staying on track to achieve her financial independence goal by age 50.

Takeaway: Clarity isn't just about knowing where you want to go–it's about creating the structures and measurements to get there. Amanda's story illustrates how a clear vision, streamlined processes, and data-driven metrics can turn chaos into a well-organized, high-performing law firm.

2. Delegation

Chaos thrives when law firm owners try to do everything themselves. Delegation isn't just a skill–it's a necessity for growth. Many law firm owners hesitate to delegate because they believe no one else can do the work as well as they can, or they fear losing control. This mindset keeps them trapped in a cycle of overwhelm, as they juggle every aspect of the business alone. By empowering your team and distributing responsibilities effectively, you create a firm that can operate without bottlenecks.

- **Empowerment**: Delegation requires trust. Equip your team with the tools, training, and authority they need to handle their roles independently.
- **Accountability**: Delegation doesn't mean abdication. Regular check-ins and clear expectations ensure tasks are completed correctly without micromanaging.
- **Scalability**: Delegation allows you to scale your firm without stretching yourself too thin. Each task you delegate frees up your time to focus on higher-value activities.

Example: James, a Litigation Attorney
James is a 45-year-old litigator who owns a firm specializing in commercial disputes. His firm generates $2.2 million annually, but James feels like he's constantly drowning. Despite having a team of four associates and three support staff, he insists on handling everything personally, from drafting pleadings to reviewing every client communication. James works 80 hours a week, and although his profit margins are a healthy 34%, he's burned out and unsure how much longer he can keep going.

Step 1: Facing the Problem

James's unwillingness to delegate stems from perfectionism. He believes that if he doesn't personally oversee every detail, the firm's quality will suffer. This belief leads to bottlenecks, as his team waits for his approval on even the simplest tasks. During a quarterly review with his accountant, James realizes that the firm's growth has stagnated because he's too busy to focus on business development or high-value cases.

Step 2: Creating a Delegation Strategy

After attending a Law Firm Mentor leadership workshop, James decides to tackle his delegation problem head-on. He starts by listing all the tasks he handles daily and categorizing them into three groups: tasks only he can do (e.g., final trial strategy), tasks he can delegate with training (e.g., drafting motions), and tasks he can delegate immediately (e.g., scheduling and administrative work).

James identifies a glaring issue: his associates are underutilized, spending more time waiting for instructions than doing substantive legal work. To address this, he creates detailed templates for common pleadings and assigns each associate specific case responsibilities. He also hires a legal assistant to handle routine filings and correspondence.

Step 3: Empowering the Team

James knows delegation requires trust, so he invests in training his team. He holds weekly meetings to review case strategies and provide feedback. He also sets clear expectations for each role, ensuring his team knows what's expected and feels confident in their abilities. To further empower his team, James updates his practice management software, allowing associates to track their own tasks and deadlines without his intervention.

Challenges Along the Way

Delegation doesn't come naturally to James. In the first few weeks, he struggles to resist micromanaging, often double-checking his associates' work or stepping in unnecessarily. His associates, initially hesitant to take on more responsibility, make a few mistakes during the transition, leading to tense moments. However, James reframes these mistakes as learning opportunities and works with his team to address the root causes. Over time, both James and his associates grow more comfortable with the new dynamic.

Results After Six Months

Six months after implementing his delegation strategy, James's workload has significantly decreased. He now works 55 hours a week, down from 80, and has reclaimed his weekends. His associates handle 70% of the firm's litigation workload, and the legal assistant manages all administrative tasks. This shift allows James to focus on high-value cases and client relationships, increasing the firm's annual revenue to $2.8 million. Despite hiring an additional team member, his profit margins remain steady at 30%, thanks to the firm's improved efficiency.

Delegation as a Catalyst for Growth

James's story illustrates how delegation can transform a law firm. By empowering his team, setting clear expectations, and holding regular check-ins, he turned a bottlenecked practice into a scalable business.

Takeaway: Delegation isn't just about offloading tasks; it's about creating a structure where everyone in the firm can contribute to its success. When done effectively, delegation frees you to focus on the work that truly matters, driving both personal and professional growth.

3. Resilience

Getting your shit together doesn't mean chaos will disappear forever, but it does mean you'll be prepared for it when it returns. Chaos is inevitable in a growing business, but resilience equips you to face it head-on without losing control. Resilience is about building systems and cultivating a mindset that allows you to adapt to challenges and disruptions with confidence. The point isn't simply to weather the storm, but to come out stronger on the other side.

- **Anticipation**: Plan for the chaos you know is coming. Whether it's a busy season, a major trial, or onboarding new staff, proactive planning minimizes disruption.

- **Adaptability**: When unexpected chaos arises, resilience allows you to pivot quickly. This requires a willingness to let go of perfection and focus on solutions.
- **Sustainability**: Resilience isn't about working harder; it's about working smarter. Build systems that support long-term success without burning out.

Example: Jessica, the Solo Practitioner Scaling to a Small Firm

Jessica, a 36-year-old solo practitioner, ran a thriving estate planning practice in a midsize city. Her firm generated $600,000 in annual revenue, and she was proud of the reputation she had built for delivering personalized service. However, Jessica wanted to scale her business to reach $1 million in revenue within three years while maintaining a 35% profit margin. She knew that growth would bring new challenges, so she set out to build resilience into her firm from the start.

Step 1: Anticipating Growing Pains

Jessica anticipated that scaling her firm would create communication challenges. She had always handled client communication personally, but as her client base expanded and she planned to hire an associate, she knew this would no longer be feasible. She worried that delegating client communication might cause her firm to lose its personal touch, potentially damaging client relationships.

To address this concern proactively, Jessica invested in a customer relationship management (CRM) system before hiring her first associate. The system allowed her to centralize all client data, including notes from consultations, communication history, and deadlines. This ensured that anyone on her team could provide seamless service without needing Jessica's direct involvement.

Step 2: Adapting to New Realities

When Jessica brought on her first associate, she faced unexpected challenges. Despite her initial training, the associate struggled to adopt Jessica's personalized approach to client communication. Some clients expressed frustration at the change, and Jessica felt tempted to step back in and handle communication herself.

Instead of reverting to old habits, Jessica adapted her approach. She implemented weekly role-playing sessions with her associate to practice client interactions and refine their communication skills. She also created templated email responses for common client questions, which the associate could customize to maintain a personal touch. These changes improved client satisfaction and boosted the associate's confidence.

Step 3: Building Sustainable Systems

Jessica's ultimate goal was to scale her firm sustainably, ensuring long-term success without burning out. To achieve this, she implemented several systems that allowed her to focus on high-value tasks while maintaining work-life balance. For instance, she hired a part-time marketing coordinator to manage her firm's outreach efforts, freeing Jessica to concentrate on client consultations and strategy.

Jessica also introduced a quarterly review process to assess her firm's performance against key metrics, such as client satisfaction scores, case completion times, and revenue growth. These reviews allowed her to identify areas for improvement and make adjustments before minor issues became major problems.

Challenges Along the Way

Scaling wasn't without its hurdles. Jessica encountered resistance from long-term clients who were accustomed to working exclusively with her. She also struggled to let go of perfectionism, often feeling the urge to micromanage her team. However, she reminded herself that resilience required adaptability and trust. By focusing on solutions rather than dwelling on setbacks, Jessica gradually built a firm that operated independently of her.

Results After Two Years

Two years into her scaling journey, Jessica's firm had grown to $950,000 in annual revenue, with a steady profit margin of 38%. Her team had expanded to include two associates and a full-time paralegal, and her CRM system ensured that clients received consistent, high-quality service. Jessica now worked 45 hours a week, down from 60, and had more time to spend with her young daughter. By prioritizing resilience, Jessica turned the chaos of growth into an opportunity for sustainable success.

Resilience as a Competitive Edge

Jessica's story highlights the power of resilience in conquering chaos. By anticipating challenges, adapting to new realities, and building sustainable systems, she transformed her firm into a scalable, efficient business.

Takeaway: Resilience doesn't mean avoiding chaos–it means being prepared for it and emerging stronger. With the right mindset and systems in place, any law firm owner can build resilience and achieve their long-term goals.

4. Continuous Improvement

Conquering chaos isn't a one-time event; it's an ongoing process. Continuous improvement ensures your firm evolves alongside its challenges, staying one step ahead of chaos at all times. Growth brings new complexities, and without regular assessments and adjustments, the systems and processes you rely on will eventually become outdated. Continuous improvement is about embracing a mindset of ongoing learning and refinement, ensuring your firm remains efficient, scalable, and adaptable.

- **Review:** Regularly assess your systems, team, and performance. What's working? What needs to change?
- **Refine:** Don't be afraid to tweak your systems as you learn. Small adjustments can have a big impact over time.
- **Recommit:** Growth comes in cycles. Every time you scale, you'll face new chaos–but each cycle strengthens your ability to handle it.

Example: David, the Business Law Firm Owner

David, a 52-year-old business law attorney, had built a successful firm generating $3 million annually with a profit margin of 32%. He prided himself on running a well-oiled operation, with strong systems in place for client intake, case management, and billing. However, as his client base grew and his team expanded to include five associates, three paralegals, and two administrative staff, David noticed cracks forming in his firm's operations. Client satisfaction scores began to dip, internal communication became strained, and profitability plateaued.

David understood that staying ahead of chaos required continuous improvement. Rather than waiting for these small issues to snowball into major problems, he committed to a structured process of regular reviews, refinements, and recommitments.

Step 1: Regular Reviews

David implemented a quarterly review process to assess his firm's performance. Each review included a detailed analysis of key performance indicators (KPIs), such as revenue growth, client satisfaction scores, case timelines, and employee productivity. He also conducted anonymous surveys to gather feedback from his team, asking questions like, "What's one process you think we could improve?" and "What's your biggest obstacle to being more effective in your role?"

During the first review, David uncovered several areas for improvement. Associates felt overburdened by administrative tasks, which limited their billable hours. Paralegals reported that unclear workflows often led to duplicative work. Clients frequently cited delayed communication as a frustration, which negatively impacted satisfaction scores.

Step 2: Refining Systems

Armed with this feedback, David began making targeted adjustments to his systems and workflows. To address the administrative burden on associates, he hired a full-time administrative assistant to handle non-billable tasks like scheduling and data entry. He also introduced a shared task management platform, allowing paralegals to coordinate their work more effectively and avoid duplication.

One of David's most significant refinements was revamping the firm's communication protocols. He created a standardized timeline for client updates, ensuring that every client received a status update at least once every two weeks. He also designated a "client liaison" role within the team to serve as the primary point of contact for routine inquiries, freeing attorneys to focus on substantive legal work.

These refinements weren't implemented overnight. David encountered resistance from some team members who were reluctant to change their workflows. However, by involving the team in the process and clearly explaining how the changes aligned with the firm's goals, he was able to build buy-in and foster a culture of collaboration.

Step 3: Recommitting to Growth

David understood that growth comes in cycles. Just as his firm had outgrown its initial systems, he knew the improvements he was making now would eventually need to be reassessed. To ensure continuous improvement remained a priority, David scheduled quarterly reviews as a recurring event and built time into his schedule to focus on strategic planning.

Over time, this commitment to recommitment paid off. David's team became more proactive in identifying potential issues, often proposing solutions during review meetings. This culture of continuous improvement not only prevented chaos but also created opportunities for innovation, such as introducing a subscription-based legal service model that generated a new revenue stream.

Challenges Along the Way

Continuous improvement required David to confront some uncomfortable truths. For example, during one review, he realized that his billing practices were inconsistent, leading to delayed collections and client dissatisfaction. Addressing this issue meant standardizing billing procedures and retraining his team—a time-intensive process that initially caused friction, but ultimately restored confidence.

Another challenge was balancing short-term demands with long-term planning. During busy periods, it was tempting to postpone reviews or rush through them without diving deep into the data. However, David reminded himself that skipping these reviews would only lead to more chaos down the line.

Results After Two Years

Two years after committing to continuous improvement, David's firm had grown to $3.8 million in annual revenue with a profit margin of 38%. Client satisfaction scores increased by 20%, and employee retention improved significantly, with fewer staff members leaving due to frustration or burnout. The firm's streamlined operations allowed David to take on more high-value cases while reducing his workweek from 60 hours to 50.

The Power of Continuous Improvement

David's story illustrates the transformative impact of continuous improvement. By regularly reviewing performance, refining systems, and recommitting to growth, he created a law firm that didn't just survive chaos—it thrived in the face of it.

Takeaway: Continuous improvement isn't about making one big change; it's about making small, consistent adjustments that compound over time. With this mindset, you can ensure your firm remains agile, efficient, and poised for success no matter what challenges come your way.

EMBRACING THE G.Y.S.T. JOURNEY

The G.Y.S.T. principle isn't about perfection—it's about progress. Chaos is inevitable in a growing law firm, but by adopting the right mindset and strategies, you can prevent it from controlling your business. Remember, conquering chaos starts with *getting your shit together:* taking ownership, building accountability, and committing to continuous improvement. With the G.Y.S.T. mindset, you're not just reacting to chaos—you're leading your firm through it with confidence and clarity.

CHAPTER 5

HOW TO USE THIS BOOK
YOUR ROADMAP THROUGH CHAOS AND CLARITY

Everything you've read so far—the journey, the stories, the emotional undercurrents, the diagnostic exercises—was designed for a single purpose: to help you see your firm with unfiltered honesty. And we've come face to face with the truth many law firm owners never slow down long enough to see: chaos isn't personal; its structural. And clarity isn't accidental trait, it's a system.

But now we're ready to shift from insight to implementation.

WHAT YOU'VE LEARNED SO FAR (AND WHY IT MATTERS)

This chapter is your roadmap for doing that. But before we move forward, it's worth pausing to acknowledge how far you've already come.

You've excavated the truth beneath your chaos.

You've seen that the overwhelm in your firm is often rooted in survival strategies that once kept you safe, but now keep you stuck. Strategies like perfectionism, avoidance, people-pleasing, or self-sufficiency.

You've diagnosed your business with precision.

Building on the diagnostic tools we discussed in previous chapters, you learned how to identify which parts of your firm are fragile, reactive, or underperforming. That diagnostic strengthens you; rather than feeling shamed, it points to your power.

You've been introduced to the G.Y.S.T. Framework

This isn't theory. It's the backbone of the Crushing Chaos methodology developed and refined by Law Firm Mentor, where we coach hundreds of law firm owners every year.

Our frameworks are living systems that work because they evolve as we learn from the patterns real firms experience and bring to us every day.

A solo coach can offer perspective, but a coaching company can offer an ecosystem.

And now, you get to use that ecosystem in book form, whenever you need it. But this book isn't one person's philosophy. It's a field-tested operating system. That's intentional and it's the advantage of learning from a coaching company, rather than a single coach or a DIY collection of resources.

Why a Coaching Company Works Better Than a Coach...And Way Better Than DIY

When chaos has become your norm, clarity feels like a fantasy. But the truth is, clarity isn't a miracle–it's a model. And the most powerful path to lasting clarity is not found in lone-wolf strategies, random webinars, or inspirational Instagram reels. It's found in aligned, expert, immersive support. That's where a coaching company–not just a coach–changes everything.

A solo coach can offer you insight. But a **coaching company** gives you infrastructure. And that distinction is everything when you're trying to move from barely managing your firm to building a thriving business that runs with or without you.

At Law Firm Mentor, we've built our company around a single, radical belief: **you don't have to choose between financial success and personal freedom. You can have both.** But only when you stop trying to do it alone. Over X years, we've worked with hundreds of clients on their path to more money, more free time, and less stress. We've heard the chaos horror stories, helped others overcome the many struggles that chaos brings, and guided law firm owners like you to achieve tremendous success. And we used all of this first-hand experience to build and refine our G.Y.S.T. Framework. Now it's time to put it to work for you.

When you hire a coach, you get one person's perspective. When you hire a coaching company like Law Firm Mentor, you get a **collective brain trust**. That means:

- **Expertise**: You're not just working with one coach; you're working with subject-matter experts in law firm operations, marketing, systems, people management, and finance.
- **Experience**: Our team has been in the trenches. We've scaled law firms, fixed broken systems, hired winning teams, and turned six-figure stress cases into seven-figure success stories.
- **Community**: You're surrounded by a network of law firm owners who are growing their firms alongside you–peers who get it, who challenge you, and who won't let you play small.
- **Structure**: Every lesson, every call, every tool we give you is grounded in our **Crushing Chaos Framework**–a proven system that eliminates overwhelm and creates space for strategic growth.

We don't just tell you to delegate–we show you how. We don't just advise you to hire–we help you write the job ad, develop interview screening tools for candidates, and onboard with precision. We're not here to give advice. We're here to build with you. And you benefit from our deep experience with proven patterns across hundreds of firms; not trial and error, not anecdotes, but data—*lots* of data—on what works in every practice area, revenue level, and personality type.

Coaching is Not a Luxury—It's a Lever

When your time is maxed out, your team is underperforming, and your systems are duct-taped together, the most expensive thing you can do is wait. Every month you operate in chaos is money lost, energy wasted, and potential left on the table.

Hiring a coaching company is not about adding another thing to your plate. It's about **crushing the chaos that's been devouring your plate for years.**

And most importantly, it's about not being alone in this anymore.

You deserve more than a moment of relief. You deserve a business that supports your life. A team that fuels your growth. A system that lets you step away and still win.

That's the path through chaos. That's the power of clarity.

And it starts the moment you decide to stop doing this alone.

How to Make This Book Work for You

This book isn't meant to be consumed once and shelved. It's a **strategic resource**—a practical, flexible toolkit to help you build a law firm that is not only more profitable and efficient, but one that supports your vision of freedom and fulfillment.

To guide you in that journey, the book is structured into five core sections:

- **Part I: The Journey**
- **Part II: The Problem**
- **Part III: The Solution**
- **Part IV: The Application**
- **Part V: The Results**

We've covered the first three sections so far, but this is only the first part of the journey. We've helped you see your chaos clearly. Now we want to help you crush it. Seeing the problem and reading about the solution is only the beginning. But real power comes in knowing what to do next. The rest of this book is about putting the solution into action. This chapter is your map for applying what you've learned to real world problems.

How to Navigate the Rest of This Book

In the remaining chapters, we'll lay out the practical playbook for crushing chaos across the six core business pillars of your firm:

- Marketing
- Sales
- Finance
- People
- Leadership
- Systems

Depending on who you are and what your firm needs there are two ways to move forward.

If You Want a Total Transformation— Read Cover to Cover

If you're the kind of person who wants to **master the art of Crushing Chaos**, you'll want to read this book **cover to cover**. You'll highlight in the margins, underline big ideas, revisit chapters, and internalize the systems that transform reactive law firms into scalable, powerful businesses. Every section connects to the others, and together they form a complete roadmap to sustainable success.

- The psychology behind overwhelm
- The mechanics of marketing
- The syncopation of sales
- The arithmetic of revenue
- The leadership patterns that create freedom or burnout
- The architecture of systems

If that resonates, read every chapter in order. You'll see in precise detail how each pillar fits with and reinforces the others, and you'll build a firm that doesn't just make money, but gives you your life back.

If You're in Triage Mode–Jump Straight to the Fire

If your firm is on fire and you need an answer fast–you don't have to wait. After the foundational sections, feel free to **jump to the implementation chapter that speaks to your biggest pain point right now.** The book is designed to give you **targeted solutions, fast.**

Need More Leads?

- Hop to *Chapter 6: Marketing Mayhem* and then continue with *Chapter 7: Marketing Magic*

Struggling to Convert Leads into Paying Clients?

- Head directly to *Chapter 8: Dominating Sales*

Worried about Revenue, Cash Flow, and Profit?

- Jump to *Chapter 9: Financial Freedom*

Overwhelmed by People Issues?

- You'll want to go first to *Chapter 10: People Power–Mastering the Challenge of Human Capital*

Challenged by Leadership Initiatives and Team Building?

- Skip to Chapter 11: The Leadership Level–Crushing Chaos from the Top Down

Is Lack of Systems, Sustainable Scaling, or Putting it All Together Your Achilles Heel?

- Go to *Chapter 12: Systems–The HEART and ART of Crushing Chaos.*

Each chapter addresses a specific pillar and provides the tools to identify the chaos (the **problem**) and the strategy to crush it (the **solution**). This structure goes beyond diagnosis and gives you both the surgical precision and comprehensiveness you need to crush chaos and find clarity.

From Insight to Action

- Use this book like a law firm **Owner's Manual**. Revisit sections as your firm grows or new challenges arise.
- Implement as you go. Don't just read–act. Each chapter offers practical steps you can apply immediately.
- Share what you learn. Use this book to lead your team. Have conversations, assign reading, and align everyone around the same systems.
- Return often. Crushing chaos is not a one-time fix. This is your playbook for every phase of growth.

Whether you're diving deep or jumping in where the fire's hottest, this book is here to guide you from burnout to breakthrough. You don't have to figure it out alone. And you don't have to settle for a business that works *against* your life.

Read strategically. Apply boldly.

And above all–keep crushing chaos.

PART IV

THE PILLARS

CHAPTER 6

MARKETING MAYHEM
TAMING THE FEAR FACTORS

Most lawyers understand that they need to market their law firms if they want to grow. The logic is simple: no clients, no revenue; no revenue, no business. And yet, despite this intellectual clarity, many law firm owners find themselves stuck–cycling through plans, dabbling with tactics, or avoiding the process altogether. Instead of confidently promoting themselves, they retreat to the safety of "doing the work," spending their energy lawyering rather than selling.

But beneath the surface, the resistance to marketing isn't just about time, resources, or even competence. It's about fear.

At Law Firm Mentor, we've seen this pattern across hundreds of firms: the struggle to market isn't a strategic problem; it's an emotional one. In every day of our coaching work we see highly skilled attorneys and law firm owners who would rather stay in the comfort of legal work than step into the vulnerability of visibility.

Marketing is one of the most emotionally triggering aspects of running a law firm. Unlike the relatively structured world of legal work–where rules, procedures, and precedent guide your every move marketing is personal. It requires visibility, vulnerability, and an openness to being evaluated, misunderstood, and judged. It asks lawyers to show up in ways they were never trained for and often in ways they've been actively conditioned to avoid.

That discomfort is not irrational. It's rooted in real, lived experiences. It's reinforced by the culture of our profession. And for many, it is baked into our identity from childhood. The fears that surface when it's time to market your firm are not surface-level anxieties. They're psychological survival mechanisms. And the only way to get past them is to understand them.

THE FIVE FEAR FACTORS

This chapter will unpack five core fears that sabotage your marketing efforts and keep your business playing small. These are not marketing problems–they are mindset problems. And until you deal with them, no tactic, tool, or script will create lasting results.

1. **The Fear of Being Seen**
   This fear is about exposure. When you put yourself out there–whether on video, in writing, or in person–you risk being evaluated. And when your self-image is tied to perfection, that kind of visibility feels threatening.
2. **The Fear of Judgment**
   Rooted in a primal need to belong, this fear reflects the pain of potential rejection. Speaking boldly or taking a stand invites disagreement, and for many lawyers, that's synonymous with exile from the professional "herd."
3. **The Fear of Underachieving**
   For those who've always been rewarded for winning, marketing feels dangerous because there's no guarantee of immediate success. And if your worth is measured by results, then trying and not excelling can feel emotionally catastrophic.

4. **The Fear of Overachieving**
   Success itself can be scary. Many law firm owners—especially women—have been conditioned to shrink, stay humble, or fear that growth will cost them control, peace, or freedom. So they self-sabotage in subtle ways to stay in the comfort zone.
5. **The Fear of Failure**
   This is the umbrella fear—the ultimate "what if." What if I do everything right and still don't succeed? What if I waste time and money? What if I prove that I'm not cut out for this? To avoid confronting that possibility, many don't try at all.

You don't need to become fearless to succeed in business. But you do need to be brave enough to face your fears head-on. In the pages that follow, we'll examine each of these fears—not just what they are, but where they come from, how they manifest in your marketing behavior, and what you can do to start shifting them.

Because you cannot crush chaos in your firm if you're still hostage to the chaos in your mind.

Problem 1: Vanquishing the Fear of Being Seen

Visibility is vulnerability—but not only because of how we look.

For many law firm owners, the fear of being seen is deeper than fear of critique over hair, teeth, posture, or voice. It's the fear that once fully visible, the world might find us wanting. Being seen is not just about appearances. It's about **occupying space, claiming authority**, and believing that what you say is **worth hearing**.

And that type of visibility—intellectual, social, and energetic visibility—is often even harder to tolerate than the aesthetic kind.

You can hide behind a good camera angle. You can outsource your wardrobe. You can edit a video. But you can't outsource *presence*. You can't edit your way out of a conversation that feels like you're out of your depth. That's the real fear. And it paralyzes more lawyers than we care to admit.

The Hidden Meaning of Visibility

Let's reframe the term *being seen*. It's not just the fear of what someone might say about your crooked teeth or your uneven smile. It's also the fear of **being perceived**—truly, deeply perceived—as less than brilliant. Less than worthy. Less than you pretend to be. It's the fear that if someone really listens to you... they may not be impressed.

And for many lawyers, especially those who've built entire identities around high performance and accolades, *that* is the more terrifying kind of exposure.

From the time we step into law school, we are groomed to be exceptional. The bell curve doesn't reward the average student. It celebrates the top performers. We are trained to compete—for grades, for clerkships, for prestigious firm offers. We learn early that our value is tied to how we *appear* to others: smart, articulate, well-prepared, and confident. It becomes second nature to manufacture that image on command.

We wear that image like armor. And in the courtroom, it serves us. In negotiations, it gives us leverage. In client consultations, it secures trust. The perception that we are knowledgeable, competent, and powerful is our **currency**. We lead with it. We sell it.

And when you are constantly in the business of selling your mind, your logic, your insight—the very idea that someone might dismiss or devalue you is not just a reputational risk. It feels like an existential threat.

So when we shift to marketing ourselves on video or social media, something jarring happens. The performance control we've mastered in person doesn't translate as neatly. On camera, there are fewer places to hide. We can't easily calibrate a facial expression or redirect a question. There is no judge to impress, no opposing counsel to outwit. There is just us. Raw. Visible. Unscripted.

Suddenly, that carefully constructed image starts to feel fragile. We fear cracks in the facade. We worry that people will see the version of us that doesn't have the perfect answer, or the ideal background, or the right lighting. And for lawyers, that level of exposure feels destabilizing.

Because if the image shatters, what happens to our value?

That question is at the core of the fear of being seen. It's not really about being seen at all. It's about being **evaluated** outside the context where we control the metrics. Where we can't rely on our case record, our credentials, or our command of precedent. Where our presence has to carry the message. And that's why it feels so risky.

And the truth is, this fear rarely presents itself openly. It often disguises itself in productivity: "I need to revise the script one more time." Or perfectionism: "I just need better lighting before I can shoot the video." Or even in a distorted humility: "No one wants to hear what I have to say anyway." But these excuses are simply elegant ways to avoid the rawness of being seen without the usual markers of success wrapped tightly around you.

Being seen in this way demands that we trust something we often haven't built up in ourselves: the belief that *we alone* are enough. Not our resume. Not our verdicts. Not our published articles. Just our presence. Our voice. Our story.

That is terrifying. And that is why so many never even press "record."

A Thought Experiment on Status-Based Comfort

Consider this:

If you walked into a networking event filled with lawyers earning **$75,000 per year**, would you hesitate to introduce yourself? Likely not.

Now, add a zero. You're now surrounded by lawyers earning **$750,000 per year.** Still comfortable?

Let's raise the stakes. What if this isn't a room of lawyers at all, but **tech startup founders** earning that same $750,000 annually?

Now add another zero. These are tech founders pulling in **$7.5 million** per year.

Still able to walk up, shake hands, and own your voice in that room?

If the answer is anything other than an immediate yes, you're not alone. Most lawyers begin to shrink inside that mental image. They start to question their vocabulary, their knowledge, their place.

Now ask yourself: why?

If your knee-jerk answer is "I wouldn't know what to say because I'm not in tech," stop right there. Because that sounds rational. Logical. A tidy, data-driven explanation.

But if we're being honest, networking is about curiosity. And the less you know about someone's industry, the **more** questions you have to ask. That should make connection easier, not harder.

So why does it get harder?

Because deep down, we fear that in those rooms, our value won't hold up. That once truly seen, we won't measure up. That those high earners will know what we earn, what we *don't* know, what we fear. That they'll see us as "just a lawyer," not a visionary, not a builder, not an equal.

We fear being seen—not because we look imperfect, but because we feel unworthy.

We worry that without our legal acumen as our shield, we don't have enough to offer. That in a room full of people who think in valuations, equity stakes, and exit strategies, our trial victories or trust documents won't impress. And in that moment, we forget that our value isn't just technical—it's human. It's in how we connect. It's in how we show up. It's in how we take up space.

CASE STUDY

A LAWYER HIDING HER POWER

Take for example a law firm owner who runs a thriving immigration practice in a mid-size city. She was earning about $400,000 annually. Her success wasn't born from flashy ads or expensive funnels. Instead, her reputation grew organically. Her sister-in-law was a Mexican woman, and through countless family gatherings, community events, and faith-based initiatives, she became known in the local Latinx community as "la abogada que ayuda" – the lawyer who helps.

Her work was trusted. Her name carried weight. And yet, she refused to market.

No videos. No social content with her face. No recorded webinars. Nothing.

When she came to Law Firm Mentor, we pressed gently to understand why, and she finally shared the truth: She hated her mouth.

Not figuratively. She literally hated the way her mouth looked when she spoke.

As a child, her family couldn't afford braces. She had visibly crooked teeth. And she was ***bullied*** *mercilessly for it–mocked, laughed at, humiliated. The teasing wasn't just a few cruel comments; it was chronic and defining. And it left a scar.*

But here's the part that goes even deeper:

It wasn't just that she had crooked teeth. It was what those crooked teeth ***represented*** *to her. They were a symbol of poverty. Of lack. Of being outside the circle of girls who were "put together," whose parents "could afford nice things."*

Her parents had done their best. But not being able to give her braces felt like a failure–to them, and ultimately, to her. She internalized the message: You're not worth fixing.

So, when she became a lawyer, she worked hard to undo that narrative. The prestige. The title. The success. It wasn't just about helping people. It was about finally ***feeling worthy****.*

And now, years later, the idea of showing her mouth–this lingering symbol of lack–on camera? It wasn't about vanity. It was about ***survival****. Because for her, video marketing wasn't about delivering a message. It was about exposing a wound.*

The Lie of Perfection, the Truth of Message

I shared something personal with her.

I sucked my thumb until I was 10. My mouth developed with a visible asymmetry. I cringe every time I watch myself on video. And yet–no one has ever said a single hateful thing about it. They've said other things, sure. But not that.

Why? Because most people don't watch you with a microscope. They watch you with a mirror. They're looking to ***see themselves*** *in your story. Not to judge you, but to connect with you.*

In a world saturated with content, the people who win aren't the flawless. They're the ***real****.*

The lawyers who show up consistently on video? Few (if any) of them are conventionally attractive or immune from critique. Many of them stumble. They ramble. They forget what they were saying. Their hair is messy. Their teeth are crooked. Their voices crack.

But they show up. And their audiences grow. And their clients trust them. Because ***authenticity always outperforms polish****.*

Reclaiming the Room

Being seen is about ***taking up space****. It's about believing your thoughts are valid, your story is valuable, and your presence is welcome.*

You can't scale your law firm by hiding. You can't build connection through silence. You can't inspire trust through invisibility.

You must walk into rooms–real or virtual–and own your value. Not because you've reached perfection, but because you're willing to lead anyway.

That means doing the uncomfortable thing: walking into the million-dollar room, hitting "record" on the camera, saying the thing you're scared to say, and risking the cringe.

Because the cringe? That's your growth signal. And the people who matter most will never notice the thing you're obsessing over. They're not watching your mouth. They're listening to your message.

Final Word: Be Seen Anyway

You don't need to be perfect to be powerful. You don't need to be polished to be profitable. You don't need a symmetrical smile to inspire trust.

But you do need to show up.

Visibility isn't the reward you get after *you feel confident. It's the road you walk* to become *confident.*

The woman with the immigration firm? She started small. A thirty-second clip. A testimonial with a voice-over. A quiet thank-you to her Instagram audience. She was scared, but she did it anyway. And as she did, her fear began to fade. Not because her teeth changed. But because her story *did.*

She saw that the message mattered more than the mouth that delivered it.

So does yours.

Takeaway: Show up. Cringe if you must. But be seen. Because every time you choose visibility over fear, you teach your brain a new story:

I am worthy of being heard.

And that belief? That's where real growth begins.

Practical Strategies to Vanquish the Fear

If this resonates, you're not alone. Here are a few ways to shift this fear:

1. **Desensitize in Private**
   Record videos daily. Don't publish them. Just record, watch, reflect. Let the discomfort surface. Then do it again. Eventually, it fades. The goal isn't to perfect your delivery–it's to train your nervous system that visibility isn't dangerous.
2. **Reframe Your Focus**
   Instead of obsessing over *how* you look, focus on *who* you're helping. Picture the client who's searching for someone they can trust. They don't need perfect. They need you. When you put your mission ahead of your insecurity, service becomes the antidote to fear.
3. **Practice Worthiness**
   Write out what makes you valuable that has nothing to do with appearance or income. Speak it out loud. Post it. Own it. This isn't about toxic positivity; it's about retraining your brain to recognize that your impact is not contingent on flawlessness.
4. **Be in Braver Rooms**
   Go to networking events that make you sweat. Practice curiosity. Ask more questions than you answer. You'll build resilience faster than you expect. Confidence isn't built in rooms where you feel superior–it's built in rooms where you feel stretched and still show up anyway.
5. **Tell the Truth**
   If you're afraid, say it. Out loud. To your coach. To your team. Maybe even to your audience. Vulnerability isn't weakness. It's magnetism. The more you normalize your fear, the less power it holds–and the more others trust you for your honesty.

Problem 2: Defeating the Fear of Judgment

There's a reason that judgment cuts so deep: we were raised to believe that being "wrong" or "bad" meant being *unworthy*. That's not an intellectual conclusion. That's a **psychological imprint**–the wiring of the nervous system. And for too many law firm owners, that wiring is still driving the show.

Let's start at the root.

From a young age, we're conditioned to associate approval with worthiness. "Good girl." "Good boy." "I'm proud of you." These phrases train us to behave in a way that wins affection. But affection, in childhood, is not optional–it's **vital**. Without it, a child feels unsafe. Unseen. Unloved.

On the other hand, when a child disobeys or fails to perform, that affection is often withdrawn. Not just the praise, but the warmth. The attention. The love. So the child doesn't just internalize the idea that they did something wrong–they internalize that *they are* something wrong.

In that fragile emotional economy, the lesson is simple and brutal:

I did bad → I am bad → I am not lovable.

And to survive that rejection, we adapt. We become pleasing. We become agreeable. We avoid risk. We try to stay inside the lines of what is "acceptable." We contort ourselves to earn love–and over time, that becomes how we try to earn *value* in the world.

This is what many lawyers carry with them into adulthood. A deep-seated fear that being judged isn't just uncomfortable–it's a **threat to their identity**. If someone disapproves, that disapproval doesn't just sting. It **confirms** their worst suspicion: that they aren't enough.

Judgment = Rejection = Exile

Maslow's Hierarchy of Needs reminds us that after food, water, and safety, the most essential human need is *belonging*. We are social creatures. Our biology evolved for tribal survival. Thousands of years ago, being excluded from the group often meant certain death. Alone, you couldn't defend yourself, find food, or stay safe.

Today, rejection doesn't lead to death—but it can still *feel* like it.

And modern rejection takes on subtler forms:

- Being ghosted.
- Being unfollowed.
- Being criticized.
- Being ignored.

For law firm owners, one of the most potent forms of rejection is **being judged in business and not chosen**—posting content that gets no engagement, speaking at an event that brings no leads, publishing a video and watching it flop. These experiences sting, and they poke at that early childhood wiring: *"They didn't pick me. That must mean something is wrong with me."*

So rather than face that pain, many lawyers retreat. They avoid marketing. They defer visibility. They tell themselves they're "waiting for the right time," or "still getting things in place," when what they're really doing is avoiding exposure.

Because judgment doesn't just mean critique—it means the possibility of being **emotionally exiled.**

The Psychology of Needing to Be Liked

One of the most common ways this fear of judgment manifests is in the **need to be liked.**

It sounds harmless—after all, don't we all want to be liked?

But for some, especially lawyers who built their lives around being the "good kid," this desire becomes a **compulsion**. The need to be liked drives decisions. It shapes communication. It dictates how they present themselves in business and personal life alike.

Here's the thing: being liked becomes a **proxy for being safe.**

If I'm liked, then I won't be judged.

If I'm liked, then I won't be rejected.

If I'm liked, then I'll be chosen, valued, included.

But if I *put myself out there*, and someone *doesn't* like me—then what? That threat is so potent, many would rather avoid visibility altogether.

This is where perfectionism takes root. It's not always about control. Sometimes it's about *insurance*—"If I look perfect, sound perfect, behave perfectly, then maybe everyone will like me." It's an exhausting, ultimately impossible standard.

And the result?

Delayed marketing. Missed opportunities. Stalled growth. Emotional burnout.

Which brings us to Steve.

CASE STUDY

STEVE, THE ESTATE PLANNING ATTORNEY

Steve came to Law Firm Mentor with a respectable but stagnant estate planning firm bringing in around $200,000 a year. By all external appearances, Steve was doing fine—he had steady client work, a good reputation, and a role in his community as the guy you called when someone's aging parent needed a will.

But under the surface, his business wasn't growing. It wasn't even trying to. Steve had **never marketed***. Not once.*

His book of business was a mosaic of connections: his parents, their friends, church members, people from his wife's friend circle. Each client led to another, until his practice had become a word-of-mouth tree with shallow roots and no new branches.

When we explained to Steve that his firm had reached the ceiling of organic growth and that deliberate, strategic marketing was required, he agreed. In fact, he loved *the idea of business building. He geeked out over systems, read business books, and even expressed a desire to become a thought leader in estate planning.*

But every time we tried to help him implement a marketing plan, Steve disappeared.

- *He attended* one *networking event... and never went back.*
- *He hired a marketing company... and then delayed every step.*
- *He missed scheduled calls.*
- *He canceled meetings with his marketing team last-minute.*
- *He took* **months** *to provide basic information for his website.*
- *He said he'd ask clients for reviews... then "forgot" or "didn't want to bother them."*

Every conversation about his marketing led to a carefully crafted, perfectly plausible excuse:

- *"I had a ton of estate plans to draft this week."*
- *"My secretary needed to vent–she's going through a lot with her abusive boyfriend."*
- *"We're interviewing for another employee and I've got to get that wrapped up before I can focus."*
- *"My church needed help organizing the retreat. I couldn't say no to Pastor John."*
- *"The house flooded last weekend, and I've been trying to meet with contractors."*
- *"We had an unexpected family issue. I'll be back on track next week."*

Always next week. Always later.

Steve's calendar had a mysterious way of "exploding" any time it was time to move the marketing ball forward. And to be clear–this wasn't laziness. This was avoidance dressed in responsibility.

Eventually, he reached a breaking point.

In a tense coaching session, Steve snapped. The frustration he had been projecting inward turned outward:

"If you had just told me to buy leads in the first place, I wouldn't be in this mess."

Of course, the idea of paid lead generation had been discussed in his initial VIP planning session. At the time, Steve didn't have the budget to support it. And more importantly, he had no website, *no client reviews, no online presence—nothing to convert the leads even if they came in. Buying traffic to a broken foundation would've been like buying a billboard that leads to an empty lot.*

So, he pivoted his blame:

"If I didn't have to pay you guys for coaching, I could afford to buy leads and solve all my problems."

That's when it became clear: this wasn't about marketing strategy. It was about **emotional self-preservation.**

Because without coaching, Steve wouldn't have hired a marketing company. He wouldn't have started building a website. He wouldn't have begun doing anything *to get visible.*

But as soon as he started inching toward visibility, panic set in. And instead of facing that panic, Steve looked for an exit.

That's when his coach cut through the fog:

"Steve... what are you avoiding by NEVER making time for marketing?"

He froze. He tried to circle back to his secretary's problems, to his clients' needs, to his jam-packed calendar.

But eventually, after enough prodding, he broke.

"If I do all this work to market—and no one buys—what does that say about me? It's easier to assume they won't *buy and say marketing isn't worth it than to put myself out there and have that* confirmed. *If I never really try, I can tell myself it wasn't my fault."*

There it was: **plausible deniability**.

If he didn't market, then his lack of success wasn't rejection. *It was strategy. It was resource management. It was logistics.*

But if he marketed–and people didn't respond? Then it would be personal.

Steve had always branded himself as the "nice guy." The helpful guy. The agreeable lawyer who didn't make waves. That image was his protection. It made him feel safe, liked, valued.

The idea of marketing–and being ignored, or criticized, or not bought from–meant that people might not like him. And for Steve, ***being disliked wasn't just uncomfortable. It was devastating.***

Why Steve Couldn't Say No

Steve's need to be liked didn't just show up in his avoidance of marketing. It showed up everywhere in his life.

- *He always bought the drinks at happy hour–even when he couldn't afford it.*
- *He always said yes to volunteer requests at church–even when he had deadlines.*
- *He never turned down unreasonable client demands–even when they violated boundaries.*

A client wanted to talk at 9:00 PM? Steve made himself available.

A prospect wanted a full estate plan in 48 hours because they feared their healthy 45-year-old sister "could die at any moment"? Steve made it happen.

Another client called during an existing client meeting "just to hear Steve's voice"? He picked up the call–right in the middle of the other appointment.

Steve wasn't just people-pleasing. He was self-erasing. *Because deep down, he believed that if he failed to accommodate someone, they would reject him. And if they rejected him, he'd be alone. Unvalued. Worthless.*

That belief didn't materialize out of nowhere.

In coaching, Steve eventually traced it back to his family.

He was raised in a home where emotional connection was conditional. If he did what was asked–no matter how unreasonable–he was praised. If he didn't, he was met with coldness, silence, or shame. Love was earned through compliance. Affection came at the cost of self-denial.

So Steve became the "good son." The agreeable one. The helpful one.

And that identity followed him into adulthood. It's why he started his firm–after his employer denied his request to join the state bar's Trusts & Estates section (a prime referral opportunity). Rather than advocate for himself, he quit.

But even then, he couldn't face rejection directly. He wrote a resignation letter and emailed it to his boss the night before his vacation–so he could avoid the discomfort of confrontation altogether.

That's how afraid Steve was of being disliked.

How Coaching Broke the Cycle

Once Steve recognized the pattern, everything changed.

He no longer saw his marketing resistance as a "time problem." He saw it for what it was: a **self-protection mechanism**.

Marketing didn't fail him. He *was failing his business by shielding himself from judgment.*

With coaching, he built a new playbook:

- *He kept his appointments with the marketing company.*
- *He wrote and uploaded content for the website.*
- *He emailed past clients asking for reviews.*
- *He committed to two networking events a month–and actually attended them.*
- *He even recorded a short, personal video about why he loves estate planning.*

> *And the result?*
>
> *In under 12 months, Steve grew his firm from $200K to $876K in revenue.*
>
> ### *Final Word: Let Judgment Come*
>
> *You will be judged. You can't escape it. But you* can *survive it–and even use it.*

Takeaway: Some people will say no. Some will critique. Some won't like you.

But some? Some will **love** you. Some will hire you. Some will *need* you. And they can't find you if you don't let yourself be seen.

Let them judge.

And let yourself rise anyway.

Practical Strategies to Defeat the Fear of Judgment

If Steve's story resonates with you, you're not broken–you're **human.** But if you let this fear go unexamined, it will sabotage your growth.

Here's how to start shifting:

1. **Name the Real Fear**
   Say it out loud: "I'm afraid if I market, and no one buys, that means people don't like me–and that makes me feel worthless." Once you name it, it has less control over you.
2. **Differentiate Value from Validation**
   Your work is valuable *even if not everyone buys it.* Not being chosen doesn't mean you're not worthy. It means you're not their fit–and that's okay.
3. **Say No on Purpose**
   Pick one unreasonable request this week–and decline it. Train your nervous system to tolerate disapproval. You'll discover that your world doesn't collapse.

4. **Reframe Rejection**
   When someone says no, say this to yourself: "That no created space for a better yes." Not all no's are losses. Some are upgrades in disguise.
5. **Anchor to Mission, not Ego**
   Marketing isn't about you. It's about who you help. If you're hiding to avoid judgment, your ideal clients are missing their solution. Don't rob them of it.

Problem 3: Overcoming the Fear of Underachieving

Among the many fears that paralyze lawyers when it comes to marketing, perhaps the most insidious is the fear of underachieving–the gnawing belief that trying and failing is worse than not trying at all.

This fear isn't just about ego. It's about identity. From the time we were little, many of us were taught–whether explicitly or through subtle cues–that our worth was tied to how well we performed. High grades meant praise. Awards meant hugs and celebration. Success meant love.

But what happened when we failed?

For many lawyers, failure wasn't met with compassion–it was met with silence, disappointment, or even punishment. Some of us were never scolded outright, but we still *felt* the withdrawal of support. A parent turning their back. A teacher moving on to the next star pupil. A mentor who suddenly had less time.

And so we learned: to be seen, to be safe, to be *loved*, we must be the best.

We must *overachieve.*

This programming runs deep. It explains why so many of us become hypervigilant about excellence. It's why we obsess over having the "right" logo before launching a website, or delay posting content until every word is flawless. It's why we prepare endlessly for that one podcast interview—and then cancel last minute out of fear we'll stumble over our words.

The Psychology Behind It

In psychological terms, what we're talking about here is conditional self-worth—the belief that our value as human beings is dependent on our ability to succeed. It's closely linked to perfectionism and imposter syndrome. And while it can drive achievement, it can also lead to chronic procrastination, anxiety, and stagnation.

Marketing—by nature—requires experimentation. You put yourself out there. You try something. It might flop. It might take months to gain traction. And that trial-and-error process feels intolerable to someone who was only ever rewarded for getting it right the first time.

When failure equals rejection—equals loss of love—we avoid it like the plague.

Enter: Latoya.

CASE STUDY

LATOYA, THE EMPLOYMENT LAW LITIGATOR

Latoya was a powerhouse in court. An aggressive litigator who could eviscerate an opposing witness with surgical precision. By day, she represented small businesses in employment disputes—defending them from wrongful termination suits, wage and hour claims, and hostile work environment allegations. She had a solid reputation in her local community, mostly fueled by word-of-mouth and referrals.

But by night? Latoya was a frustrated business owner. She knew she was capable of more. Her dream was to represent larger companies—national brands and franchises whose complex legal needs could support long-term, lucrative engagements. She didn't want to chase one-off cases anymore. She wanted predictability. Scalability. Prestige.

When Latoya came to Law Firm Mentor, she had no idea how to break into that market. And worse–she was terrified to try.

Her LFM coach made a simple suggestion: start networking with more successful business owners.

Up until then, Latoya's marketing was confined to her local Chamber of Commerce–an organization filled with solopreneurs, mom-and-pop shops, and mid-six-figure businesses. She liked those people. She enjoyed the familiarity. But she also knew they couldn't get her where she wanted to go.

So she researched. She made a list of industry events, trade shows, and CEO groups where her ideal clients gathered. And then…she did nothing.

For months, *Latoya sat on that list. She'd open the email with upcoming events and feel her stomach drop. Her mind would race:*

"What if I go and I can't hold a conversation?"

"What if they ask me who I've worked with and I don't have a big-name client to mention?"

"What if I say something stupid and blow my one chance?"

She rationalized her inaction. "I'm too busy right now," she told herself. "I'll go once I land just one bigger client. Then I'll have something to talk about."

But deep down, she knew what was really going on.

Latoya didn't fear rejection. She feared underperforming. She feared not being good enough in front of people who, in her mind, were better than her. Richer. Smarter. More powerful. She feared the look in their eyes when they realized she didn't belong.

And so she stayed small.

Until the day she didn't.

The Turning Point

Her former colleague invited her to a local event hosted by the National Association of Women Business Owners. Latoya hesitated, but curiosity won out. She RSVP'd. She got dressed. She showed up.

The room was buzzing. These were serious businesswomen—founders of multi-million-dollar companies. Women with staff. Infrastructure. National reach.

Latoya tried to blend in.

But then it happened.

A woman from a major toy manufacturing company—one of Latoya's dream clients—struck up a conversation. They chatted casually for a moment, and then the woman asked the fateful question:

"So, who are some of your representative clients?"

Latoya froze.

Her mind went blank. Her throat tightened. She panicked. After stammering out a half-sentence, she smiled awkwardly, mumbled something about needing the restroom—and bolted.

She hid in that bathroom for twenty minutes. And then?

She slipped out the back door and drove home.

No goodbyes. No follow-ups. Just shame.

For weeks after that event, Latoya berated herself. She felt embarrassed. Ashamed. Frustrated. She started questioning whether she was even cut out for higher-level clientele.

But somewhere inside, the embers of ambition were still burning.

She regrouped.

She reviewed her past cases and created a "success metrics" list—actual dollar amounts she had saved her clients, lawsuits she'd defeated, settlements she'd negotiated. She practiced talking about them. She didn't need to lie or inflate—just reframe her value in ways that powerful business owners would understand.

When a colleague invited her to a meet-and-greet with a Vistage group—an exclusive community of CEOs and business owners with companies ranging from $10M to $90M+—Latoya said yes.

This time, she was ready.

She rehearsed how she'd talk about herself. She leaned into the outcomes *she produced rather than the size of the companies she'd worked with.*

At the event, she spoke with calm confidence. When one CEO asked her about prior results, she shared:

"I helped one company avoid an $80 million exposure in wage and hour claims. We never even went to court. I found enough evidence to persuade the plaintiff's attorney to walk away. In another case, I defended a $20 million lawsuit all the way to verdict. And we won."

Her voice didn't shake. Her hands didn't sweat. She smiled as she spoke.

That CEO? He wasn't just impressed–he introduced her to three other CEOs in his network.

And within months, Latoya landed her first "whale"–a division of a major pharmaceutical company. The engagement? Worth over $200,000 in the first year alone.

But it took eight and a half months *from her first attempt to that signed contract.*

Eight and a half months she could have shaved off, had she faced her fear sooner.

Why the Delay?

Latoya's delay didn't come from laziness. It came from **perfectionism**–*a deeply rooted need to protect herself from being anything other than the best. And that need wasn't new. It had shaped her entire life.*

In high school, Latoya loved music. She'd grown up listening to her dad's jazz records and secretly practiced the alto saxophone in her room after school. Her band teacher begged her to audition for the marching band–she had real talent. But Latoya declined. Not because she didn't want to. But because she wasn't sure she'd earn ***first chair****. In her mind, anything less than being "the best" was synonymous with failure. If she couldn't guarantee the win, she wouldn't play the game.*

In her junior year, the drama department announced the spring production: **Les Misérables**. *Her friends were auditioning. She* *knew every song. She'd acted before–had even gotten praise in a middle school play–but this time, she didn't even show up for the tryouts. Why? Because she knew she wouldn't be cast in lead roles as Éponine or Fantine. And if she couldn't be the lead, she decided it wasn't worth trying at all.*

In college, Latoya chose classes not by interest, but by the perceived likelihood of securing an A. When she considered applying for a competitive internship at a national law firm, she talked herself out of it because she wasn't in the top 5% of her class–never mind that she was easily in the top 10%. She couldn't face the possibility of being rejected.

This pattern continued into her legal career. She only volunteered for high-visibility cases when she already knew the subject matter cold. She'd review briefs ten times before filing. She once delayed launching her website for six months because she couldn't decide between two shades of navy blue for the background.

So when her coach asked her to start attending events with CEOs and C-suite executives–when the possibility of failure became **real, visible**, *and potentially* **humiliating**–*it wasn't just nerves that kicked in. It was the emotional machinery of a lifetime of perfectionism, roaring to life like a security system. Her brain told her: "If you don't show up, you can't mess up."*

That belief is the enemy of progress.

Perfectionism disguised itself as preparation. As "just needing more time." As "not quite ready." But what it really was? **Fear**. *Fear of looking inexperienced. Fear of being laughed at. Fear of being found out as a fraud. Fear of underachieving.*

That fear cost her time. And more than that, it cost her money. For every month she held back, there were clients she never met. Referrals she never received. Retainers she never earned. And she knew it.

The irony was painful: she had **already** *done the hard things. She'd litigated high-stakes cases. She'd stood up to judges and opposing counsel. She'd won trials that other attorneys were afraid* *to take. But because she couldn't guarantee she'd be "the best" in a new room–the room of business owners, not lawyers–she almost didn't enter.*

Final Word: Confidence Comes from Doing

It wasn't until she saw the pattern clearly–until she recognized that this was the same script *she'd been running since childhood–that she could start to rewrite it.*

When she finally walked into that Vistage event, it wasn't that the fear had disappeared. It's that she brought her preparation with her, instead of letting it keep her on the sidelines. She acknowledged her need to feel confident–but she gave herself permission to **build** *that confidence through action, not wait for it to arrive as a prerequisite.*

Her perfectionism hadn't vanished. But it no longer dictated her behavior.

She learned what every high-achieving lawyer needs to know:

You don't have to be the best. You have to be visible.
You don't have to be flawless. You have to be present.
You don't have to be ready. You just have to be willing.

Takeaway: Latoya succeeded not because she changed who she was–but because she stopped waiting to be perfect before she showed up.

Practical Strategies to Move Through the Fear

If you're stuck in this loop–here's how to start breaking free:

1. **Reframe "Failure" as Data**
   Every failed pitch, awkward introduction, or botched marketing campaign is not a reflection of your worth. It's information. Learn from it.
2. **Define Success Broadly**
   Don't measure success solely by dollar signs. Measure it by action taken. Did you show up? Did you pitch? Did you publish that blog? That *is* success.

3. **Visualize the Outcome**
   Picture yourself landing that ideal client. Speaking at that event. Being invited into that boardroom. Let that vision drive your action.
4. **Borrow Confidence from Your Results**
   Can't name-drop clients? No problem. Talk about outcomes. Dollars saved. Time reduced. Claims prevented. *Value* translates.
5. **Take Imperfect Action—Publicly**
   Post before you're ready. Pitch before you're perfect. Go to the event even if your elevator pitch is still rough. Confidence comes from reps, not rehearsals.

Latoya's story is more than a case study. It's a mirror. How many clients have *you* not met yet because you're waiting to be "ready"?

Let this be the case that sets you free. You do not have to be perfect to succeed. You just have to begin.

Problem 4: Slaying the Fear of Overachieving

If underachieving keeps us safe from failure, then overachieving threatens to expose us to attack.

That may sound counterintuitive, especially to high-performing lawyers. After all, isn't overachievement what we're striving for? Bigger firms. Bigger clients. Bigger stages. Bigger bank accounts.

But there's a dark undercurrent to that drive—a hidden fear most won't admit.

Because the moment you start winning too much, too fast, too visibly—you become a target.

This fear doesn't usually sound like fear. It masquerades as "I'm just not ready to grow." Or, "It's safer to keep the firm small and lean." Or, "I just want to practice law—I don't want all the drama that comes with scaling."

But the truth is, many lawyers are subconsciously sabotaging their growth—not because they're afraid to fail, but because they're afraid to succeed **too much**.

Welcome to the *Upper Limit Problem*.

The Upper Limit Problem: A Gay Hendricks Classic

In *The Big Leap*, Gay Hendricks introduces the idea of the *Upper Limit Problem*—the belief that there is a limit to how much success, love, money, or happiness we're allowed to experience. When we surpass that threshold, we unconsciously do things to bring ourselves back down.

We pick fights. We procrastinate. We micromanage. We avoid taking the next step.

We do it not because we're incapable—but because we're afraid of what might happen *if* we keep rising.

What if more visibility brings more scrutiny? What if more income brings more responsibility? What if more power brings more isolation? What if people come for us?

For lawyers, the fear of overachieving is rarely articulated, but it manifests in real and costly ways.

Let me tell you about Marcus.

CASE STUDY

MARCUS, THE CRIMINAL DEFENSE ATTORNEY

Marcus built his solo criminal defense practice from the ground up. He was charismatic in court, relentless in advocacy, and respected by his peers. After seven years in practice, he was clearing over half a million dollars annually and had a client base that trusted his strategic brilliance.

And yet—he stayed small.

He didn't want associates. He didn't market aggressively. He didn't create automated systems. He didn't build infrastructure.

He said it was because he "liked being hands-on." That he "wasn't ready for the stress" of running a bigger firm. That he "wanted to preserve quality."

But the real reason?

He was scared.

You see, Marcus had already experienced what it felt like to rise—and get knocked down.

The Ethics Complaint

A few years back, Marcus hired a marketing firm to revamp his law firm website. They were specialists in legal marketing—or so they claimed. As part of their deliverable, they created web copy that described Marcus as an "expert in criminal defense," along with language that emphasized his "specialization" in trial work.

Innocent enough, right?

Except in Marcus's jurisdiction, using terms like "expert" or "specialist" without formal certification is a violation of the Rules of Professional Conduct.

He didn't write the copy. He didn't even approve it. But someone—likely a competitor—found the site, took screenshots, and filed an anonymous complaint with the Office of Attorney Ethics.

Marcus was contacted and informed that the language violated ethical standards. He immediately forwarded the notice to the marketing firm and asked them to scrub the site of anything even remotely close to a violation.

They assured him it was handled.

A few weeks later, he received formal notice of a disciplinary proceeding.

Why? Because the offending language was **still** *on the site—in a few hidden metadata tags and alternate page versions the marketing firm failed to remove.*

Marcus was livid. And terrified.

"I had to spend tens of thousands defending myself," Marcus told me. "It was complete B.S., but it shook me. I thought: **That could be me.** *All it takes is one jealous lawyer, one bitter client, one board member who doesn't like how visible you are..."*

The process dragged on for months. Even though he wasn't ultimately sanctioned, the investigation and reputational risk were traumatic. He felt exposed. Vulnerable. Hunted.

After that, Marcus stopped all outbound marketing. He pulled back from speaking engagements. He told his paralegal to stop posting on the firm's social media. He even declined media interviews on high-profile cases.

He didn't want the attention. Attention, in his mind, equaled danger.

The irony? His fear of being too successful was now the very thing capping his growth.

The Cost of Staying Small

Eventually, Marcus reached a breaking point. His case load was unmanageable. He needed help. So he did something he'd resisted for years–he hired an associate.

His new hire, Jake, was a rock star. Quick thinker. Great in court. Clients loved him. He hit his billable hours, collected fees on time, and brought calm energy to the team.

Within a few months, Jake started getting referrals–from a local prosecutor he'd befriended, and even from one of Marcus's long-standing clients.

It was everything Marcus had hoped for in a hire.

And yet...he panicked.

Marcus started recalling his own rise to prominence as a young attorney. Back then, his mentor had promoted him to everyone–judges, clients, other lawyers. That visibility turned Marcus into a rising star.

And it also made him a recruitment target.

He remembered how firms from across the region had reached out, trying to lure him away. The only reason he didn't leave was because he genuinely loved his boss–and that boss had announced his retirement a year in advance, encouraging Marcus to launch his own firm.

But now? Marcus didn't trust Jake would be as loyal.

He worried that if he praised Jake too much, it would inflate his ego. If he let Jake network, he'd become seduced by other offers. If he gave Jake room to grow, he'd grow **out** *of the firm.*

So Marcus did the only thing he could think of: he suppressed him.

He stopped introducing Jake at bar events. He took Jake's name off client case summaries. He told the receptionist to route all calls through him. He pulled Jake from big trials and reassigned him to research.

He kept him hidden.

Jake, of course, noticed. At first, he thought Marcus was just busy. Then he started feeling iced out.

After a few months, Jake sat Marcus down and said, "I feel like I'm being smothered. I want to grow here, but I'm not sure I can."

Marcus reassured him. Told him he was valued. But made no changes.

And a few weeks later, Jake quit.

Not for more money. Not for better perks. But for a shot at building a name.

The exact thing Marcus feared had come to pass–not because he promoted Jake too much, but because he didn't promote him at all.

By trying to protect his firm, Marcus had poisoned it.

The Myth of "Safe" Success

Fear of overachieving isn't about humility. It's about protection.

We fear scrutiny, so we stay invisible.

We fear envy, so we downplay our wins.

We fear abandonment, so we suppress our talent.

But the truth is, you cannot hide and grow at the same time.

You want a better life? You have to expand your capacity to be seen, known, and talked about.

Will some people be jealous? Yes.

Will some come for you? Maybe.

Will you make mistakes as you grow? Absolutely.

But the alternative–staying small, shrinking your potential, withholding your light–is a death by a thousand cuts.

You're not protecting yourself. You're suffocating yourself.

The Breakthrough

After Jake left, Marcus spiraled. His revenue dropped. His team morale tanked. His confidence eroded.

But eventually, he did what lawyers are trained to do–he analyzed the facts.

He saw the common thread: he was the one pulling the brakes. Every time the firm hit a stride, he found a reason to stall. Every time an opportunity arose, he'd say, "Maybe next year."

He realized he was afraid of being too *successful.*

He feared the ethics board, so he stopped marketing.

He feared losing staff, so he stunted their growth.

He feared judgment, so he silenced his voice.

Marcus had hit his upper limit–and he was keeping himself there.

So he made a decision.

He rehired a marketing firm–but this time, one with legal ethics counsel. He launched a podcast on criminal defense reform. He promoted another associate, a brilliant Latina trial lawyer, and featured her on every major case.

He stopped trying to be invisible–and started building an empire.

> ### *Final Word: No More Playing Small*
>
> *You are allowed to be powerful. To be rich. To be visible. To be joyful. To be free.*
>
> *You don't owe anyone a smaller version of you to make them feel more comfortable.*
>
> *And you don't have to apologize for your ambition.*

Takeaway: The only thing standing between you and the next level... is your willingness to claim it.

Practical Strategies to Overcome the Fear of Overachieving

If you see yourself in Marcus, here's how to push past the upper limit:

1. **Name the fear.**
   Ask: What's the worst that could happen if I succeed wildly? Say it out loud. Put it on paper. Shine light on the shadow.
2. **Conduct a Post-Mortem Before You Die.**
   What would you regret more—being too visible and getting criticized, or staying small and never living your potential?
3. **Promote your people.**
   Celebrate your staff. Develop your team. If someone leaves because you built them up, you can build again. Your value isn't in hoarding talent—it's in being a leader who attracts it.
4. **Build compliant systems.**
   If ethics complaints scare you, don't avoid growth—grow smarter. Vet your vendors. Hire legal consultants. Automate with oversight.
5. **Redefine Safety.**
   Safety isn't hiding. Safety is being so rooted in your integrity that no one can knock you off course. You don't need to be invisible. You need to be bulletproof.

Problem 5: Conquering the Fear of Failure

Failure.

It's a word most lawyers avoid at all costs.

Not just dislike–*avoid*. Strategically. Systematically. Almost obsessively.

Because in the practice of law, failure doesn't just mean a bruised ego or a botched attempt. It can mean real harm. High stakes. Unforgiving consequences.

How Lawyers Learn to Fear Failure

In law school, we learned this early. One misstep on an exam could plummet your GPA, cost you your shot at law review, or knock you out of the running for clerkships and summer associate offers. Law school didn't reward effort–it rewarded perfection. Not process–just results. Show your work? Only if the final answer was right. And the cost of being wrong wasn't just academic; it was existential. For many of us, our self-worth became tied to how close we were to the top of the class. We weren't just trained to succeed–we were indoctrinated to fear failure.

Then, we entered the profession.

And the stakes got higher.

In law, failure isn't theoretical. It's consequential. It means a mother may lose custody of her children. A wrongly-accused man might go to prison. A grieving family might be denied compensation after a fatal accident. It means the victim of domestic violence might return to an unsafe home. That a client's life savings could be drained in probate. That a corporation may be exposed to liability because someone didn't understand the nuance of an employment clause.

Failure isn't just personal–it's professional, ethical, reputational, financial. It means real people get hurt. Real dollars are lost. Real lives are altered.

So, we armor up.

We become hyper-vigilant. Meticulously prepared. Exhaustively cautious. We triple-check our citations, re-read every brief, agonize over every word in an email. Because we know that even a small mistake—something seemingly insignificant—could result in a grievance, a malpractice claim, or worse: a public shaming in court or the disciplinary board calling your number.

The message is clear, if unspoken:

There is no margin for error. There is no tolerance for failure.

And it doesn't stop at the courtroom door.

How Fear Masquerades as Professionalism

This cultural wiring bleeds into every other area of our professional lives. Want to try a new intake process? Better make sure it's flawless. Thinking of filming videos to promote your firm? Only if you can do it perfectly. Want to build a course, host a webinar, pitch to speak at a conference? Only if there's a guarantee it will succeed.

Which, of course, there isn't. And so, we don't.

We stick to what we know.

We avoid what we don't.

We convince ourselves that caution is wisdom. That our reluctance is simply a product of experience. That hesitation is prudence. That we're not *avoiding* anything—we're just being responsible.

But here's the truth:

Most lawyers don't fail because they try and fall short.

They fail because they never try at all.

They stay in the zone of mastery—the area where they already know they'll win. They don't launch the new program, explore the niche practice area, or pitch the media opportunity. Not because it's not a good idea. But because the idea of putting something into the world that could be judged—and possibly fall flat—is unbearable.

Beneath the Excuses

We rationalize our inaction with clever excuses:

It's not the right time.

I need to do more research.

I'm already so busy.

I need to get through this next trial, this next hire, this next vacation, then *I'll focus on it.*

But often, underneath all of that is a quieter, more vulnerable truth:

We're scared.

Scared that if we give it everything we've got and still fall short, we'll have to confront the terrifying possibility that maybe we're not good enough. That maybe our success so far has been luck. That we've reached the edge of our capability and there's nothing left to grow into.

And that's not strategy.

That's fear.

And fear, in the legal profession, is often camouflaged. It wears the mask of professionalism, of restraint, of "responsible decision-making." But really, it's chaos in disguise–undermining growth, eroding innovation, and quietly convincing some of the brightest minds in the profession to play small.

Failure is not just a professional hazard for lawyers. It is a personal threat. A challenge to our identity. A risk to our sense of safety and control. And until we confront it–not just intellectually, but emotionally–we'll remain trapped by it.

Not moving forward.

Not taking risks.

Not becoming who we're actually capable of being.

Because fear doesn't always look like panic.

Sometimes it looks like perfectionism.

Sometimes it looks like procrastination.

Sometimes it looks like prudence.

But it always feels the same:

Stuck.

And you can't build a future from a stuck place.

The Myth of Safe Inaction

Fear of failure often disguises itself as logic:

- "I don't want to waste money on marketing that doesn't work."
- "I don't want to embarrass myself in front of colleagues."
- "I'm not tech-savvy."
- "I just don't have the time right now."
- "Things are fine the way they are–I don't need to push."

These sound reasonable. They *feel* rational. But most of the time, they're not actually strategic choices. They're fear-based justifications–internal arguments that soothe your anxiety while slowly sabotaging your potential.

Here's the uncomfortable truth:

Doing nothing is not neutral. It's a decision. And often, it's the most expensive one you can make.

Every time you delay action–whether it's launching a new offer, creating content, trying a new intake system, or hiring that next key team member–you are making a choice to stay behind. In business, there is no standing still. The market moves forward with or without you. Your competitors are evolving, your clients' expectations are shifting, and your relevance is decaying–unless you're actively feeding it.

You're not *saving* money by avoiding visibility. You're *losing* opportunity by default.

It might feel safer to stay in your comfort zone–continuing to operate only in the ways that feel familiar, predictable, and well-rehearsed. But that kind of safety is an illusion. Comfort is not security. In fact, in business, comfort is often the breeding ground for stagnation.

Let's look at a few real-life "safe" choices:

- **Tried and True.** A lawyer refuses to try Facebook ads because they don't understand them. Instead, they keep investing in outdated print ads that yield no measurable return–spending more over time for less impact.
- **Business as Usual.** A solo practitioner won't delegate intake calls because she believes "clients want to talk to the lawyer,

not staff." So she spends half her week playing phone tag instead of doing high-value legal work–and ends up burned out and underpaid.

- **Missing the Boat.** A mid-career partner avoids doing videos because "it feels weird" to be on camera. Meanwhile, a less experienced competitor floods YouTube with helpful explainers and becomes the go-to expert for the region.

Each of these choices feels cautious. But none of them are safe. In fact, they're actively harmful.

Avoiding action doesn't protect your reputation.

It slowly dissolves your relevance.

And that erosion happens quietly. Not with a bang, but with a slow fade: declining inquiries, fewer referrals, waning engagement, a steady sense that something's slipping but you can't quite name what.

There is no future in invisibility.

Clients don't hire the best lawyer. They hire the lawyer they *see*. And if you're not visible–online, in person, in content, in conversation–you become irrelevant, no matter how skilled you are.

Inaction may keep you from making mistakes, but it also keeps you from making momentum. And momentum–not perfection–is what builds businesses.

Growth doesn't live in the comfort zone.

And neither does leadership.

Leaders *move*. Even when it's messy. Even when it's awkward. Even when they don't have every detail figured out.

Lawyers often cling to the safety of what they've always done. But your law degree, your years in practice, your accolades–those are not shields against irrelevance. They're *tools*. And tools don't work unless you pick them up and *use* them.

The world has changed. Marketing has changed. Law has changed. What hasn't changed is that success still belongs to those who are brave enough to try, to stumble, and to grow anyway.

So, yes–it might feel risky to step forward. But the real risk? Standing still.

Reframing Failure: Data, Not Identity

In business, failure is not a verdict. It's feedback.

- If your ad doesn't convert, you don't suck–the ad needs tweaking.
- If your video gets no engagement, it doesn't mean you're boring–it means the hook missed.
- If your consult didn't close, it's not a sign to quit–it's a signal to adjust.

Failure is simply **data**.

Smart business owners collect it. Lawyers often fear it because they think it reflects on *them*.

It doesn't.

The best marketers in the world fail all the time. They test headlines. They test subject lines. They tweak button colors.

You know what they don't do?

They don't stop.

They iterate. Because every failure gives them information to get closer to what works.

You're not building perfection. You're building clarity.

And clarity is what drives consistent, replicable results.

Failure is inevitable. But it's also invaluable. It's how you get better, faster.

Every failure contains a lesson. The only question is: will you be brave enough to learn it?

Identity Versus Outcome

One of the most paralyzing fears lawyers face is not "what if this fails?"

It's "What does it mean about *me* if this fails?"

This is where perfectionism and ego collide.

Lawyers are used to being the smartest person in the room. The trusted voice. The fixer.

So when they try something new—something outside of law—and it doesn't work perfectly, they don't see it as iteration.

They see it as failure of identity.

But that mindset is a cage.

You are not your outcomes. You are your willingness to evolve.

The most powerful lawyers aren't the ones who never fall. They're the ones who bounce.

Resilience isn't just recovering after failure. It's anticipating that you will fail, and preparing to learn from it instead of hiding from it.

Your growth depends on your ability to fail forward. To see a rough launch not as a mistake, but as a starting point. To treat resistance not as a stop sign, but as a checkpoint for progress.

The Real Risk

Let me be clear:

The risk isn't that you'll try something and it won't work.

The risk is that you'll do **nothing** and expect your world to stay the same.

It won't.

Your competitors aren't hesitating. Your prospects aren't waiting. Your market isn't freezing.

If you want to stay safe, that's fine. But safety isn't security.

Security comes from adaptability. From momentum. From being the kind of leader who learns fast, adjusts fast, and keeps going.

The longer you wait, the harder it becomes to re-enter the conversation. The world is evolving. You have to evolve with it.

Fear of failure is not a sign to stop. It's a signal to prepare.

CASE STUDY

JIM – THE INVISIBLE SUCCESS

Jim was a known quantity.

He'd been practicing for nearly 30 years. Mid-50s, married, two kids in college, deeply rooted in a suburban community. He handled divorces, estate planning, real estate closings. A classic generalist. Not flashy, but deeply respected. The kind of guy whose name showed up on charity auction banners and Rotary Club plaques.

The Cost of Standing Still

His firm was steady. Not booming, but not struggling. Jim drove a Lexus, owned a colonial on a cul-de-sac, and took two weeks off every summer to vacation with his wife.

But his business was quietly eroding. Fewer referrals. Flatter revenue. Younger attorneys were marketing online, taking up more digital space. Jim saw it. He dismissed it.

"I built my business on relationships," he'd say. "I'm not some desperate lawyer chasing clicks."

That was the story he told himself.

But the truth? He was afraid.

He didn't know how to do online marketing. He didn't understand SEO, pixels, reels, or webinars. And rather than admit that, he hid behind dignity. Told himself that putting himself out there made him look like he was struggling.

What he didn't want to admit was this:

He was afraid that if he tried, and it didn't work, everyone would see him fail.

So he did nothing. And things got worse.

The First Win Changes Everything

When Jim first joined Law Firm Mentor, he said he wanted systems. What he needed was confidence. We worked slowly. We asked better questions. Eventually, he cracked open.

"I feel like I missed the window," he said. "Like, I should just ride out the rest of my career as I am."

That's what fear does. It convinces you that your future is behind you.

So we started small. One video. Just a story about a client's custody case. He posted it with a $50 boost.

It got 13 likes. 8 comments. One consultation.

And everything changed.

That small win chipped a crack in his armor. Jim started posting weekly. Then biweekly. Then he raised his rates. Then he delegated more. Then he hired a marketing assistant.

Today, he's not just known at the Rotary Club. He's known on Google.

And he's free.

Because once you stop letting failure define you, you start letting growth reshape you.

Jim has now embraced a completely different leadership identity. He talks openly about the fear he felt, the resistance he harbored, and the shame that had kept him stuck. And because he did the thing he feared most–publicly putting himself out there and letting people judge–he became more magnetic, not less.

He's attracted clients who say, "I hired you because I saw your video and felt like you were the kind of lawyer who really cares." He's had former colleagues reach out and ask, "How did you get comfortable doing this kind of thing?"

Jim didn't just conquer his fear of failure. He transformed it into a platform for growth, visibility, and purpose.

> *Final Word: Don't Believe the Fear*
>
> *Fear of failure is a liar. It whispers that you're not ready. That you'll embarrass yourself. That you should wait until you have more time, more knowledge, more money, more courage.*
>
> *Don't listen.*
>
> *Start small.*
>
> *Start scared.*
>
> *Start now.*
>
> *Because nothing changes if nothing changes.*

Takeaway: The only true failure is the one you never gave yourself permission to outgrow.

Practical Strategies to Conquer Your Fear of Failure

Ask yourself:

1. What action have I been avoiding out of fear it won't work?
2. What story have I been telling myself about why I haven't done it?
3. What would it look like to try and *learn*, instead of try and *win*?
4. What data could I gather with a simple, small test?
5. What's the cost of waiting?
6. What if failure was proof you're doing something brave?
7. What message would it send to your team if you led with courage?

CONCLUSION

Marketing is much more than a business tactic. It's a battleground of emotion, identity, and fear. And for lawyers, few endeavors are more emotionally charged than putting yourself out there for public consumption. In this chapter, we explored the hidden forces that keep even the most ambitious attorneys playing small, despite their aspirations for impact and growth. These aren't just hesitations. They are deeply embedded fears, trained into us by a profession obsessed with perfection and paralyzed by risk.

You've confronted your fears. Now, let's build your magic.

FEAR FACTOR INDEX

The five fear factors discussed in this chapter are paired with The Fear Factor Index, a diagnostic tool found in **Appendix A**. The index will help you surface the specific fears that are most likely driving your current outcomes, with brief guidance on how to interpret your results. Before moving on, you may find it helpful to assess how the fear factors discussed in this chapter are currently showing up in your firm. In addition, expanded, interactive versions of all our decision-support tools are available online, accessible via links and QR codes included in the Appendix.

CHAPTER 7

MARKETING MAGIC
CRUSHING CHAOS AND FINDING SUCCESS

There's a moment every business owner reaches—when the adrenaline of launching wears off, and you realize: no one is coming to save you.

No magical referral partner.

No genius strategist with the golden funnel.

No "one viral post" that catapults your brand to glory.

If you want to grow, you have to market.

And if you want to market, you have to be seen. Fully.

That's where the chaos begins.

Marketing is one of the most systematizable, scalable parts of any business—but it's also the most emotionally chaotic. Because it's not just about putting out a service or a story. It's about putting out *yourself.* Your voice. Your face. Your ideas. Your value.

In Chapter 8, we unpacked the five most common fears that lawyers experience when it comes to visibility and growth. We tackled the deeply ingrained internal scripts—the fear of being seen, the fear of being judged, the fear of underachieving, the fear of overachieving, and the fear of failure itself.

Now, we shift.

This chapter isn't about what's holding you back.

It's about what's going to push you forward.

MARKETING ISN'T MAGIC— BUT IT CAN FEEL LIKE IT

Here's a truth most gurus won't tell you: marketing isn't about the latest trend, tool, or tactic. It's not about hacking the algorithm or copying what worked for someone else.

It's about creating *alignment.*

When your marketing reflects your voice, your values, your vision—and it's delivered through systems that work even when you're tired, distracted, or unavailable—that's when things start to feel like magic. Not because the work disappears, but because it flows.

Magic is the natural byproduct of clarity, confidence, and consistency. And the key to *Crushing Chaos* is building all three into your marketing foundation.

THE LAW OF VISIBILITY: YOU CAN'T SERVE WHO CAN'T SEE YOU

There are people in your community, your network, and your industry right now who are searching for exactly what you do—and they're hiring someone *else* because they don't know you exist.

This is the tragedy of invisibility.

And it's why marketing isn't optional for law firm owners. It's not a bonus activity for when you have "extra time." It's not a luxury to outsource when you "get more clients." It's the engine. The *heartbeat.* The pulse of sustainable business.

So let's be blunt: if your marketing is inconsistent, chaotic, fear-based, or non-existent—you're not building a business. You're running a side hustle that's dependent on referrals, reputation, and random luck.

You deserve more than that.

You deserve a machine that feeds itself. A strategy that builds month after month. A brand that attracts not just *any* clients—but the right clients.

That's what this chapter is going to teach you.

A CHAPTER IN FIVE SOLUTIONS

This chapter is structured around five transformative solutions—each designed to address and reverse the fears explored in Chapter 8. These aren't vague mindset hacks. These are tactical shifts paired with strategic implementation. And yes—each one comes with stories, systems, and scripts you can start using *now*.

Here's what we're going to cover:

1. Embrace Visibility: Your Path to Success

You'll learn how to build a marketing identity that feels safe, powerful, and authentic. We'll dismantle the "visibility is vulnerability" myth and replace it with strategies that honor your voice *and* grow your reach.

2. Judgment-Free Zone: A Journey to Confidence

We'll talk about how to develop a content strategy that invites connection without crumbling under the weight of what others might think. You'll learn how to lead with value—not validation.

3. Achieve with Assurance: Balancing Ambition

Perfectionism has a sneaky way of looking like professionalism. In this section, we'll talk about "launching ugly," testing ideas before they're ready, and getting momentum even when your inner critic is screaming.

4. Growth: The Key to Marketing Triumph

This is where you'll learn how to stretch your comfort zone without snapping your sanity. We'll explore how to make your next-level vision *safe* for your nervous system—and build a strategy that lets you scale without imploding.

5. Marketing Strategies for Chaos Crushers

This is the tactical wrap-up. Think of it as your Marketing Chaos Survival Kit. We'll dive into specific campaigns, content structures, automation tips, and decision filters that help you keep your strategy simple, streamlined, and scalable.

THIS CHAPTER IS ABOUT EMPOWERED EXECUTION

You're not here because you lack ideas.

You're not here because you're lazy.

You're not even here because you don't know how to market.

You're here because chaos has kept you from executing consistently.

You're here because fear has made you pause when you needed to publish.

You're here because you've waited for certainty—when all you needed was clarity and courage.

That's what *Marketing Magic* gives you.

No more chaos. No more confusion.

Just clarity, commitment, and a system that sells your value without selling your soul.

Because here's the ultimate marketing truth:

People don't buy what you do. They buy who you are.

And they can't buy it—if you're too afraid to show them.

Welcome to *Marketing Magic*.

Let's make your message unmissable.

Solution 1: Embrace Visibility – Your Path to Success

Visibility isn't just about being seen.

It's about *letting* yourself be seen.

It's about taking up space—not just in the minds of potential clients, but in your own identity as a business owner, a thought leader, and a force in your industry. And for lawyers—especially solo and small firm owners—visibility is more than marketing strategy. It's personal. It's emotional. It's *existential.*

Because here's the uncomfortable truth: you cannot grow what you will not own.

And many lawyers are hiding in plain sight.

They have the credentials. They have the results. They have the satisfied clients and the glowing reviews. But if you scroll their social media feed? Silence. If you Google their name? Crickets. If you ask them what they do at a networking event, they'll say "I practice law" or "I'm in family law" or "I work with clients"—as if that somehow masks the fact that they run a *business*.

Visibility is not just the concept of being seen.

It's the *decision* to let people know who you are.

You are not "just" a lawyer.

You are a law firm *owner.*

And when you say that out loud—when you *own* it in how you speak, post, share, pitch, and publish—something incredible happens: people begin to see you not just as a practitioner, but as a *leader.*

Visibility is also about being heard.

It's about finding and using a voice that may have been buried under years of legalese, courtroom decorum, or fear of judgment. It's about moving from generic legal content to thought leadership—sharing not just what you do, but *why* you do it, how you think, and what you believe.

People hire you for your *expertise*, but they connect with you because of your *energy*. Your essence. Your vibe. If they don't hear it, they won't feel it. And if they don't feel it, they won't hire you.

This is where so many lawyers get stuck.

They think visibility is about ego. Or self-promotion. Or that it's only for the "influencer" types. So they shrink. They tell themselves that being quiet is professional. That being reserved is humble. That the work should "speak for itself."

But let me be blunt: your work can't speak.

You have to.

Visibility is not vanity–it's viability. It's how you grow. It's how you scale. It's how you build a brand that people trust, remember, and refer.

And it starts with giving yourself permission to *be visible*.

In the next several pages, we're going to unpack what visibility looks like when it's done with intention and integrity. We'll explore how to move past the fear of exposure and into a state of empowered expression. We'll talk about strategy, storytelling, systems–and how to make visibility feel less like a risk and more like a responsibility.

Because in a world full of noise, the most courageous thing you can do is *let yourself be heard*.

The Invisible Armor: Why Lawyers Resist Visibility

Lawyers are trained to advocate for others.

We speak *on behalf of*. We represent. We argue cases with precision and passion–for our clients. But when it comes to advocating for ourselves–our businesses, our perspectives, our worth–we often freeze.

Why?

Because visibility feels *vulnerable*.

It means stepping out of the safe, neutral zone of "professionalism" and into the messy, unpredictable world of *public perception*. It means risking judgment. Criticism. Rejection. Misunderstanding.

It means risking *being known*.

And for many lawyers, that risk feels too high. So instead, we stay in the shadows. We hide behind logos. We outsource our voice. We convince ourselves that if we just do excellent legal work, the business will come.

But here's the emotional truth: many of us were *rewarded* for invisibility.

We were praised for being the quiet student, the diligent associate, the one who didn't rock the boat. We learned that humility meant silence. That deference was professionalism. That boldness was arrogance. And so we buried our ambition under layers of politeness and polish.

But the problem is—*you cannot grow a business in hiding.*

You cannot lead from the background. You cannot scale by whispering.

Visibility is an emotional act. It requires courage. Not just to be seen, but to *stand for something.* To say: "This is who I am. This is how I help. This is why I matter."

CASE STUDY

NEIL – THE LAWYER BEHIND THE CURTAIN

Neil is a real estate attorney in his mid-40s. He lives in the suburbs of a major metropolitan area and owns a small but steady solo practice. His days are packed—closings, contract reviews, client hand-holding, the usual. From the outside looking in, Neil appears to be doing just fine.

But underneath the surface, Neil is in turmoil.

He's divorced, with four kids under the age of 16. He splits custody 50/50 with his ex-wife, who works in corporate finance and lives a lifestyle that, quite frankly, outpaces his. There's no overt competition between them, but Neil feels the pressure. Not just to keep up—but to **catch up.** *To prove he can build something real. Something lasting. Something* **better.**

And while he tells himself it's about "providing for the kids," part of him—if he's being honest—is still trying to prove his worth to his ex. To show her he was never the underachiever she accused him of being during their fights. That he **can** *be successful, respected, and self-sufficient.*

That pressure manifests as obsession with perfection. Neil is a good lawyer—meticulous, honest, methodical. But he's a ghost in the marketplace. His website is basic. His online reviews are few. He hasn't posted anything on social media in over a year. He avoids networking events, ignores speaking opportunities, and flat-out refuses to do video.

He tells himself it's a matter of time. "When things slow down." "When I get the website redesigned." "When I finally find the right copywriter."

But the truth? Neil is afraid to be seen.

When Visibility Feels Like a Threat

The idea of being the **face** *of his law firm terrifies him. He's convinced that putting himself out there will open him up to criticism—especially from people who knew him "before." Before the divorce. Before the debt. Before the low points he's fought to recover from. He fears people will see right through the suit and tie and realize he doesn't have it all together.*

But the more Neil hides, the harder things get.

His revenue is flatlining. His referrals are inconsistent. He's constantly stressed about money—juggling kids' expenses, trying to keep the mortgage paid, and dipping into savings to keep the business afloat during slow months. And all the while, he's watching competitors with far less experience lap him in visibility. They're showing up online. They're creating content. They're hosting workshops and podcasts and webinars. They're owning their space.

And they're growing.

Neil knows he can't afford to stay invisible—but he also can't shake the belief that visibility will expose his vulnerabilities.

The turning point came during a lunch with a former colleague—someone Neil once mentored at a large firm years ago. She had recently launched her own practice and was growing quickly. During their conversation, she casually mentioned that two clients had hired her because they'd seen her short Instagram videos explaining the closing process. Neil was stunned. Not by the fact that video worked–but by how ***simple*** *the videos were. She wasn't slick. She wasn't flashy. She was just herself–confident, clear, and* ***visible****.*

That night, Neil looked at his own social media. Crickets.

No one knew who he was. Not because he didn't have something valuable to say–but because he wasn't saying anything.

That's when it clicked.

Neil didn't need to be perfect to be seen. He just needed to be ***present****. He needed to show up as the person his clients already trusted–knowledgeable, calm, and competent. Not a performer. A professional.*

Showing Up, Publicly

Law Firm Mentor coached Neil to start small. The very next week, he posted a photo of himself at a closing table with a first-time homebuyer. They were grinning, holding a set of keys, standing in front of a stack of papers and a bottle of sparkling cider. The caption read:

"Another first-time buyer crosses the finish line. Proud to help folks make smart, informed decisions in one of the most important transactions of their lives."

Before he hit "post," Neil sat staring at the screen, heart pounding. It felt... vulnerable. Exposed. What if someone thought it was cheesy? What if his ex saw it and rolled her eyes? What if his law school buddy commented some sarcastic jab?

But he did it anyway.

Within an hour, the post had ten likes. Then twenty. A comment from a realtor he hadn't spoken to in years:

"Love this! You were the smoothest closer I ever worked with. Let's grab coffee soon."

Then another comment from a former client:

"Neil was AMAZING. Highly recommend if anyone is looking to buy or sell!"

His stomach flipped. It was like a high. A mix of relief and adrenaline. Someone **saw** *him—and it wasn't scary. It was empowering.*

Over the next few weeks, Neil started showing up more. He shared a quick LinkedIn post about three things every investor should ask before buying a rental property. He recorded a 2-minute video explaining why title insurance mattered. He posted a photo from his son's soccer game with a caption about the balancing act of being a solo lawyer and a full-time dad.

And yes—he stumbled. His first video had bad lighting and his voice cracked. He misspelled a word in a caption once. He second-guessed himself constantly. But he kept going.

He got a private message from an attorney he respected, saying, "Man, I've been thinking of doing videos but I've been too scared. You inspired me." That one floored him.

He also got a snide comment from an old colleague: "Look who's an influencer now." It stung—but Neil realized something: the people who mocked him weren't his clients. They weren't paying his bills. Their opinions were irrelevant.

Visibility wasn't just growing his audience. It was ***shrinking his fear.***

Final Word: You Can't Grow if You Hide

Within a few months, he was invited to speak on a local business podcast. Then a realtor asked him to lead a webinar. Then he was asked to be on a panel at a real estate investor networking event.

Clients started calling him directly, saying "I saw your post" or "I heard you on that podcast." Referrals doubled. His schedule was still full—but now it was full of **the right people**. *People who knew him, liked him, trusted him—before they ever picked up the phone.*

> *But most importantly, Neil was showing his kids something new.*
>
> *They saw their dad standing tall, being proud of who he was, not just working to survive–but building something. Not hiding.* ***Leading.***
>
> *And that changed everything.*

Takeaway: Visibility didn't expose Neil's weakness. It revealed his *strength.*

Choosing Your Visibility Lane: Match the Method to Your Mindset

One of the biggest mistakes lawyers make when trying to "get visible" is assuming there's *one right way* to do it. You look around and see someone killing it on TikTok, someone else hosting a legal podcast, another person writing long-form blog posts, and yet another who seems to live on the rubber chicken dinner circuit giving CLEs and workshops.

Here's the truth: **Visibility is not one-size-fits-all.**

To build sustainable visibility that aligns with who you are, you need to choose the right *platforms*–the ones that fit your energy, your strengths, and your *clients' behavior.*

Below is a blueprint you can use to match your personality to the best visibility method for you:

1. If you're a natural speaker:

Best platforms: Live video (Facebook Live, Instagram Live, YouTube), webinars, podcasts (as a guest or host), in-person networking and CLE speaking.

Practice areas that benefit most: Family law, criminal defense, immigration, personal injury–any area where clients make high-emotion decisions and want to feel connected to the *human* behind the firm.

Strategy tip: Start with short, unscripted Q&As. Record 2–3 minute videos answering questions you hear all the time. Don't overproduce. The more real you are, the more trust you'll build.

2. If you're a natural writer:

Best platforms: Blog articles, email newsletters, LinkedIn posts, Medium articles, client guides.

Practice areas that benefit most: Estate planning, elder law, business law, IP—any area where clients are detail-oriented and want thoughtful, educational content.

Strategy tip: Set a rhythm. One post a week on LinkedIn or your blog, and one monthly newsletter. Make it personal *and* practical. Educate, but tell stories too. People remember stories more than statutes.

3. If you're great in conversation but not on camera:

Best platforms: Podcast guest appearances, networking groups (Business Network International, Chamber of Commerce), bar associations, joint webinars with referral partners.

Practice areas that benefit most: Real estate, business transactional law, trusts, and estates—areas where relationships drive referrals.

Strategy tip: Get on other people's platforms first. Reach out to local CPAs, realtors, or financial advisors and offer a joint webinar. You don't have to "sell"—just have a conversation that adds value.

4. If you like structure and consistency:

Best platforms: Email marketing, monthly educational webinars, pre-recorded video series, firm-branded YouTube playlists.

Practice areas that benefit most: Any. But especially powerful for firms that want long-term SEO, brand authority, and evergreen content.

Strategy tip: Batch your content. Record 4 videos in one day. Write 3 newsletters in one afternoon. Systematize visibility so it doesn't feel like a chore—it feels like a calendar item.

5. If you're highly visual or creative:

Best platforms: Instagram (especially Reels), Pinterest (yes—lawyers *do* get traction here), slide decks or carousels on LinkedIn, behind-the-scenes content.

Practice areas that benefit most: Family law, personal injury, immigration, and any practice that serves everyday consumers who engage with visuals.

Strategy tip: Focus on *human moments*—closing day, court wins, team photos, client gifts, handwritten thank-you notes. Your community wants to see your firm's personality. Show it.

Final Tip: Match Platform to *Client Behavior*, Not Just Your Personality

While your personality plays a big role in what you'll *enjoy* doing (and thus, *stick with*), you also need to consider where your clients actually *are*.

- If you serve high-net-worth professionals → LinkedIn and email marketing win.
- If you serve working-class families → Facebook and YouTube are king.
- If your referrals come from other professionals → Podcasting, webinars, and live CLEs will keep you top of mind.
- If you serve younger clients (Gen Z or Millennials) → Instagram, TikTok, and short-form video matter more.

You're not trying to become an influencer. You're building *trust*. And visibility—when done authentically—lets people *know*, *like*, and *trust* you before you even pick up the phone.

Solution 2: Judgment-Free Zone: A Journey to Confidence

Confidence is not the absence of fear; it's the decision to move forward anyway.

CASE STUDY

DHERICA

Dherica knew how to move forward. She'd done it her whole life. A triple minority–Black, female, and gay–she'd never walked into a room where she wasn't, on some level, the outsider. And yet, she had risen.

Raised by a single mother in inner-city Detroit, she was taught to "be twice as good for half the credit." And so, she became exceptional–graduating top of her class in college and law school, earning a federal clerkship, and then taking a job at a mid-sized white-shoe firm where she did what she always did: outperform expectations. She knew how to make herself indispensable. She knew how to win.

But excellence isn't immunity.

The Armor that Kept Her Safe - and Small

At firm dinners, she smiled through microaggressions. She ignored the jokes that danced around her Blackness, her womanhood, her queerness. She heard them–and buried them. When a partner once joked, "We got diversity points with you, huh?" she laughed along, though inside, she shrank.

Still, she pressed on. She didn't climb the ladder. She built her own.

Six years ago, she left that firm and started her own commercial litigation boutique. Armed with loyal clients and a sterling reputation, she scaled quickly. Within three years, she hit the million-dollar mark. Two years later, she passed $4 million in annual revenue. She had five attorneys, a staff of eight, and a book of business anyone would envy.

But it wasn't enough.

As market trends shifted, so did her clients' spending. The pandemic had ushered in belt-tightening. General counsels became more risk-averse. Longtime corporate clients began renegotiating retainers and outsourcing less litigation. Her revenue flatlined.

And Dherica panicked.

For years, she hadn't marketed. She hadn't needed to. Clients came to her from relationships she'd nurtured at her old firm, or from referrals by happy general counsels. She'd never had to sell *herself–and frankly, that was fine with her. Because marketing felt* dangerous.

She didn't say that out loud–not even to herself at first. But the truth was, the idea of putting herself out there, intentionally becoming more visible, felt like peeling back armor she wasn't sure she could survive without. She'd spent her entire career proving she was safe. *That she wasn't the angry Black woman. That she was polished, palatable, precise.*

Learning to Own the Space

But marketing–especially the kind her Law Firm Mentor business coach suggested–meant leaning into presence. *Not just being seen, but owning the space she occupied. Entering rooms she'd always politely waited to be invited into.*

That meant networking. *Not passively.* Deliberately.

She joined Law Firm Mentor with skepticism in year six of her practice. On her very first coaching call, the topic was marketing–and she nearly left the Zoom room. But something pulled at her. She had invested to grow. And growth meant discomfort. So she leaned in.

Dherica's coach didn't hand her a list of SEO tricks or tell her to make TikToks. Instead, the suggestion was strategic, simple, and terrifying: **high-end networking.**

"I want you to start meeting decision-makers," the coach said. "General counsels. CEOs. Board chairs. The people who decide where legal spend goes."

Dherica blinked.

"You mean... cold reach-outs?"

"I mean warm introductions. You already have the network. You just haven't activated it."

She resisted. Not because she couldn't do it. Because she was scared.

"I don't want to feel like I'm begging," she said.

"You're not. You're presenting a solution."

"But what if they think I'm bragging?"

"Then you're not their lawyer. You're not a fit for everyone. That's a feature, not a flaw."

It took three weeks before she made the first call.

It was to a former GC she'd worked with years ago. They had mutual respect. She asked him for lunch and practiced the pitch in her car for 45 minutes before walking into the restaurant.

She nearly bailed three times.

But once the conversation started, she relaxed. She explained how her firm had grown. How her team's capabilities had evolved. How they'd won a major arbitration in New York and expanded into regulatory compliance. The GC listened. Then he said:

"I've got someone I want you to meet. Our portfolio company needs litigation support in Dallas."

And just like that, she had a lead.

One lunch led to another. Then an executive dinner. Then a private roundtable hosted by a local tech incubator. Each event was a fresh arena for the same self-doubt. She picked her outfits carefully. She adjusted her language. She took mental inventory of every gesture and phrase, terrified she'd "overshare" or come off as too confident–or not confident enough.

One night, at a formal reception, she found herself at a table with four white men in blue suits. They were swapping law school war stories and corporate acquisition gossip. For ten minutes, she smiled and nodded, unseen.

Then one asked, "So what kind of law do you practice?"

And she said it.

"I run a commercial litigation boutique. We handle high-stakes business disputes for regional banks and mid-market tech companies. I've got a team of five lawyers, and we've tried over twenty cases in the last four years. And our win rate is excellent."

No qualifiers. No deflections. Just truth.

The room quieted, then nodded. One man leaned forward and asked for her card.

She got a new client three weeks later.

It didn't happen overnight. But confidence, like a muscle, grew with every rep. Every time she walked into a room where she didn't feel *like she belonged but stayed anyway, she grew. Every time she introduced herself not as "a lawyer" but as* the founder and managing partner of a high-performance litigation boutique, *she took back power.*

Her revenue rebounded. But more importantly, she changed.

She stopped needing external validation. She no longer shrank herself to fit the comfort of others. She stopped apologizing for her ambition.

And in coaching, she became a beacon for others.

Final Word: The Courage to Be Seen

Dherica now mentors new women in the LFM community. She shares her story with brutal honesty–the fear, the armor, the choice to shed it.

She tells them: "You don't have to wait until you feel confident to act confident. Action births confidence. Show up. Stand tall. Take the mic. Let them see *you."*

Takeaway: Visibility without confidence is hollow. But confidence without visibility is wasted.

This is the journey. Not just to more clients, but to deeper self-worth. The judgment is real. But it isn't final. You get to write your story—and tell it on stages, in boardrooms, and across every negotiating table you sit at.

Just like Dherica.

How to Build Confidence and Crush Judgment—Your Concrete Action Plan

Dherica's story proves that confidence is cultivated, not inherited. But if you're waiting for confidence to arrive before taking action, you'll wait forever. Confidence grows through doing. The key is not to eliminate judgment—yours or others'—but to *navigate it skillfully.*

Here are **five proven action steps** you can implement *this week* to strengthen your confidence muscle and dissolve judgment paralysis:

1. Start with a Confidence Inventory

Tool: "Evidence List" Exercise

Before you show up, remind yourself why you belong in the room. Make a list of 10 tangible accomplishments from your legal career—cases won, clients retained, contracts negotiated, crises managed. Keep this list on your phone. Before any networking event, pitch, or client meeting, read through it to anchor yourself in *fact-based confidence.*

LFM Coaching Outcome: After using the Evidence List for 90 days, one solo family law attorney reported a 40% increase in successful consultations because she started presenting her value more assertively.

2. Identify Your "Judgment Triggers"

Tool: The "Inner Critic Log"

Every time you hesitate to put yourself out there—whether it's skipping an event, declining to speak up on a call, or not submitting your firm for an award—write down what stopped you. Was it fear of seeming arrogant? Fear of being judged by others? Fear of stumbling?

Naming the fear disarms it.

LFM Coaching Outcome: One estate planning lawyer realized she avoided podcast invitations because she feared sounding "too salesy." Once identified, we helped her write an authentic intro pitch. She now books 2–3 podcast guest spots per month.

3. Create a "Safe Room" Network

Tool: Confidence Circle

Dherica found strength by entering high-stakes rooms, but she didn't do it alone. She had a LFM coach. She had community. You need a "Confidence Circle"–a small group of other law firm owners (ideally 3–5) who are actively marketing their firms. Meet monthly. Share fears. Give feedback. Hold each other accountable. It's not just support. It's strategy.

LFM Coaching Outcome: A group of women litigators from three different states formed a circle and began pitching each other for speaking engagements. Each one booked a paid CLE within 6 months.

4. Take One Bold Visibility Action Each Week

Tool: Weekly Visibility Tracker

Set a simple weekly goal: one visibility action per week. Examples:

- Post a case success story on LinkedIn (even anonymously).
- Send a warm email to a former client.
- Attend one in-person business networking event.
- Ask to speak at a Chamber of Commerce meeting.
- Pitch a local journalist on a relevant news story.

Track your activity and reactions. Celebrate the wins. Learn from the misses. Repeat.

LFM Coaching Outcome: One commercial real estate attorney went from zero events to 12 in three months. Result? 4 new clients and 2 strategic partnerships.

5. Master Your Pitch – Without Apology

Tool: "No Shrinking Bio" Script

Many lawyers diminish their brilliance with vague intros: "I'm just a lawyer," or "I do a bit of litigation." No. No more shrinking. Instead, memorize a *bold* 30-second intro that says:

"I run a firm that helps [X clients] solve [Y problem] through [Z services]."

Practice it. Use it everywhere—from Zoom calls to Uber rides.

LFM Coaching Outcome: One tax controversy attorney landed a corporate client after giving her new "No Shrinking Bio" at a women's bar event. The GC said, "That intro made me want to know you more."

Your Journey to Confidence Starts with One Step

You don't need to change everything overnight. You just need to do *one thing* today that future-you will thank you for. These five strategies work. They've helped hundreds of LFM clients step into their power, dismantle the fear of judgment, and attract the clients they deserve.

Confidence is a Practice, not a Personality Trait.

Every email you send.
Every handshake you offer.
Every room you walk into.

Each one is a vote for the lawyer—and the leader—you're becoming.

Now let's keep going.

Solution 3: Ambition Permission

There's a tension that lives deep inside most high-achieving lawyers—particularly women, people of color, and those from underrepresented groups, though it exists within many lawyers regardless of their demographic profile. It's the unspoken question:

"Is it okay to want more?"

More money. More recognition. More impact. More influence. More time. More freedom. More *everything*.

For many, the ambition is there. It's hardwired. You wouldn't have gotten through law school without it. You wouldn't have built a practice, served demanding clients, survived in courtrooms, or juggled your way through twelve-hour days if it weren't.

But somewhere along the journey, ambition starts to feel... dangerous.

Too much ambition makes you "greedy." Or "arrogant." Or "never satisfied." The moment you dream bigger than the room you're in, someone–your peers, your team, your family, even your inner voice–suggests you're going too far. "Aren't you doing enough already?" they ask. And you wonder: *Am I pushing too hard?*

This is where **chaos sneaks in**–not in the goal-setting, but in the **self-silencing** that follows. You want more, but you fear losing respect. You crave freedom, but worry that outsourcing or automating too much makes you lazy. You want to scale, but you're afraid that public growth invites private criticism.

You try to play small and still feel big. That's where burnout brews.

Let's be clear: **There is nothing wrong with wanting more.**

Wanting to double your revenue isn't greedy. Wanting to become a thought leader in your field isn't self-absorbed. Wanting to be a millionaire, or speak on international stages, or exit your firm with a fat buyout is not "too much." It's called *vision*. And when ambition is paired with alignment, it becomes *leadership*.

The problem isn't your ambition. The problem is the *lack of permission* you give yourself to pursue it fully.

At Law Firm Mentor, we see this pattern constantly in our coaching community. Brilliant lawyers who built six- or seven-figure firms... and then stalled. Not because they ran out of ideas. But because they hit an *internal ceiling*. They were afraid that having more meant being seen as less likable. Or less relatable. Or less loyal. Especially if they came from humble beginnings or are surrounded by people who are content with less.

Here's what you need to know:

Ambition does not make you selfish. It makes you *stewardship-minded*.

Your ambition, when directed with clarity, can create jobs, uplift communities, revolutionize industries, and build generational wealth. When you allow yourself to own your desire, without shame or apology, your decisions become sharper. Your leadership becomes cleaner. And your impact? It expands exponentially.

But to achieve with assurance, you must first dismantle the guilt that keeps you playing small. You must challenge the cultural narratives that say success must come at the expense of peace, humility, or belonging. You must develop **new systems and new mindsets** to support bigger dreams–without burning out or isolating yourself.

This isn't about wanting "it all." It's about choosing *what matters most*, and building a practice and life that reflects *your definition* of success.

The next story we'll explore is about a man who almost let his ambition die quietly... until he realized that scaling wasn't selfish. It was *liberating*.

Let's meet him.

CASE STUDY

NIXON – FROM SURVIVAL TO SIGNIFICANCE

At first glance, Nixon looked like the American Dream in a suit.

Tall, fit, clean-cut. A conventionally attractive, straight white man with a warm, approachable demeanor and the kind of smile that made clients instantly feel at ease. He lived in a mid-century modern home in a good school district with his wife and two kids. His calendar was always full, his website was polished, and he was doing steady business as the owner of a boutique estate planning firm.

From the outside looking in, people thought Nixon had it easy.

But looks are deceiving.

Because what no one saw—what even Nixon *tried to forget most days—was the fire he walked through to get where he was.*

The Trauma Behind the Calm

Nixon grew up in a storm of chaos.

When he was just three years old, his mother took him and his six-year-old brother Chandler and fled the man they called Dad after a night of alcohol-fueled rage left her with a split lip and a shattered arm. They spent the next two years in and out of shelters, sleeping in borrowed beds, relying on food pantries, and clutching to survival like a lifeline. Nixon, barely old enough to form sentences, learned to be quiet, compliant, invisible.

His mother remarried quickly—on the fourth date—with a man who, while not violent, had his own demons. His stepfather was kind but chronically unemployed, cycling through jobs as easily as he did six-packs. His presence was a step up from chaos, but never a step toward security.

So Nixon grew up hardwired for survival.

He worked two jobs in high school. Paid his own way through a state college. Applied for law school with the hope—not the certainty—that he'd get a full ride, and then did everything he could to stretch the scholarship once it came. Even after graduation, when most new lawyers dreamed about climbing the BigLaw ladder or buying their first condo, Nixon just wanted one thing: ***safety****.*

He defined success the way a war survivor might define peace—not as abundance, but as the absence *of fear.*

By the time he opened his estate planning firm, Nixon had already defied the odds. He was married to a wonderful woman, father to two healthy children, and the owner of a profitable law practice. His income was steady, his clients loyal, and his Google reviews glowing.

But Nixon had no idea he was stuck. Because from where he stood, just not being afraid anymore *felt like a miracle.*

And yet, deep down, he was restless.

He would scroll LinkedIn and see colleagues building million-dollar firms, speaking on stages, hosting podcasts, and creating digital courses. He'd shut the app and tell himself, I don't need all that. *But something gnawed at him in the quiet hours.*

He'd look at his bank account and see **enough**, *but wonder if it could be* **more**.

He wanted to scale his practice. He wanted to bring on another attorney. He wanted to start offering trusts and probate litigation services, and even had the idea to write a short book for families navigating end-of-life planning.

But every time he got close to making a bold move, his chest tightened. A voice from his past whispered, Don't get greedy. Don't tempt fate. Don't fly too close to the sun.

Teaching a Survivor How to Dream

He brought this to his first coaching session with Law Firm Mentor.

When we asked Nixon about his goals, he said, "Honestly, I just want to stay comfortable. I'm not trying to become some empire builder."

But then we dug deeper.

He admitted that he'd put off hiring help for over a year, even though he was drowning in client work. He confessed that he'd wanted to niche into elder law, but worried he didn't know enough. He revealed that his email list had grown to nearly 2,000 people—but he'd never sent out a single newsletter because he didn't want to "bother" anyone.

What Nixon really feared wasn't growth. It was collapse.

He believed—at a cellular *level—that scaling would disrupt the delicate balance of safety he'd spent his whole life constructing. In his mind, staying small was the price of staying alive.*

This fear wasn't logical. It was primal.

So we started there—with his nervous system.

We helped Nixon see that his fear of ambition was a trauma response masquerading as pragmatism. It wasn't that he lacked ability. He lacked permission. *Permission to want more than survival. Permission to trust that stability wouldn't disappear just because he took a risk.*

We didn't tell him to leap. We coached him to **step.**

That's the difference between Law Firm Mentor and most coaching companies that serve lawyers. We don't glorify the big leap if the nervous system isn't ready for it. Because here's the truth: when a lawyer who is already afraid takes a massive, high-stakes risk, and it goes sideways? The wound left behind doesn't just slow them down. It can kill their momentum for years–or worse, permanently.

And that's what Nixon was terrified of. Not the failure itself–but what he would believe about himself if he failed.

So, we started small. One habit. One mindset shift. One courageous act. Because big wins don't come from big moves. They come from small moves done consistently–then scaled with confidence.

For Nixon, the first step was to stop white-knuckling his pricing.

His flat fees were painfully low. And he knew it. But every time we gently nudged him toward an increase, he gave the same answer: "I can't afford to lose anyone."

That wasn't just about marketing fear. That was survival fear. That was 7-year-old Nixon watching his mom ration milk between him and his older brother. That was 10-year-old Nixon reading eviction notices and pretending not to be scared. That was 14-year-old Nixon quietly packing his backpack with groceries at his after-school job, just to make sure his mother didn't go hungry.

He wasn't just avoiding conflict with clients. He was avoiding the possibility of being punished for wanting more.

So we didn't say, "Double your fees." We didn't say, "Burn your existing pricing structure to the ground." We said, "Let's look at your most time-consuming package and raise that by 10%. Just that one. For the next two weeks. Let's see what happens."

He agreed, reluctantly. "But if I lose clients..."

"You won't," we said. "But if you do, it's because they were never going to grow with you anyway."

The first client he quoted at the new rate didn't flinch. Nixon called us immediately after, stunned.

"They didn't even ask why the price was different," he said. "They just said okay."

That moment gave him something far more important than the extra $500 in revenue.

It gave him evidence.

That's what a single step provides. Not just movement. But proof. It tells your nervous system: "Hey, you did something hard. And nothing bad happened." That's how you earn trust with yourself. That's how you build the foundation for ambition that's rooted in resilience, not adrenaline.

That small victory unlocked a domino effect. He raised another price. Then another. We coached him through difficult conversations, showed him how to confidently present value without apologizing, and taught him how to write emails and proposals that sounded like the version of Nixon who already believed in his worth.

He began to see the pattern for what it was: a trauma response disguised as business logic. He wasn't just underpricing. He was hiding. Because staying small felt like staying safe.

But playing small has its own cost.

Nixon had always believed that his background made him more "grateful" than his peers. That he wasn't greedy–just practical. But what he hadn't realized was that he was living in a form of financial and professional repression, perpetuated by the belief that reaching too far meant risking everything.

He had to rewrite the narrative.

So we introduced a new exercise: the "Safe to Stretch" inventory. Nixon began journaling weekly about every time he resisted doing something ambitious. Every time he hesitated to attend a networking event, avoided submitting a CLE proposal, or declined an opportunity to be interviewed on a local news segment. Then, he documented what he told himself in those moments.

Most of it boiled down to: "Don't stick out. Don't attract attention. Don't tempt the universe."

This was magical thinking. The childlike belief that striving for more would bring cosmic retribution. But once he saw it on paper—day after day, week after week—he couldn't unsee it.

It was never about money. It was never about risk. It was about identity.

He didn't think he deserved to lead a wildly successful firm because no one in his family had ever done it. Because "men like him" didn't have the luxury of thriving. Because he feared becoming someone even his mother wouldn't recognize—someone who stopped working himself to the bone and started enjoying the fruit of his labor.

That's when we gave him permission.

We said, "You don't owe the past anything. It already made you. Now you get to choose."

From there, Nixon's evolution was rapid. Not because he suddenly became fearless—but because he built the capacity to act in spite of fear. He rewrote his entire operations plan in 90 days. Started hiring from a place of strategy, not desperation. Built out a referral network of financial advisors. Got featured in a national estate planning blog. He even created a podcast—just five episodes, but it was his.

Final Word: Finding His Permission

By the end of that year, he had tripled his personal income, doubled the size of his team, and more importantly, stopped apologizing for wanting things.

> *That's the real transformation. Not the revenue. Not the team. Not the podcast.*
>
> *It's the internal permission slip. The moment when a lawyer no longer feels guilty for dreaming big–and no longer waits for the world to tell them it's safe.*
>
> *Because here's what we've learned coaching hundreds of lawyers like Nixon:*
>
> Big leaps scare small identities.
>
> *That's why we don't ask you to leap. We ask you to step. And step again. And again.*

Takeaway: When you master small steps, you expand your capacity. Your dreams get bigger, but so does your belief in your ability to hold them. Your nervous system stops panicking every time you make a bold move. You stop expecting punishment for prosperity. You stop thinking it's arrogant to want more.

And you start becoming the kind of lawyer–the kind of leader–who changes everything. For your family. Your team. Your community. Yourself.

That's what Nixon learned.

And now, he doesn't just lead a firm.

He owns his ambition.

Practical Steps to Achieve with Assurance

Balancing ambition doesn't mean shrinking your goals. It means building the *emotional infrastructure* to carry them. Here's how we help lawyers like Nixon move from fear-based restraint to grounded, confident growth:

1. Name the Fear Behind the Goal

Ambition is never the problem. Fear is. And fear thrives in vagueness. The first step is to ask:

- What outcome are you afraid your ambition will create?

- Who will judge you if you become more successful?
- What punishment are you unconsciously expecting?

Try this: Journal for 15 minutes about the *worst thing* that could happen if your biggest professional goal came true. Then write a second entry about the *best thing* that could happen. You'll start to see which version you're more emotionally connected to–and why.

2. Create Your "Safe Stretch" Ladder

At LFM, we don't push people into the deep end of their fear. We build stairs.

- Make a list of 5 growth actions that feel slightly uncomfortable but not overwhelming.
- Choose *one* and commit to it this week.
- Once completed, choose the next.

Examples might include:

- Raising one fee by 10%.
- Speaking up in a professional group where you usually stay quiet.
- Asking a satisfied client for a testimonial.
- Applying for an award or recognition.

These actions build "evidence equity"–proof that discomfort isn't danger and success won't break you.

3. Uncouple Your Past from Your Future

Your childhood, your money story, your fears of being "too much" or "not enough"–they are *context*, not *truth*. We can honor the survival strategies that got you here without letting them define where you go next.

Try this mindset reframe:

"That fear protected me before. I don't need it now."

Write it. Repeat it. Believe it.

4. Surround Yourself With Ambitious Voices

You will *not* outgrow fear in isolation. Nixon's real progress began when he heard other lawyers normalize what he was experiencing–especially the successful ones. Whether it's a coaching community, a mastermind group, or a circle of trusted peers, you need others who are willing to say:

"Wanting more doesn't make you ungrateful. It makes you ready."

5. Build Systems That Reinforce Growth

Scaling without structure leads to chaos. So if your ambition includes a bigger team, more clients, or higher-level services, your internal systems need to evolve accordingly.

- Review your org chart. Where will pressure build as you grow?
- Look at your pricing model. Is it scalable?
- Consider your time. Are you working ON the business, or still stuck IN it?

Don't just chase more. Create the conditions where more is *manageable.*

6. Set Success Thresholds That Don't Involve Self-Betrayal

This one's crucial: Growth shouldn't cost you your health, family, or joy. Define what *balanced ambition* means for you.

- How many hours per week do you want to work?
- How many clients can you serve with excellence?
- What's your "enough" number for income, lifestyle, and savings?

LFM helps lawyers get clear on *where they're going*–so they don't arrive somewhere that looks good but feels like hell.

Bottom line?

Ambition is sacred. It's not a flaw. It's not arrogance. It's the divine pull toward your purpose–and it *must* be honored with care.

You don't have to go big fast.

You just have to go.

Step by step. System by system. Belief by belief.

And when you do, the chaos doesn't crush you.

You crush it.

Solution 4: Growth: The Key to Marketing Triumph

Growth isn't just a result of successful marketing–it's the *fuel* that keeps marketing working. Too often, lawyers get stuck in a loop of waiting until they've "arrived" to start sharing. They think, *"Once I'm successful, once I hit that number, once I get those cases–then I'll tell people about it."* But here's the truth: **Marketing is not about arrival. Marketing is about momentum**. And momentum only happens when you're in a constant state of visible growth.

This section is about embracing the simple truth that *showing your growth is your marketing*. If you are working on getting better–at the law, at managing your firm, at building your brand, at showing up–you already have something to market. People are inspired by progress. They don't need you to have it all figured out. They need to see that you're in motion. That you're not stagnating. That you're building something worth paying attention to.

And here's the kicker: growth is attractive. Not just in the motivational-poster sense, but in a *hardwired-human-behavior* kind of way. If you've ever read *The Science of Getting Rich* by Wallace D. Wattles, you've encountered the concept of the **Impression of Increase**. Wattles teaches that people are inherently drawn to those who radiate growth. When others see that you are *increasing*–your success, your energy, your opportunities–they associate you with abundance. And we all want a piece of that.

Let me bring it down to Earth with one of my favorite analogies: **No one wants the Captain of the Parcheesi Club. Everyone wants the Captain of the Football Team.**

Why? Because everyone wants him *because everyone wants him.*

He's not necessarily the smartest, the kindest, or even the best partner for a long-term relationship. But he *looks* like he's winning, and that's enough to make people look twice. In business, that principle holds just as true. Visibility + momentum = magnetism. You don't have to be the best lawyer in town to attract the best cases—you just need to show that you're growing, that you're active, and that people are paying attention.

This is what I call *organic status marketing*. You're not faking success. You're narrating your journey through it. You're showing up and saying, "Here's what I just learned," or "We just hired our second paralegal," or "We just wrapped a big case and here's what I took away." When you're relentlessly focused on growth, you have endless material to promote. And that promotion doesn't come off as self-congratulatory—it comes off as inspiring, aspirational, and energizing. It makes people want to align themselves with your brand. It says, *"This person is going places."*

And here's the thing—even sharing your struggles can create this same effect. When you are open about how you're working to get better, people root for you. They invest emotionally in your story. This is the energy that drives referrals, client loyalty, speaking opportunities, and press. They don't just want to *see* the win—they want to be *part* of the win.

So let's be clear: marketing your growth is not about ego. It's about engagement. It's about connection. It's about signaling that your business is alive, evolving, and expanding. And that creates a gravitational pull—one that brings people in and keeps them watching.

In the next section, you'll meet Terrence, a lawyer who wrestled with the fear of promoting his growth—until he realized that hiding his evolution was costing him the one thing he craved most: influence. Through his journey, you'll see how growth-focused marketing doesn't just build credibility—it builds community.

Let's dive in.

CASE STUDY

THE RELUCTANT RISE OF TERRENCE MARTIN

Terrence Martin never intended to be seen. He wasn't hiding, exactly–he was just trained by the culture of law to believe that professionalism meant invisibility. Be good, stay quiet, do the work, and the work will speak for itself. That was the gospel he'd followed since graduating top of his class from a mid-tier law school and opening his solo criminal defense practice in Philadelphia.

He was smart, precise, and deeply committed to his clients. He won tough cases, negotiated even tougher deals, and slowly built a modest reputation as a solid, trustworthy attorney. But his revenue plateaued. After nearly a decade in practice, he was making around $275,000 a year–just enough to keep the firm afloat, keep one legal assistant on payroll, and pay himself a decent, but far from life-changing, salary.

The Beliefs that Kept Him Quiet

Terrence came to Law Firm Mentor during a low moment–his father had just been diagnosed with early-onset Alzheimer's, and Terrence was struggling to keep up with the emotional toll of caregiving while holding together his caseload and cash flow. He was exhausted and feeling guilty. He wanted to take care of his dad, to be present for his teenage son, and to give his wife more than drained leftovers at the end of the day.

When we reviewed his business, the issue was clear: Terrence had become the best-kept secret in Philadelphia law.

His SEO was weak, his intake pipeline was almost entirely referral-based, and he hadn't posted on social media in over two years. He had no newsletter, no blog, no community engagement–and no real visibility strategy. Yet when we looked at his client outcomes and satisfaction scores, they were stellar. He had stories worth telling. He had wins worth celebrating. But he didn't think any of it mattered *in the way marketing "should."*

"I just feel like if I start talking about myself, people will think I'm bragging," he told me during one of our early coaching calls.

That fear ran deeper than marketing. It was wired into his upbringing.

Terrence had grown up in a working-class Black family where humility wasn't optional–it was a survival strategy. His mother had drilled into him the dangers of being "too loud," of attracting attention, of looking arrogant. "Don't make yourself a target," she'd said a hundred times when he was a kid. And in a world that often punishes confident Black men for simply existing with pride, Terrence had learned early on to shrink, to blend in, to let others shine while he quietly did the work.

So when I suggested he start sharing more about his growth–posting when he hired someone, celebrating a trial win, sharing a quick insight from a CLE he attended–he flinched.

"Isn't that... I don't know, kind of performative?" he asked.

"Only if you're faking it," I replied. "But you're not. You're doing the work. You're learning. You're improving lives. Why keep that locked in a drawer?"

Showing Up

It took months of gentle but consistent coaching to get Terrence to take action. His first step was an internal victory–he began documenting what he was proud of each week. Not publicly, just for himself. At first, the list was thin: "Didn't yell at the opposing counsel who tried me." "Prepped for court while dad was in the hospital." "Closed out my Monday task list by Friday."

But that ritual unlocked something. Terrence started to see that he was growing. Even in chaos. Even while grieving his father's mental decline. Even while parenting and lawyering and caregiving and hurting.

And then something unexpected happened: his assistant posted a photo of the firm's new reception area after they'd redecorated. Nothing special–just a clean, modern look and a caption that read, "New space, new energy. #MartinLaw #LevelUp." Terrence didn't know she'd posted it until a local colleague tagged him in the comments.

The post got dozens of likes and a few congratulatory comments. Then a former client messaged, "Wow, I didn't realize you had grown so much. Are you taking on new matters?"

Within two weeks, Terrence got three new consultations directly from that post.

His eyes widened in our next session. "I didn't even post it," he said. "But people noticed. It's like... they care."

"They do," I said. "They're watching. And they want a reason to root for you."

That was the shift. Not a dramatic leap, but a subtle reorientation of identity. Terrence started sharing more–but always in his voice, on his terms. A snapshot of his desk with a caption about managing chaos during trial prep. A short reflection after losing a tough case, where he honored his client's dignity and his own learning. A selfie with his son on college tour day with the caption, "Building legacies in and out of court."

These weren't "ads." They weren't lead-gen campaigns.

They were proof of growth. *Proof of commitment. Proof of humanity.*

And the growth that followed was exponential.

Final Word: Visibility Isn't Vanity; It's Leadership

Within a year, Terrence had hired another associate, doubled his support staff, and tripled his revenue. His social media presence remained modest–no viral videos, no gimmicks–but his referral base exploded. Colleagues reached out for co-counseling. Judges complimented his professionalism. His old law school invited him to speak on a panel about ethical criminal defense.

But what Terrence valued most was the emotional freedom he gained. The ability to show up as himself–not a version of success that fit someone else's mold. He'd been afraid of looking arrogant. What he found instead was that authentic visibility *doesn't alienate people. It draws them in.*

When his father passed the following spring, Terrence wrote a heartfelt post thanking his team for holding the firm together while he grieved–and acknowledging how much his dad's lessons shaped the man and lawyer he had become. That post was shared over a hundred times.

Takeaway: Growth is never just about the firm. It was about the lives you touch by being willing to be seen.

Step-by-Step Strategy: How to Market Through Growth

Ready to do what Terrence did–without the months of resistance? Here's a practical roadmap to start building your own "impression of increase":

Step 1: Create a Weekly Wins Ritual

Every Friday (or whatever day your workweek winds down), write down 3-5 things that reflect your growth. They could be:

- New client matters
- Hiring decisions
- Lessons learned from mistakes
- Personal milestones
- Leadership breakthroughs

This practice builds awareness of your own momentum—and gives you a bank of authentic content to pull from.

Step 2: Share the Journey, Not Just the Trophy

Most lawyers only post when they "win" something: a verdict, an award, a speaking gig. But the magic is in the *journey*. Your followers want to see:

1. What you're learning
2. What you're building
3. What challenges you're navigating

Try posting about:

- A system you just implemented (and why)
- How you trained a team member this week
- Something a client said that reminded you *why* you do this work

Step 3: Use the "3S" Visibility Formula

If you're nervous about what to post, use this simple formula:

- **Simple** - Keep it easy to understand. No legalese.
- **Specific** - Ground it in your real life. "Just onboarded our 100th client" hits harder than "Business is booming."
- **Soulful** - Make it human. Let people connect with the person behind the post.

Step 4: Choose Your Playground

Don't try to be everywhere. Pick one platform where your people are already engaging—Instagram, Facebook, LinkedIn, or even YouTube if you're a talker—and commit to **one post per week**. That's it.

Step 5: Let Growth Be the Hook

Your marketing doesn't have to scream, "Hire me!" It just has to whisper, "I'm going somewhere." That subtle magnetism draws clients, referrals, and opportunities your way without ever feeling like a sales pitch.

Final Note: Stop Waiting to Be Impressive

Let me say this plainly: **you do not have to be perfect to be powerful.**

The idea that you need to "arrive" before you can share is a lie that's keeping you broke, invisible, and stuck. Marketing is not a highlight reel–it's a conversation. And if you're only willing to show up when everything is polished, you'll spend your whole career waiting for a day that never comes.

You are growing. You are building. You are becoming.

And your audience isn't looking for a finished product–they're looking for someone they can relate to, trust, and cheer for. Someone who shows up. Someone who's real. Someone who's *moving forward.*

That someone is you.

So stop hiding your growth. Start narrating it. That's how you crush chaos in marketing–not by becoming louder, but by becoming more alive. More visible. More *you.*

The world is watching.

Let them see you rise.

Solution 5: Marketing Strategies for Chaos Crushers

The legal world is changing. Fast. And if you're not keeping up, you're falling behind.

We are living in a moment of marketing disruption unlike anything we've seen in the last twenty years. TikTok has dethroned Google as a search engine for the next generation. Instagram isn't just for pictures anymore–it's where Gen Z goes to search for everything from vacation spots to criminal defense lawyers. Podcasts are more trusted than billboards. And AI? It's not a futuristic buzzword anymore. It's in your office. On your phone. Writing your emails. Scanning your contracts. Managing your intake.

Welcome to the new marketing frontier.

To be a Chaos Crusher in this era—to build a law firm that stands out, grows fast, and commands attention—you must become not just a practitioner of law, but a student of **attention**. Because attention is the currency of our digital economy. Without it, your skills, your service, your brand? They go unseen.

The AI Awakening

Let's talk about the elephant in the room: **AI**.

The widespread adoption of tools like ChatGPT, Gemini, Copilot, and others has given even the smallest law firms superpowers. The question is no longer *whether* you should use AI—it's *how effectively* you'll wield it. Let's break down exactly how these tools can revolutionize your marketing.

- **Draft blog posts in minutes**: AI can take a single idea—like "how child custody is decided in New Jersey"—and spin it into a fully structured blog post in under five minutes. The draft won't be perfect, but it'll be 80% of the way there. For lawyers like Latoya, who struggled with the fear of writing something that wasn't perfect, this was a game changer. Once she saw that ChatGPT could produce a first draft, her anxiety melted away. Suddenly, writing became editing. And editing was manageable.
- **Generate SEO-optimized web content with a single prompt**: Tools like Gemini and ChatGPT-4 can research trending keywords in your practice area and embed them naturally into content. Instead of guessing what your clients are Googling, you can build blogs, service pages, and FAQs that *meet them where they are*. Nixon used this method to rebuild his estate planning website around terms like "trusts for blended families in Georgia" and "how to avoid probate taxes." His web traffic more than doubled within six months.
- **Brainstorm video scripts**: Hate staring into a camera with nothing to say? AI can help you write short scripts tailored to

your tone, audience, and platform. Want to sound confident but compassionate? Formal but modern? Prompt the AI with your style and topic, and it can generate a script you can tweak and record. This helped Marcus, who struggled with the fear of being seen, start filming 60-second videos without freezing up. AI gave him a jumping-off point—he brought the authenticity.

- **Automate client follow-ups**: Imagine sending a thoughtful, customized follow-up to every client who reaches out, even at 2 a.m. With AI-powered CRMs and email workflows, you can. These tools can be trained to respond to FAQs, schedule consultations, and drip information to potential clients while you sleep. This is how Nixon's firm converted 21 new leads in a month—by using AI to follow up consistently and intelligently, without sounding robotic.
- **Create detailed marketing plans**: AI doesn't just generate content. It can also act like your virtual marketing director. Input your firm's goals, niche, and ideal client avatar, and it can produce a 90-day strategy complete with topics, formats, and platform suggestions. For overextended solo attorneys, this kind of guidance is worth its weight in gold. When Terrence felt too overwhelmed to plan content, ChatGPT helped him build a weekly structure he could actually stick to.

In short, AI is not the enemy. It's the assistant you didn't know you needed. The firms using it aren't cheating—they're outpacing the competition by being smart, fast, and agile. AI can't replace your expertise. But it can amplify it. The longer you resist it, the further behind you'll fall.

And yet... many lawyers are *still not using these tools.*

Why? Fear. Overwhelm. Skepticism.

But here's the reality: AI is not replacing lawyers. It's replacing lawyers who **refuse to leverage it.**

Just like Westlaw and LexisNexis replaced digging through books, AI is the next evolutionary step. Your competitors are using it to scale faster, reach more people, and position themselves as thought leaders. If you ignore this shift, you do so at your peril.

The Rise of the Sound-Bite Culture

Text is not dead. But it's definitely been demoted.

Today's consumer doesn't want to read a wall of words. They want:

- **60-second reels** that break down big ideas
- **10-minute podcast clips** that speak directly to their pain
- **TikToks** that blend humor with helpful legal tips
- **YouTube Shorts** that deliver answers, fast

And you know what? That consumer is your *client*. Not some teenager dancing online. Your actual client–a divorcing parent, a small business owner in litigation, a person injured in a car accident–they're scrolling just like everyone else.

They are looking for answers. And if you're not the one giving them in a format they can *digest*, then someone else is.

That's the massive opportunity–and the massive threat.

So, how do we crush chaos in this new marketing era?

With a plan. A strategy. And a commitment to staying informed, nimble, and creative.

Here are 15 powerful strategies that will make you not just visible–but *magnetic*. Now, let's break each of these down with depth and purpose.

1. Weekly Video Tips

Why: Video builds visibility and trust faster than any other format. Clients see your face, hear your voice, and begin to develop a relationship with you before they ever call. Remember Dherica from Solution #2? Her fear of being judged on social media kept her from getting visible. But when she began sharing 30-second videos from her car in the courthouse parking lot, engagement tripled, and referrals followed. Why? Because she didn't just tell people she was relatable. She *showed them.*

2. Podcast Guesting

Why: Podcasts have long-tail value. Once you're interviewed, that content lives forever—and can be repurposed across platforms. Nixon from Solution #3 leveraged podcast guesting as a low-stakes way to build visibility. He was scared of seeming "too ambitious" because of his trauma history, but podcasting allowed him to ease into visibility while speaking with empathy and depth. His vulnerability became his superpower—and listeners turned into clients.

3. Repurposed Content Strategy

Why: One idea shouldn't live in just one place. Marcus, the criminal defense lawyer from Problem #4 in Chapter 8, was terrified to market at all. Once he started documenting wins internally, we helped him turn those insights into short-form content, email snippets, and team shoutouts. His visibility exploded—not because he created more, but because he *used more of what he already had.* Repurposing isn't just efficient—it's powerful.

4. SEO-Optimized Blogging

Why: Blogging isn't dead—it's just changed. As we saw in Problem #3 from Chapter 8, Latoya feared underperforming and therefore avoided blogging for years. Once she started writing with specific Google search terms in mind (like "NYC discrimination lawyer for women"), her traffic doubled. Blogging still works when it's specific, consistent, and localized. Don't blog about "employment law"—blog about "your rights if your boss fires you while pregnant in Atlanta."

5. Email Marketing with Personalization

Why: Email is the highest-converting marketing tool—if you use it to tell stories, not push promos. Remember Jim, the lawyer who feared failure? He started writing weekly emails sharing real cases (anonymized) and his lessons from them. It humanized his brand. Clients don't want perfection—they want to see how you think.

6. Instagram Stories Behind the Scenes

Why: Today's consumer doesn't trust a perfect feed. They want to know *who* they're hiring. When Terrence from Solution #4 allowed his assistant to post his office redesign on Instagram Stories, he didn't expect much. But that post led to three consults in two weeks. Why? Because it signaled *growth*. People want to associate with momentum. And behind-the-scenes content says: I'm real, I'm relatable, I'm rising.

7. Google Business Profile Posts

Why: It's free, underutilized, and powerful. Posting here improves your local ranking and adds fresh relevance to your listing. We had one solo in Texas post weekly "FAQ Friday" updates. In 90 days, his Google listing jumped above competitors who'd been paying for ads. If SEO is digital real estate, your Google profile is your front porch. Decorate it weekly.

8. YouTube Educational Videos

Why: YouTube search often outranks even law firm websites. Nixon's estate planning firm added a YouTube channel where he explained topics in plain English—no jargon, no pitch. Just trust-building content. One of his videos—"Can my kids kick out my second wife if I die?"—got thousands of views. It wasn't fancy. It was just *real*.

9. Strategic Collaborations

Why: You don't have to do this alone. Terrence partnered with a Black male therapist to co-host a "Protecting Black Fathers" Facebook Live. The therapist shared trauma recovery tips. Terrence shared family law strategies. Together, they reached more than either could alone. This is the power of aligned values and cross-pollinated audiences.

10. Client Video Testimonials

Why: Your clients are your best marketers. But written testimonials are skimmed–*video sticks*. Latoya asked one of her clients to record a 45-second iPhone video about her experience. That clip, posted to her website and social media, led to the highest engagement she had seen all year. Nothing sells your services like a real voice and real results.

11. Live Q&A Sessions

Why: Engagement drives visibility–and nothing engages like "ask me anything." Marcus, still afraid of overexposure, decided to do a "3 Myths About Criminal Defense" Instagram Live. It was short, messy, and perfect. People asked questions. He answered authentically. And four consults came in that week. Don't wait to be polished. Go live and be *present*.

12. Google Review Campaigns

Why: Reviews aren't vanity–they're conversions. People trust what others say more than what you claim. Dherica was hesitant to ask clients directly, but we helped her build a follow-up email asking for feedback *and* giving a direct review link. Her reviews tripled in 60 days–and so did her inquiries.

13. Paid Ads with Retargeting

Why: Paid ads without retargeting is like handing out flyers in a windstorm. Retargeting shows your ad again to those who clicked or visited. One small firm in North Carolina implemented a basic Facebook retargeting campaign after running video ads on "Child Custody 101." Their second-touch clickthroughs converted 4x higher than the first. Don't waste your budget–*recapture your audience.*

14. AI-Powered Intake + Follow-Up

Why: You are losing leads at night, on weekends, and during lunch breaks. AI bots fill that gap. Nixon's firm installed a smart intake chatbot that screened leads, answered FAQs, and scheduled consults while his team slept. In the first month, they booked 21 new consults without lifting a finger. That's not "futuristic." That's *today*.

15. Legal Lead Magnet Funnels

Why: Give first. Ask second. When Marcus started offering a free "5 Things to Know Before You Hire a Criminal Defense Lawyer" PDF, opt-ins doubled. That freebie built credibility. It also filtered out price-shoppers. People who read it were better informed—and more ready to retain him.

You Can Do This

You don't need to do all 15 of these at once. You don't need a film crew, a copywriter, or a marketing degree. What you need is the **willingness to try.**

Because the firms that will thrive in the next 10 years aren't the ones with the biggest marketing budgets. They're the ones with the most **marketing courage.**

Courage to experiment. To speak up. To be visible. To learn tools that feel foreign. To admit what you don't know and lean into what you can master.

That's where Law Firm Mentor comes in. We don't just hand you a list of strategies—we walk you through them. We help you customize them. And most importantly, we help you **crush the fear** that keeps so many lawyers from marketing at all.

Marketing is no longer optional. Neither is evolution.

The good news? You're not alone. You've got the tools, the tech, and the team to do this.

Now is the time. Let's crush this.

Bonus Implementation Tip: Choose just **three** of the strategies above to begin with. Execute those consistently for 90 days. Then evaluate, iterate, and expand. Marketing is not a one-and-done—it's a discipline that rewards commitment and visibility over perfection.

And remember: no matter how fast the landscape changes, your willingness to adapt will always be your biggest advantage.

Chaos crushers don't chase trends. They create results.

Marketing gets people to the door. But what happens *after* they knock determines whether your firm grows—or just spins its wheels. Visibility is essential, but it's not enough. You also need to know how to **sell your services with confidence** and **manage your money with clarity**. In the next chapter, we're going to shift from attraction to conversion, and from revenue to profit. Because if marketing is the magnet, then sales and finance are the engine—and it's time to build one that hums.

CHAPTER 8

DOMINATING SALES

If there is one skill that determines the trajectory of your law firm more than any other, it's sales—yet it's also the skill most lawyers are least willing to claim. We dress it up with softer language: consultations, strategy sessions, evaluations. But underneath all the semantics lies a simple truth: every consultation is a moment where someone decides whether to trust you with their problem. And that decision is made through a sales process, whether you acknowledge it or not.

SALES: THE UNSUNG SKILL THAT UNLOCKS YOUR LAW FIRM'S GROWTH

Most law firm owners avoid the word "sales" like it's a bad Yelp review. They prefer to think of what they do in consultations as "advising," "educating," or "screening." But make no mistake: every consultation is a sales conversation—and the outcome of that conversation determines the growth, stability, and financial health of your business.

The problem is that most lawyers were never taught how to sell. And worse, they picked up habits that actively repel clients—like overloading prospects with information, surrendering control of the consultation, avoiding objections, and ghosting follow-up opportunities. These aren't harmless missteps. They are revenue leaks. And they're keeping you from building the firm you want.

In this section, we'll walk through the five biggest sales problems law firm owners face:

1. **Treating Sales Like An Audition**–Overwhelming instead of enrolling.
2. **Failing To Frame The Consultation**–Allowing the prospect to lead.
3. **Lacking Structure**–Talking instead of selling with strategy.
4. **Panicking At Objections**–Missing the chance to guide the decision.
5. **Skipping Follow-Up**–Abandoning the sale before it's closed.

Each of these problems will be explored in depth–with case studies, tactical corrections, and the mindset shifts needed to crush chaos in your consultations and convert more prospects into paying clients.

Let's start with the first–and most costly–mistake.

Sales Problem 1: The Mind is a Minefield: Why Your Legal Consultations Aren't Converting

Most lawyers treat the sales consultation like an audition.

They come in rehearsed, prepared, and ready to put on their best performance–not realizing the audience is too overwhelmed to follow the script. Instead of guiding the prospective client to a confident yes, they flood them with information, options, strategies, and legal analysis. And then they wonder why those clients walk away saying, "I need to think about it."

The truth is, your prospect is not looking for an education. They're looking for relief. They are burdened by fear–fear of spending too much money, fear of being scammed, fear of losing their case, and fear of the emotional fallout of facing the problem in the first place.

When you overload an already-fearful brain with more information than it can process, you create decision paralysis.

And in paralysis, people don't move forward. They retreat.

In this section, we'll dig into the real psychological reasons why your consultations aren't converting. You'll learn how the human brain behaves under legal stress, why the data-dump method backfires, and how to shift from performing to guiding. This isn't about saying less—it's about saying what matters. It's about creating emotional clarity in the middle of mental chaos.

When you stop treating the consultation like a courtroom argument to be won, and start treating it like a leadership moment to be navigated, you'll see your close rate climb—and your client relationships deepen.

Let's unpack the problem.

Legal Consultation as an Audition

Lawyers are not taught how to sell. We are taught how to advocate. And when the time comes to secure new clients for our firms, we often fall back on what we know best: persuading through information. The problem is, legal sales isn't a closing argument in a courtroom—it's an emotional exchange with a person who is often overwhelmed, confused, and afraid. And in that vulnerable space, many lawyers do the exact opposite of what's effective. They data-dump. They "audition."

The legal consultation becomes a performance—one where the attorney unconsciously tries to prove their worth by offering insight after insight, strategy after strategy, hoping the prospect will be impressed enough to say yes. But legal consumers aren't usually looking to be impressed. They're looking for safety. For clarity. For permission to believe that the mess they're in can be handled. And when you drown them in data, you don't create confidence—you create paralysis.

This problem goes deeper than just poor communication. It stems from a fundamental misunderstanding of how the human brain processes uncertainty and fear. When someone is facing a legal issue—be it a custody battle, a criminal charge, a lawsuit, or the death of a loved one—they are not operating from a calm, analytical place. Their brain is in threat response mode. They are already overwhelmed by the implications of the problem they're facing. And instead of soothing that mental state, most lawyers pile more pressure on by offering a buffet of legal theories, possible outcomes, and war stories.

This overload does not move people to action. It traps them in indecision.

To understand why, let's look at a familiar real-world example: The Cheesecake Factory menu.

The Cheesecake Factory has become a running joke in American culture—not just for its enormous portion sizes, but for its menu, which is longer than some novellas. With over 250 menu items spanning dozens of cuisines, it overwhelms the diner with choices. And what do most people do when they sit down? They panic. They scan the menu for ten minutes and still have no idea what to order. Some avoid the restaurant altogether. Others show up with a plan, having already Googled the menu at home to avoid the anxiety of choosing on the spot.

This is the paradox of choice. Social scientists have studied this phenomenon extensively. Too much choice doesn't liberate us—it paralyzes us. In one famous study, shoppers at a grocery store were offered samples of jam. One group saw 6 flavors. Another saw 24. The larger group attracted more curiosity, but the smaller group generated 10 times more purchases. Why? Because fewer choices made the decision easier. When the brain is overloaded, it defaults to avoidance.

Now think about how this shows up in modern dating culture. Apps like Tinder, Bumble, and Hinge give people access to tens of thousands of potential matches. You're no longer choosing from your community or social circle. You're choosing from an endless sea of options. And what's happening? Fewer people are coupling. Commitment is declining. Why? Because the brain, once again, becomes overwhelmed by possibility and defaults to non-decision. "What if there's someone better?" "How do I know I've chosen right?" "Maybe I'll wait and see."

This is exactly what happens in legal consultations.

When a lawyer offers every possible solution, every variable, every hypothetical, it feels like they are being thorough. In truth, they are giving the client a reason to delay. The client leaves with more to think about, not more to act upon. And that is the death of sales.

Legal consumers are not looking for a menu of services. They are looking for leadership. They want someone to say, "Here's the problem, here's how we solve it, and here's what I recommend you do next." They want decisiveness, not data. They want certainty, not complexity.

At Law Firm Mentor, we teach lawyers to shift from auditioning to advising. From overwhelming to orienting. We show you how to lead a consultation with clarity and emotional intelligence–because the person in front of you isn't just evaluating your credentials. They are trying to survive their own story. If you make their next step easier, they will take it with you.

And if you don't, they'll keep looking–not because you weren't good enough, but because their brain wouldn't let them decide.

CASE STUDY

RACHEL PORTER – THE EXPERT WHO COULDN'T CONVERT

Let's now turn to a case study of one law firm owner who learned this lesson the hard way–and transformed her consultations from chaos to clarity.

Background and Challenge

Meet Rachel Porter, a seasoned family law attorney in Connecticut with 17 years of experience. She was known for her polished presentations, robust client packets, and encyclopedic knowledge of divorce law. Clients who hired her loved her. The problem? Not enough people did.

Her consultation-to-client conversion rate hovered around 30%–well below the national average. Rachel couldn't understand it. "I give them everything they need," she'd say. "They get the roadmap. The reassurance. The real deal. Why aren't they hiring me?"

Rachel took immense pride in her ability to evaluate legal problems. It made her feel powerful, competent, and accomplished. When she could look at someone's story, analyze their facts, and produce a legal roadmap, she felt like she was delivering real value. That moment–where she got to be *the expert, where she saw the light bulbs go off in a client's eyes–made all the years of education and effort feel worthwhile. She didn't see herself as selling. She saw herself as helping. Helping people understand the process. Helping them feel less afraid. Helping them see the path forward.*

But underneath her confidence was an unspoken fear: she didn't want to come off as "salesy." She hated the idea of being pushy. Her worst nightmare was a prospect feeling manipulated. So she overcorrected. She focused entirely on delivering value, believing that if she just gave enough, clients would naturally say yes. She didn't pay attention to the client's body language or emotional state. She paid attention to herself–Was she coming across as confident? Did she sound authoritative? Was she demonstrating her worth?

It was during this season that a prospect came to see her–a woman who had been in a 20-year marriage, childless, and unemployed since college. She held a now-obsolete degree in computer science and was completely financially dependent on her husband. She wasn't in love with him anymore, and while she was having an affair with a married neighbor, she didn't want to break up his marriage. She wasn't in love with him either. But the sneaking, the shame, the feeling of stagnation–it was all suffocating. Still, she wasn't ready to leave.

Rachel did what she always did.

She listened. Then she launched.

She began with a summary of Connecticut's equitable distribution laws. Then pivoted to alimony guidelines. She covered the factors courts consider in long-term marriages. Discussed vocational evaluations. Talked about forensic accounting in the event of undisclosed assets. She shared three case examples and printed out a five-page intake roadmap. She mentioned her Martindale-Hubbell rating. Her court appearances in three counties. Her negotiation wins. Her trial experience.

The prospect nodded. Took notes. Even smiled once.

And then said it: "I need to think about it."

Rachel never heard from her again.

Breakthrough and Transformation

During her next coaching call with Law Firm Mentor, Rachel unpacked the conversation. Her coach asked: "What was she afraid of?"

Rachel paused. "I don't know," she admitted. "I was so focused on educating her that I didn't ask."

That was the turning point.

With LFM's help, Rachel restructured her consultations. She began asking more questions. Sitting in silence. Holding space. She learned to recognize when someone wasn't ready to hear strategy—because they hadn't yet faced their own truth. She trained herself to listen beyond the words.

But change didn't come easily.

The next time a similar prospect walked in, Rachel started strong. She asked open-ended questions. She nodded with empathy. But about ten minutes in, she slipped. The silence got uncomfortable. The urge to perform took over. And before she knew it, she was back to giving a legal masterclass.

No sale.

Rachel was devastated. She called her coach in frustration. "I blew it," she said. "I just couldn't sit in the discomfort."

Her coach reassured her: "Sales is a skill. You're unlearning decades of conditioning. Keep practicing."

So she did.

Rachel realized that part of her resistance came from a deeply personal place. Delivering legal information made her feel safe. Smart. Worthy. It was her armor. It was her identity. Her legal knowledge was the thing that always earned her respect, admiration, and confidence. Letting that go–even temporarily–felt like dismantling a part of herself. It made her vulnerable. And that vulnerability felt threatening.

But she pushed through it.

She brought in her staff and role-played consultations. She recorded herself and reviewed the footage. She practiced sitting with silence in everyday conversations–at home, with friends, even at the grocery store. Slowly, the fear subsided. The urge to prove herself quieted. She began to trust the process.

And eventually, she didn't have to try so hard. It felt natural.

Within three months, her conversion rate jumped to 62%.

Not because she learned new legal facts–but because she stopped trying to prove herself and started showing up to serve.

She became a guide instead of a lecturer.

And that changed everything.

Final Word: Learning to Listen and Mastering Sales

The first step to mastering sales isn't learning how to pitch–it's unlearning the urge to perform. When you shift from teacher to leader, from explainer to listener, you create the space for prospects to move forward. You don't have to push. You just have to stop overwhelming.

Takeaway: This shift doesn't just serve your prospects—it serves your peace. You stop walking away from consultations second-guessing yourself, wondering what you could've said differently. Instead, you leave grounded, knowing that your job was to create clarity, not to deliver a TED Talk. And from that grounded place, your confidence grows—not from how much you know, but from how much you helped.

In the next section, we'll look at a second pitfall that sabotages law firm sales: skipping the emotional journey. Because even when you simplify the message, if you don't connect with the heart of the client's fear, you'll still struggle to close.

Let's dive in.

Sales Problem 2: Failing to Set the Frame

If the first rule of sales is "don't overwhelm," then the second is "take the lead." Yet, time and time again, law firm owners walk into consultations and immediately hand the reins to the prospect. Not intentionally—but by default. They open the meeting with, "So, how can I help you today?" or "Tell me what's going on," and suddenly they're no longer the leader in the room. They're reacting. Responding. Chasing the conversation. From there, it's hard to recover authority, let alone close a sale.

The problem is that most lawyers confuse being client-centered with being client-led. In an effort to seem approachable, helpful, and service-oriented, they let the prospect dictate the pace, the flow, and the structure of the meeting. But legal sales isn't about being agreeable—it's about creating clarity. And clarity requires leadership. If you're not setting the frame, you're letting fear, confusion, and emotional chaos run the show.

Here's the real danger: when the conversation lacks structure, the prospect's mind fills in the blanks. They create meaning where there was none. They follow emotional rabbit holes. They interpret silence as judgment, vagueness as dishonesty, and complexity as risk. Without a clear, direct path from problem to solution, their brain will default to stalling tactics—"I'm not sure," "Maybe later," or the ever-familiar, "Let me think about it."

In this section, we're going to dismantle the myth that being a passive listener makes you more trustworthy. We'll show how setting the frame early—clearly and confidently—actually makes prospects feel safer. Because when you take the lead, you give their mind a map. And people don't follow uncertainty—they follow strength. Let's explore what that leadership looks like in the context of legal sales.

When You Don't Set the Frame, Chaos Sets It for You

Every sales conversation has a frame—even if it's not the one you intended.

In law firm consultations, the frame is the unspoken structure that defines *who leads*, *what matters*, and *how decisions will be made*. It's the energetic container that determines whether the prospect feels guided or lost, whether the conversation builds momentum or fizzles into confusion. And when you fail to set that frame consciously and clearly, the consultation takes on a life of its own.

Let's start with what most lawyers do by default. They begin consultations with some variation of:

"So, what brings you in today?"

"Tell me what's going on."

"What can I help you with?"

It sounds polite. Client-focused. Warm. But those openers are more than just casual conversation—they are cues. They signal to the prospect: *you're in charge here.* You set the agenda. You determine the pace. You decide what's relevant.

That would be fine—if prospects were showing up to consultations in a calm, rational, focused state of mind.

They're not.

Prospects come to you in chaos. Emotional chaos. Financial chaos. Internal chaos. Even the most composed person sitting across from you is battling an invisible storm: fear of the unknown, shame over their situation, anxiety about money, worry about the future, guilt about hurting someone they love, lack of clarity about how their issue will be resolved or rage at someone who hurt them. They're looking for relief, but their brain is running in ten different directions. When you hand them the reins, you're giving that chaotic mental state the power to drive the consultation. And chaos never leads to clarity. It leads to paralysis.

Think of it like handing the steering wheel to a toddler mid-highway and saying, "Where do you want to go?" You're not being generous. You're being irresponsible.

Worse, you're abdicating your role as the leader.

And prospects feel it. Subconsciously, they sense that no one is in control. And when that happens, the primal brain takes over and searches for safety. Often, that "safety" comes in the form of retreat—back to the comfort of indecision, postponement, or ghosting.

Contrast that with a framed consultation.

When you start by confidently stating, "Here's what we're going to cover today," you immediately take command of the room. You tell the prospect: *I've got you. You're not alone in this. There is a plan.* You give their brain the roadmap it's desperately craving. And suddenly, their cortisol levels start to drop. Their breathing slows. They stop clenching their jaw. They start to trust you—not because you've dazzled them with credentials, but because you've demonstrated leadership.

This is not just sales theory. This is neuroscience.

The human brain loves structure. It needs sequence. We feel safest when we understand what's coming next and how we fit into it. It's why people enjoy assembly instructions, recipes, and itineraries. It's why chaotic environments—like emergency rooms, crowded airports, and even kids' birthday parties—trigger stress responses. In uncertain environments, we crave authority. Someone to take the wheel. When you set the frame, you become that authority.

Let's use an everyday example: imagine you walk into a new fitness class for the first time. You're nervous. Unsure where to put your bag. You don't know the instructor, the other attendees, or the format of the class. But then the instructor steps up and says: "Welcome! Here's how today's class will go. We'll start with a warm-up, then we'll do three circuits. I'll demo each move first, and you can modify if needed. We'll finish with a cooldown and stretch. Let's get started."

Instantly, you feel better. Why? Because you know what's coming. You feel safe. Supported. Seen.

Now imagine the opposite: you walk in, and the instructor just starts doing burpees. No intro. No roadmap. No context. You're lost, stressed, and already planning your escape.

That's what an unframed consultation feels like.

Let's go deeper.

When lawyers don't set the frame, the conversation becomes reactive. The prospect's emotions steer the dialogue. If they start crying about how their spouse is a narcissist, the consultation becomes a therapy session. If they start venting about money, it becomes a financial advisory call. If they want reassurance, you give it. If they ask legal questions, you start performing. The conversation becomes a series of detours—none of which lead to a sale.

Even worse, you risk skipping the emotional journey entirely. You never get to the real pain. You never learn what they're truly afraid of. You miss the moment where they reveal that their real fear isn't the divorce—it's being alone. Or that their biggest worry isn't the custody schedule—it's their child growing up to hate them.

These emotional reveals are where buying decisions are made. If you don't structure the consultation to guide prospects through those moments, you'll never access the truth behind the "I need to think about it."

The irony is, many lawyers believe setting the frame is too aggressive. They think it sounds rigid, cold, or overly scripted. But the opposite is true. Structure creates safety. Boundaries create trust. And framing the consultation isn't about boxing people in–it's about giving them a container to find their way out of chaos.

It can be as simple as saying:

"Thanks for being here today. Here's how we typically structure these meetings. I'll start by asking you some questions to get a sense of what's going on. Then I'll explain how the law applies to your situation. If it seems like a good fit, we'll talk about next steps. Sound good?"

That one script changes everything. It sets expectations. Establishes control. Calms the nervous system. And reclaims your role as the leader.

Because in the end, legal sales isn't about being liked. It's about being trusted. And trust begins with leadership. Always.

Let's look at two examples of attorneys who struggled with setting the frame–and what changed when they did.

CASE STUDY

DANIELLE, THE ADOPTION ATTORNEY

Danielle Lopez had been practicing adoption law in Georgia for over a decade. Her favorite matters were stepparent adoptions, because she believed in the beauty of legally securing the bonds already formed in blended families. She was warm, nurturing, and deeply invested in her clients. Her reputation for being compassionate had earned her a steady stream of referrals.

Losing the Frame

One Friday morning, a prospect walked into Danielle's office, eager but unhurried. The woman explained that her husband adored her child from a previous relationship and had been raising her for years. They'd casually discussed the idea of making the relationship official through adoption. But there was no pressing urgency–no court order, no upcoming relocation, no legal conflict. It was more of a "someday" goal.

Danielle did what she always did. She warmly welcomed the prospect and opened the floor with, "So tell me what's going on." The prospect smiled and began sharing her story. Danielle listened intently, interjecting gentle affirmations. As the conversation flowed, they shared a few laughs–especially when the prospect detailed her husband's over-the-top efforts to win her daughter's affection, like building a treehouse with working electricity and a snack pantry. At one point, they even bonded over their shared love for cheesy '90s sitcoms.

The energy felt effortless. Danielle felt they were clicking. She was genuinely enjoying the exchange. She validated the woman's journey and explained the legal process in detail–timelines, consent requirements, background checks, and court appearances. She shared her personal story of being adopted herself and how that shaped her approach to law. The woman was receptive and engaged, nodding often and asking thoughtful questions.

When the prospect said, "I'll talk to my husband and get back to you," Danielle wasn't worried. In fact, she was certain this one was a done deal.

But the follow-up never came.

Leading with Structure

Danielle waited days, then weeks. She sent a friendly check-in email. Nothing. She finally admitted to her team that she was stunned. "It went so well," she insisted. "She even hugged me at the end!"

When Danielle brought this to her LFM coach, the response was firm: "You never set the frame."

It was true. Danielle had let the prospect lead the consultation. She hadn't created structure. She hadn't explained what they were going to cover, how the meeting would flow, or what decisions needed to be made. Instead, she let the rapport carry the moment, believing that connection alone would drive conversion.

Her coach explained that emotional bonding is not a substitute for leadership. "You gave her a therapy session," the coach said. "Not a sales conversation."

At first, Danielle resisted the feedback. "But I let her talk because I wanted to understand her!" she protested. Her coach replied, "You can do that–and still lead. Frame first. Guide second."

So Danielle began to shift. She adopted a new consultation script:

"Thanks for being here. Here's how today's meeting will go. First, I'll ask you a few questions to understand your situation. Then I'll explain the process and how it applies to you. Finally, if it feels like a good fit, we'll discuss what next steps look like. Does that sound okay?"

It felt awkward at first. Danielle worried she sounded robotic. But over time, her consultations began to feel more focused. More efficient. Prospects showed up better prepared. And most importantly, more of them started to say yes.

Her conversion rate jumped 20% in just two months.

Final Word: Connection Isn't Conversion

Danielle's warmth and empathy built instant connection–but she let the conversation unfold without direction. The rapport was genuine, yet without structure or a clear purpose, the prospect left feeling heard but not guided.

Through coaching, Danielle learned that leadership in a consultation doesn't diminish compassion–it amplifies it. By framing each meeting with clear steps and expectations, she created a sense of direction that reassured clients and increased conversions.

Takeaway: Connection opens the door–but leadership invites clients to walk through it.

CASE STUDY

DEMETRIUS, THE EMPLOYMENT LAWYER

Demetrius Patel was a sharp, strategic employment defense attorney based in Chicago. His firm focused on helping small businesses stay compliant and out of court. He was logical, detailed, and deeply risk-averse–traits that served him well in litigation but sometimes made him stiff in consultations.

When Logic isn't Leadership

One afternoon, Demetrius met with a business owner who'd recently avoided a lawsuit from a disgruntled ex-employee. The business owner was rattled and wanted to prevent future problems. He spoke about needing help with contracts, anti-harassment training, and general compliance.

But the conversation quickly went off-track.

The prospect began sharing the saga of the ex-employee: text message screenshots, secondhand gossip from staff, and even speculation about the former employee's mental health. Demetrius, unsure how to redirect, listened patiently. He took notes. He offered legal insights when asked. But he never set the frame.

The meeting meandered. By the end, Demetrius had covered three possible service models, mentioned his retainer options, and even offered to review the company handbook–gratis. The prospect smiled, said he'd "run it by the team," and left.

Demetrius felt deflated.

Reclaiming Authority

When he brought the story to LFM, his coach asked, "Who was leading that meeting?"

"I guess... he was," Demetrius admitted.

His coach replied, "Exactly. He brought chaos. You let it steer the meeting. That's why he walked out with no clarity–and no urgency."

Demetrius started practicing a stronger frame. He opened meetings with a clear agenda. He stopped taking the bait on emotional detours. He redirected when prospects wandered.

Most importantly, he reclaimed authority.

And as a result, his retainer sales doubled in ninety days.

Final Word: Control the Conversation, or It Controls You

The lesson here is unmistakable: prospects want to be led. They may not say it, they may not even know it–but when they walk into your consultation full of emotion, confusion, and fear, they're subconsciously scanning for someone who can restore order. If you don't step up and frame the conversation with authority, you're effectively handing the steering wheel to a panic-stricken passenger and hoping they'll drive you both to safety. That's not client-centered; that's client-abandonment dressed up as kindness. And in legal sales, it's a surefire path to stalled decisions, ghosted follow-ups, and consultations that "felt great" but produced nothing.

Takeaway: These examples make it clear: when you don't set the frame, chaos does. And chaos never leads to commitment.

Fortunately, the solution is simple–though not always easy. Setting the frame is a learnable skill, and once implemented, it fundamentally transforms the trajectory of your consultations. You move from passive pleaser to trusted advisor. You guide the emotional journey instead of reacting to it. And you begin to hear fewer "I need to think about it" and more "Where do I sign?"

But even with a strong frame in place, there's another hidden danger that can sabotage your sales process–letting your own discomfort drive the consultation. In the next section, we'll explore how lawyers accidentally slow down or stall the sale when they feel awkward talking about money.

Let's dig in.

Sales Problem 3: Not Knowing What to Ask

By the time most lawyers sit down for a consultation, they're already switching into "problem-solving mode." Years of legal training and practice have wired us to listen for the facts, connect them to the law, and deliver sound advice as quickly and efficiently as possible. We think we're being helpful–showing our knowledge, building trust, proving we're the best option. But here's the truth: solving legal problems isn't what makes the sale.

Selling is not about giving the right answers. It's about asking the right questions.

And that shift–from answering to asking–is one of the hardest transitions for lawyers to make in the sales process. When you sit down with a prospective client, you are not conducting a legal consultation. You are leading a legal sales conversation. And those are two completely different things. A legal consultation is designed to diagnose legal problems. A legal sales conversation is designed to uncover emotional pain, urgency, and desire–then build a bridge to a better future. That bridge is you.

If you rush to deliver value, you skip over what motivates the buying decision. You miss the chance to identify the true afflictions and aspirations. You gloss over what they've tried before, what they fear will happen next, and what's truly at stake if they do nothing. Those questions don't just build connection–they build commitment.

In this section, we'll walk through how to reframe your consultations with curiosity. You'll learn how to lead with questions that guide prospects to sell themselves. Because when you ask the right questions, the answers they give will close the sale for you.

Description Of The Problem

At the heart of every successful legal sale lies a series of well-crafted, emotionally resonant, and logically sequenced questions. These questions aren't random–they're rooted in human psychology and buyer behavior. But most lawyers have never been trained to think this way. Instead, we rely on our instincts, which often lead us astray. Rather than guiding prospects through the emotional and practical journey that drives a sale, we revert to what we know: asking about facts so we can supply legal answers. That's not a sales conversation. That's a legal assessment.

To shift into true sales leadership, we must reorient our questioning around four key areas: the affliction, the aspiration, the attempted solution, and the anticipated consequence. These four pillars form the architecture of every buying decision. And when you fail to explore even one of them, the entire structure wobbles.

The Affliction: What's Really Going On?

The affliction is not just the legal issue–it's the human experience of that issue. Too often, lawyers stay at the surface: "You're going through a divorce," or "You're facing a discrimination claim." But that doesn't tell us what's happening emotionally. Are they scared, angry, embarrassed, overwhelmed? Do they feel powerless or betrayed? What's it like to live with that uncertainty every day? What's the cost of doing nothing?

When you only ask fact-based questions, you miss the opportunity to tap into the emotional drivers that fuel urgency. Facts rarely sell. Feelings do. A woman might want a divorce, but the real pain could be the fear that her children will grow up thinking emotional abuse is normal. A business owner might want to avoid a lawsuit, but the true affliction is his paralyzing anxiety that one misstep could destroy the company he built from scratch.

Sales questioning starts with empathy. When you ask, "What's been the hardest part of this for you?" or "How is this impacting your day-to-day life?" you move the conversation from intellect to emotion. And once you're there, you've tapped into the well of motivation that actually drives decisions.

The Aspiration: Where Do They Want to Be?

Once you've uncovered the affliction, the next step is to paint the vision. This is the future state the prospect wants to live in. It's not enough to say, "You want custody," or "You want compliance." You have to understand what that future *feels* like. What will change when the problem is solved? How will they sleep better, breathe easier, show up differently in their lives?

Many lawyers gloss over this part because it feels vague or impractical. But skipping the aspiration is like trying to sell a GPS without asking where someone wants to go. If you don't know their destination, how can you chart a path to it?

Asking, "What would a successful outcome look like for you?" or "What would it mean to you if this were resolved?" opens the door to emotionally compelling answers. You'll hear things like, "I'd finally feel safe," or "I'd have peace of mind for the first time in years." That language creates emotional stakes. It transforms a transaction into a transformation. And people don't buy legal services–they buy the transformation.

The Attempted Solution: What Have They Tried Before?

Prospects aren't blank slates. By the time they get to you, they've usually tried something–whether it was hiring a different lawyer, Googling answers, asking friends, or simply doing nothing. Understanding their past efforts tells you how badly they want change, what didn't work, and where the emotional residue still lives.

When you ask, "What have you tried to fix this so far?" or "Have you spoken to any other professionals about this?" you gather context.

But more importantly, you build credibility by listening. You show respect for their journey. You let them explain why they're still stuck.

And their answers give you gold. Maybe they hired a bargain lawyer who ghosted them. Maybe they spoke to five firms who all scared them into inaction. Maybe they did nothing because they were in denial. Each answer is a roadmap for how to position your solution—not just as a service, but as the service that finally moves them forward.

The Anticipated Consequence: What Happens if They Don't Fix It?

This is the urgency question. It's also the one most lawyers skip. We assume the risk is obvious. But prospects aren't always logical. They may minimize the stakes. They may believe they have time. They may be frozen in fear. Unless you explore the consequence of inaction, they'll stay in limbo.

Ask: "What happens if you don't do anything about this?" or "What are you most afraid could happen if this continues?" These questions surface the stakes. They force the prospect to consider the cost of delay. And often, that cost is emotional, not just financial or legal.

A parent might realize that their child's well-being is at risk. A business owner might admit that stress is affecting their health. These are buying triggers. When a prospect says, "I can't keep living like this," you're no longer selling. You're helping them make a life-changing decision.

Mastering sales questioning isn't about manipulation. It's about illumination. You're shining a light on what matters most, connecting the dots between pain, desire, and possibility. And when done well, the prospect doesn't feel sold to. They feel seen.

That's what creates conversions. And that's the difference between legal advising and legal sales.

CASE STUDY

PEDRO, THE DWI ATTORNEY

Pedro Alvarado ran a solo criminal defense practice in a mid-sized town in Texas. A former public defender turned private practitioner, he had carved out a niche focusing almost exclusively on DWI cases. With a sharp mind and courtroom swagger, Pedro was known for being tenacious in trial and compassionate toward clients. But there was one area where he repeatedly fell short: converting consultations into paying clients.

Winning the Legal Battle, Losing the Emotional One

It wasn't that prospects didn't like him. In fact, most left the consultation praising his professionalism and warmth. He'd answer every question thoroughly, anticipate legal pitfalls, and reassure them they were in capable hands. But when it came time to hire him, many would say, "Thanks, I just need to think about it," and then disappear.

Pedro was baffled. "I'm giving them gold," he told his LFM coach during a group sales training. "They leave knowing exactly *what to expect legally. How is that not value?"*

That's when the coach stepped in and challenged him: "Pedro, you're solving the wrong problem. They're not coming to you for answers–they're coming to feel understood. You're winning the legal argument, but losing the emotional sale."

Pedro was defensive at first. "I ask them why they were pulled over. I ask if they took a breathalyzer. That's relevant, right?"

"It's legally relevant," the coach replied, "but not emotionally compelling. You're treating it like a deposition. This isn't cross-examination. It's a sales conversation. And that means leading with curiosity, not control."

Pedro sat back, quiet.

Reframing Consultation

So the coach introduced him to the four core questions–questions designed not just to gather facts, but to uncover pain, urgency, desire, and impact:

1. ***Why now?***
2. ***What have you tried already?***
3. ***What are you most afraid will happen if this doesn't get resolved?***
4. ***How will your life be different when this is over?***

At first, Pedro couldn't believe it. "That sounds like therapy," he said, half-joking. "My clients just want to stay out of jail."

"No," the coach corrected. "Your clients want to stop feeling like criminals. They want their freedom, their dignity, their peace of mind. You need to ask questions that get them there."

To help him bridge the gap, the coach walked Pedro through a mock consultation. The coach played Pedro, and Pedro played the role of a DWI prospect–a 42-year-old father who'd been pulled over leaving a friend's birthday dinner. No prior offenses, but he was terrified of losing his license and, with it, his ability to drive his kids to school.

The mock went like this:

Coach: *"So, why now? What made you decide to come in today rather than wait until your court date?"*

Pedro (in character): *"Because... well, I don't want to screw this up."*

Coach: *"What have you already done about it?"*

Pedro: *"Nothing yet. I've just been reading online... and speaking of which, is it true that I could be thrown in jail for this, rather than just lose my license?"*

Coach: *"I understand you're concerned about that, and we'll definitely address this very valid question shortly. Right now, though, I just want to make sure I understand how you're processing what's* *happening. So, you've said you've been reading information online. What else have you done?"*

Pedro: *"Not much, honestly. I talked to a buddy of mine who went through something similar, but his case was totally different. And I keep going down these internet rabbit holes, and every article contradicts the last one. I feel like I'm spinning."*

Coach: *"That makes sense. It sounds like you're overwhelmed with too much information and no clear plan. Let me ask–what are you most afraid will happen if this doesn't get resolved the way you hope?"*

Pedro: *"I mean, losing my license would suck–but the worst part? I'm divorced. I do the school runs. If I can't drive, I can't have my kids. My ex is already looking for any excuse to get full custody. This would hand it to her."*

Coach: *"That's a heavy weight to carry. And when this* is *over–when it's handled and behind you–what changes for you?"*

Pedro: *"I'll be able to sleep again. Right now, I'm waking up at 3 a.m. with my chest tight, picturing myself being cuffed in front of my daughter. I know that's extreme, but... it's where my head goes."*

Pedro sat back, stunned. "I've never heard a client talk like that before."

"That's because you've never asked them to," the coach said. "Your job isn't to fix the legal problem–it's to help them imagine the outcome and feel safe choosing you as the path to get there."

Leading With Curiosity And Compassion

Pedro committed. He wrote the four core questions down and taped them to his desk. He practiced them out loud. He used them in team role-plays. At first, it felt awkward. He had to fight his impulse to jump in and reassure. But over time, something shifted. Prospects began opening up. They got emotional. They thanked him–not for answering their questions, but for asking them.

A few weeks later, a man came in for a consult–a small business owner who'd been pulled over after a networking dinner. He was embarrassed, anxious, and already defensive.

Pedro opened the meeting differently. "Before we get into the details," he said, "I want to understand where you are. Why today? Why now?"

The man blinked. "Because I haven't slept in a week."

Pedro nodded. "Tell me what you've tried already to manage the situation."

"I called two lawyers. They just told me their price and said they'd see me in court. I need someone who actually gives a damn."

Pedro leaned in. "What are you most afraid will happen if this doesn't go your way?"

The man exhaled, then whispered, "I've worked my whole life to build my business. If I get a conviction, my commercial insurance will triple–or worse. This could bankrupt me."

And finally: "When this is over–when we've handled it–what will that mean for you?"

The man choked up. "I'll be able to go home and look my daughter in the eye without shame."

By the end of the consultation, the man pulled out his card and said, "You're the guy."

Pedro didn't even have to pitch.

From that point forward, consultations felt different. He wasn't proving himself. He was connecting. And the sales followed.

His close rate rose 40% over the next 60 days.

He didn't change his pricing. He didn't change his credentials. He changed his questions.

And that changed everything.

Final Word: Transforming Conversations

The real magic of a sales consultation doesn't happen when you give the perfect legal answer–it happens when the prospect hears themselves say something they've never admitted out loud. When they confront the fear they've been avoiding. When they articulate the cost of doing nothing. And when they envision, often for the first time, what it would mean to finally be on the other side of the chaos. That kind of clarity doesn't come from telling–it comes from asking. Purposefully. Strategically. Compassionately. And it's those questions–not your resume, your courtroom wins, or your Ivy League degree–that move a prospect to say yes.

When lawyers make the shift from diagnosing to discovering, from solving to selling, they don't just improve their close rate–they transform the consultation into a profound moment of insight for the prospect. You become the first person who really sees them. And in that space, trust is born. In the next section, we'll show you how to build on that trust by communicating your value in a way that's clear, compelling, and worthy of investment.

Takeaway: Once you've uncovered the truth, your next job is to show them why you're the only one who can deliver the solution.

Sales Problem 4: Mishandling Objections

Objections. The word alone is enough to make most lawyers tighten their jaw and brace for conflict. Whether it's "I can't afford it," "I need to think about it," or "I have to talk to my spouse," objections often feel like rejection wrapped in polite conversation. And for many law firm owners, this is the exact moment where a solid consultation suddenly collapses. You can feel the energy shift. You freeze, or you retreat. You backpedal. You soften the terms, lower the price, or worse–end the meeting with a meek, "Well, just let me know."

Here's the truth: **objections are not rejections. Objections are buying signals.** They only show up when the prospect is mentally wrestling with a real decision. Objections mean they're considering it seriously enough to start troubleshooting their own fears. But when you panic, avoid, or mishandle those objections, the conversation stalls and the prospect walks.

This isn't conflict. This isn't debate. Handling objections isn't about winning. It's about leading.

Most lawyers were never taught how to respond without getting defensive or crumbling under discomfort. So they either argue ("Well, our rates are fair for the value") or they retreat ("Okay, no worries, think about it"). Neither response serves the prospect–and neither leads to a sale.

In this section, we're going to demystify objections. You'll learn that objections are not barriers–they're opportunities. When handled with confidence and compassion, objections become the final stepping stone toward a yes. We'll show you exactly how to move from awkward tension to graceful leadership using a simple, repeatable process. And when you master this skill, closing becomes not just easier–but inevitable.

When Objections Derail the Sale

It happens every day in law firm consultations across the country. Things are going well. The prospect is nodding, engaged, asking questions. You've built rapport. You've set the frame. You've asked the right questions. You can feel them warming up, picturing their life after this legal mess is handled. You start to lean in toward closing the sale.

Then it happens.

They cross their arms. They shift back in their chair. Their voice drops just a hair when they say, "Yeah...this all sounds good. But honestly, I didn't expect it to be this expensive." Or worse, "I need to talk to my spouse." Or the dagger of all daggers: "I just need to think about it."

Cue the pit in your stomach.

Everything about the energy changes in that instant. The warm, collaborative conversation suddenly feels awkward, heavy, charged. You feel the tightness in your chest. You glance down, shift in your chair, scramble for the right words. And whether you realize it or not, your brain is screaming one thing: **DANGER**.

Because that's what objections trigger—your nervous system's fight-or-flight response. You're no longer the composed professional leading the conversation. You're the kid getting picked last in gym class. The associate being dressed down by a judge. The teenager being ghosted after a promising date. Your mind translates an objection as rejection, and rejection hits the primal part of the brain like a threat to your survival.

And so, like any threat, you react. Some lawyers go into **fight mode**. They stiffen, defensively justifying their fees or policies.

Well, this is standard in the industry.

Our rates are fair given the complexity of your case.

If you value doing this right, this is the cost.

Others drop into **flight mode**. They backpedal. They soften their stance.

I totally understand. Take your time.

We can follow up in a few weeks.

If you want, I can email you a recap so you can think it over.

In both cases, what's really happening is the same: you've abandoned the leadership role. You've let the objection become the end of the conversation instead of the bridge to the close.

Here's what most lawyers completely misunderstand about objections:

Objections are not the problem. Objections are part of the process.

In fact, an objection means you're doing something right. It means the prospect is considering hiring you seriously enough that their brain has moved into "problem-solving" mode. They're trying to figure out:

Can I afford this?

Can I justify this?

Will my spouse agree?

Am I making the right decision?

If they weren't considering hiring you, they wouldn't bother objecting at all. They'd nod, thank you for your time, and walk out without ever raising a concern.

The real problem isn't the objection.

It's how you respond to it.

When you freeze, panic, or retreat at the moment of an objection, the prospect experiences something subtle but devastating. They feel the leadership energy drain out of the room. They were looking to you as the person who could guide them through the scariest, most uncertain problem in their life–a custody battle, a criminal charge, a lawsuit, the risk of losing their home, their marriage, their business.

And if you collapse at the first sign of discomfort, what you're unconsciously telling them is: *If I can't handle this tough conversation about money, how am I going to handle the much tougher conversations coming with your opposing counsel, your ex, the prosecutor, the judge?*

The objection isn't just about money. It's a test–whether they realize it or not–of your capacity to lead under pressure.

What most lawyers don't realize is that objections are never really about money.

It might sound like money. It might present like money. But peel back the layers, and it's rarely the true barrier.

When a prospect says, "I can't afford this," what they often mean is:

I'm scared this won't work.

I don't trust that I can handle the consequences if this doesn't go right.

I'm afraid to make a mistake and look foolish.

I've never invested this much in myself or my problems before.

When they say, "I need to think about it," it often means:

I'm overwhelmed and don't have enough clarity to make a decision.

I'm waiting for someone else to give me permission.

I'm afraid of committing because then it becomes real.

And when they say, "I need to talk to my spouse," sometimes it's true. But sometimes it's code for:

I need an escape hatch from this decision because I'm uncomfortable"

What makes it worse is that lawyers are socialized to avoid discomfort.

The same professionalism that teaches us to remain calm in court, to be measured with clients, to avoid confrontation at networking events also teaches us to default to politeness in sales. *And polite avoidance kills conversions.*

But here's the beautiful flip side:

When you realize that objections are simply part of the buying decision–not barriers–you start to meet them with curiosity instead of fear.

Imagine if, instead of tightening up when a prospect says, "I can't afford this," you leaned in and calmly asked, "I hear you. Can you help me understand–is it that you didn't expect legal fees at this level, or is it that you're not sure about the return on investment?"

Or when someone says, "I need to talk to my spouse," you could reply, "Absolutely–I'd want my spouse involved, too. What's important for them to know about why you're considering moving forward?"

This isn't arguing. It's guiding. It's coaching someone through the fear that naturally comes with making a serious decision about their life, their family, or their business.

Because here's the thing–if a prospect gets cold feet over a sales conversation and you let them retreat without helping them work through it, you're not serving them. You're letting them stay stuck. You're letting their chaos win.

And your job–the reason they came to you–is to help them *out* of chaos.

Sales Problem 5: Failing to Follow Up

You wrapped the consult. It went well. The prospect seemed engaged—maybe even enthusiastic. They nodded at the right moments, asked smart questions, and didn't flinch (too hard) at the price. They said they needed to "think about it," "check with their spouse," or "sleep on it." You smiled, thanked them for their time, and told them to reach out when they were ready.

And then... nothing.

A day passes. Then a week. You think about following up but feel awkward—don't want to seem pushy. You've already had a great consult. If they want to hire you, they will... right?

Wrong.

Here's the hard truth: **failure to follow up is a silent killer of law firm revenue**. It's not that the consult didn't go well. It's not that the prospect changed their mind. It's not even that they didn't want to hire you. It's that they're human—and humans need help making decisions when emotions fade and chaos creeps back in.

Most lawyers assume that silence after a consult means "no." In reality, it often means "not yet"—and you just let the moment pass. You surrendered your leadership role the second you left the next move up to them.

In this section, we're going to unpack why follow-up is one of the most neglected (and profitable) parts of the sales process. You'll learn how to reconnect with prospects without being needy, how to revive interest even weeks after the initial meeting, and how to follow up with confidence, compassion, and conviction—so you don't just have good consults, you have closed deals.

When the Follow-Up Falls Flat

Let's talk about the biggest sales killer no one ever thinks is the problem: **the silence that follows a consult.**

You know the moment. The consult ends. You've shared your insight, built rapport, walked them through what it would look like to work with your firm. You feel that buzz—that momentary high of having done your job well. The prospect smiled, thanked you, said all the right things. "This was really helpful," they said. "I'll be in touch." You smiled back, shook their hand, and maybe even felt a little rush of confidence that you had this one in the bag.

And then... they disappear.

No email. No call. No signature on the retainer agreement. Just *ghosted*—as if that great consult never happened. Days pass. Then a week. You think about following up. You think about calling. But the voice in your head whispers: *If they wanted to work with me, they would have reached out. I don't want to be annoying.*

So you sit. You wait. You move on to the next consult, hoping this time things will be different.

But here's the harsh, unfiltered truth: **your job wasn't over when the consultation ended.** In fact, for many prospects, the *real* sales conversation only begins after that first meeting. The quiet that follows a consult isn't a closed door—it's a wide-open window. And if you're not following up, you're not closing. You're leaving opportunity, revenue, and service on the table.

The Myth of the One-Call Close

Most lawyers have unconsciously bought into the fantasy that great sales happen in a single, magical consult. One conversation, and the client eagerly signs. And sure—sometimes, that happens. But often, it doesn't. Why?

Because your prospect is dealing with **emotional chaos.**

Maybe they just learned their spouse is filing for divorce. Maybe they were just arrested. Maybe their parent died and now they have to sort out an estate, or their ex is trying to take their child across the country, or they just got sued by a former business partner. Whatever the crisis is, it's *raw*. It's overwhelming. Their nervous system is on overdrive.

So they come to your consult in fight-or-flight mode. They're nodding, they're listening—but their brain is scrambling to process information while simultaneously trying to make a high-stakes decision. They might understand that hiring you is the right move, but the magnitude of that decision hasn't fully landed yet.

They leave the consult and enter what we call **the emotional vacuum**—a space where the sense of urgency starts to fade, and logic and fear start to take over. In that vacuum, chaos reasserts itself. Their friends start giving unsolicited advice. Their cousin's wife's neighbor who "went through something similar" starts feeding them horror stories. And if you're not there—if your voice is absent in the days that follow—then someone else's voice fills that void.

That someone else might be another lawyer. Or a spouse. Or even just their own self-doubt.

Your follow-up is the bridge between emotion and decision. It's your opportunity to anchor their attention back to what matters—why they came to you in the first place. And if you're not showing up in that critical window, you're not just losing the sale—you're failing to lead.

Why Lawyers Resist Following Up

The reasons lawyers resist following up are as varied as they are emotionally charged. For some, it's fear. *What if they say no? What if they didn't like me? What if I come across as desperate or salesy?*

Others mask that fear with self-righteousness: *If they're not motivated to move forward, they're not my ideal client.* Or they tell themselves, *I'm too busy to chase people. I don't have time to play cat-and-mouse.*

But let's call it what it is: **avoidance.**

Avoidance dressed up as professionalism. Avoidance rooted in discomfort with rejection. Avoidance fueled by the lie that follow-up is harassment.

In truth, when done with skill and service, follow-up is not desperate—it's **devoted**. It says to your prospect: *I haven't forgotten you. I still believe I can help you. And I care enough about your outcome not to let you drift back into crisis without a lifeline.*

You don't need to beg. You don't need to chase. You need to **lead**.

Follow-Up is a System, Not a Feeling

Too many law firm owners treat follow-up as a feeling–*I'll know when I should reach out again*–instead of what it truly is: **a system.** You don't wait to "feel" like sending out your retainer agreement. You don't "feel" your way into discovery responses. So why are you treating follow-up like a maybe instead of a must?

The truth is, **80% of sales are closed after the fifth point of contact.** And yet, most lawyers give up after one or two. That means you're leaving tens–if not hundreds–of thousands of dollars on the table every year simply because you don't have a follow-up protocol.

Prospects are busy. They're emotional. They forget. They get distracted. Life pulls them in another direction. But that doesn't mean they don't need you. It just means you need to stay in their world *long enough* to help them take action.

This doesn't mean daily calls and emails until they block you. It means having a clear, compassionate, and consistent system:

- A set schedule for follow-up points: 24 hours after, 3 days later, 1 week later, etc.
- A system to document and track where they are in the decision cycle
- A tone that feels supportive, not pushy
- A mindset rooted in service, not desperation

And perhaps most importantly: **you need to believe that following up is part of your duty as their potential lawyer.** Because if you *can* help them–and you *don't* follow up–you've left them at the mercy of their chaos. You let them drown when you could have thrown the lifeline.

The Consultation is Not the Close

So many lawyers treat the consult like a finish line. It's not. It's the starting gun. Everything that happens after the consult is where the sale actually gets made–through intentional follow-up, persistent leadership, and compassionate reminders that you haven't forgotten them and you still believe in their outcome.

Sales isn't about who makes the flashiest pitch. It's about who stays in the conversation long enough to earn trust.

And if you're not following up?

You're not just missing out on clients. You're surrendering your role as a guide–and leaving people stuck in the very chaos they came to you to escape.

CASE STUDY

RECLAIMING THE SALE AFTER THE SILENCE – VANESSA'S STORY

Vanessa Cortes was the kind of lawyer every client wanted in their corner. Smart. Steady. Seasoned. A former public defender turned private practitioner, she'd spent the better part of a decade fighting fiercely for people caught in the crosshairs of the criminal justice system. Her boutique law firm in Houston had a loyal client base, a hard-earned reputation for excellence, and a small but dedicated team that believed deeply in their mission.

But if you looked under the hood, Vanessa's business was quietly bleeding. Not from bad service. Not from malpractice. But from an invisible wound that cut her cash flow to the bone.

She wasn't closing nearly enough consults.

More specifically–she wasn't following up after them.

When Silence Feels like Rejection

Vanessa had always prided herself on running a "non-salesy" firm. Her consultations were educational, compassionate, and human. She gave clients real value in that initial meeting, often outlining their best- and worst-case scenarios, breaking down potential outcomes, and explaining her legal strategy without sugarcoating a thing. And her consults felt *good. People thanked her, often tearfully. They told her how much clarity she had given them. They left hugging her. But they also... left.*

And they didn't always come back.

At first, she chalked it up to the nature of the business. "Not everyone's ready," she told herself. "Some people are shopping around. Some just can't afford it. That's not on me."

But the pattern continued. Her calendar stayed full, yet her conversion rate hovered stubbornly around 25%. That meant three out of four people who met with her didn't hire her. And while her team kept generating leads, the firm wasn't growing. It was surviving. Barely.

That's when Vanessa came to Law Firm Mentor. During her intake call with one of our coaches, she rattled off the usual suspects: not enough time, too many low-quality leads, burnout from doing it all herself. But when we dug into her sales process, the issue was glaring:

She had no follow-up system. None.

She'd send a single email after the consult–"Let me know if you have any other questions"–and then move on. If the prospect didn't reply, that was the end of it. She'd write them off as a "no" and focus on the next person. Her CRM was basically a glorified address book, and her team wasn't even trained to track consult outcomes.

"You realize you're sitting on a goldmine of almost-clients, right?" we asked.

Vanessa blinked. "What do you mean?"

We pulled up a report of everyone who had come in for a consult in the past 90 days but hadn't hired her. There were seventy-two people *on that list.*

Seventy-two people who had been vulnerable enough to share their legal crisis with her.

Who had taken time out of their lives to seek her out.

Who, at some point, thought Vanessa might be the solution to their problem.

And not a single one had received a second point of contact.

Building a System That Works

Vanessa flushed. "But I don't want to pressure them," she said. "If they want to hire me, they will. I don't want to seem desperate."

We nodded. "What if it's not about pressure? What if it's about leadership?"

That was the turning point.

We walked Vanessa through a simple reframe: follow-up is not pestering–it's service. If someone comes to you in crisis and you know you can help them, letting them drift back into chaos without support isn't noble. It's negligent. They came to her for guidance, not just information. And she had left them in limbo.

Of course, the fix wasn't just about mindset–it was about systems.

We helped Vanessa design a ***5-touch follow-up sequence:***

1. *A warm, personalized email within 24 hours of the consult.*
2. *A short check-in call or voicemail on Day 3.*
3. *A second email on Day 5 that revisits the pain points discussed.*
4. *A value-driven touchpoint on Day 8–an article, checklist, or FAQ that speaks directly to their concerns.*
5. *A final email or call on Day 12, framed with gentle urgency and invitation.*

We also built simple automations in her CRM so her assistant could track every consult, schedule follow-ups, and escalate warm leads back to Vanessa for re-engagement.

*But here's the truth–***Vanessa didn't love it at first.**

She felt awkward leaving voicemails. She hated the sound of her own voice in follow-up videos. She second-guessed whether she was bothering people. There were days she almost pulled the plug.

But then the responses started coming in.

Clients she thought were gone forever suddenly emailed back:

"I'm so glad you reached out. Life's been crazy, but I do want to move forward."

"I've been thinking about our meeting every day. Thanks for the reminder."

"You know what? I'm ready."

Within the first 30 days of using the new follow-up sequence, Vanessa closed nine consults that otherwise would have gone cold. That's over $45,000 in booked revenue from leads she had previously written off.

By month two, her conversion rate had jumped to 46%. By month three, it hit 61%.

And something even more surprising happened: ***Vanessa started to feel proud of her sales process.*** *She realized that following up didn't make her pushy–it made her powerful. It reminded prospects that she wasn't just another lawyer. She was the one who didn't forget them. The one who stayed in the conversation. The one who cared enough to call back.*

Final Word: Follow-Up is Where the Sales Lives

Now, every consult ends with a clear next step. Her team knows exactly when and how to re-engage. Her prospects don't fall through the cracks. And Vanessa? She no longer confuses silence with rejection. She sees it for what it really is: hesitation that needs a nudge.

Vanessa's follow-up game didn't just rescue her revenue. It restored her confidence.

Takeaway: In a world where chaos is loud and legal problems are scary, **being the voice that doesn't disappear is one of the greatest services you can offer.**

Conclusion: The Fortune *Is* in the Follow-Up

Sales doesn't end when the consult does. It ends when the prospect makes a decision—and far too often, that decision never comes because you vanished too soon. By mastering the art and science of follow-up, you transform from a helpful voice in a moment of crisis into a trusted guide who sees them through the fog. That's not being pushy. That's being present. That's being a professional. That's being the leader they need.

When you adopt systems of follow-up rooted in service—not scarcity—you stop leaving your revenue to chance. You reclaim the power to close with integrity, consistency, and confidence. And you begin to experience the beautiful compounding effect that comes from converting more of what you already have.

But as your sales numbers rise, so too does your financial complexity. More clients means more money. More money means more decisions. And more decisions without a strategy can turn windfalls into waste.

In the next chapter, we'll leave the world of sales and step fully into the realm of finance. Because real freedom isn't just about making more—it's about managing wisely, planning intentionally, and mastering the flow of money in and out of your firm.

Let's turn your financial success into lasting sustainability.

Conversion Scorecard

The challenges to converting consultations to sales discussed in this chapter are paired with a Conversion Scorecard in **Appendix A**. The scorecard will help you assess your consultation process and identify where your challenges may be, with brief guidance on how to interpret your results. Before moving on, you may find it helpful to assess how the conversion challenges described in this chapter are currently showing up in your firm. In addition, expanded, interactive versions of all our decision-support tools are available online, accessible via links and QR codes included in the Appendix.

CHAPTER 9

FINANCIAL FREEDOM

FROM FINANCIAL MANAGEMENT TO FINANCIAL MASTERY

Let's be honest—most law firm owners don't want to think about money unless they're swimming in it or drowning under it.

When things are going well, we don't question it. The bank account looks healthy, the bills are paid, and we assume we're "doing fine." But when things tighten—when payroll is looming, a big retainer doesn't come in, or the tax bill hits like a sucker punch—that's when panic sets in. That's when we realize we've been **managing money emotionally**, not strategically.

Here's the truth: most lawyers weren't taught how to think like business owners. We were taught how to bill. How to track time. How to get the work done. But no one handed us a playbook for building a business that actually **functions** financially—let alone thrives.

That ends here.

This chapter is your financial reckoning—but the empowering kind. We're not here to beat you up over bad decisions or overwhelm you with spreadsheets. We're here to show you how to think, plan, and act like a financially free entrepreneur—one who runs the numbers instead of being run by them.

We're going to cover five key areas that unlock true financial mastery: knowing your One Number, forecasting your future (not just reacting to the past), avoiding the lure of fast but fatal debt, budgeting like a strategist–not a martyr–and creating compensation models that motivate your team *without* bleeding your bottom line.

You don't have to become an accountant. But you do have to become accountable.

Because financial freedom isn't just about making more money. It's about learning how to **keep it, use it, and grow it–on purpose.**

Let's begin.

WHEN THE NUMBERS DON'T ADD UP

I started my law firm with a partner. We quickly realized that we wanted different things and could not both create what we wanted if we pursued the preferences and passions of the other. So, over pizza one Friday, with our accountant, we peacefully divvied up our law firm and went our separate ways.

In my first year alone, I had grown from 43 to 55 clients. I was practicing law 60+ hours a week in 12 counties across New Jersey *and* fitting in another 20-30 hours per week ordering supplies, negotiating contracts, shopping for essentials, setting up digital profiles, and more. it was mentally and physically fatiguing at a level that is still traumatic to recall. I was exhausted.

I barely had time to meet with my accountant, let alone "balance the books." I did have him set me up on QuickBooks so I could write checks directly from the software and track transactions. But I didn't know how to pull any reports, see how much money I had spent, or even know how much I needed each week to run the firm. My accountant tried to explain it to me, but I felt horribly ignorant of the process and was too frustrated and embarrassed to tell him I had not one clue what the f$*k he was saying! So, I just nodded along. And returned to my willfully blind ignorance after he left.

The one thing I did need to know was how much money I needed to make every week to keep the lights on and to pay my assistant. QuickBooks was terrifying, so I resorted to a much simpler method: the back of the napkin approach to accounting. In a nutshell, I realized that I DID need to understand forecasting, cash flow projections and budgeting–but I didn't need to know it RIGHT NOW. What I needed to know RIGHT NOW was how much I needed to make this month. And so, I did some fuzzy math and arrived at my "One Number."

That's the thing about chaos–it thrives in ambiguity. And nothing feels more ambiguous, more slippery and stressful, than money you can't quite define. If you don't know what your law firm costs to operate each month–if you don't have a hard number that includes every overhead cost, every recurring expense, every salary (including your own)–then you're not running your business. You're guessing at it. You're surviving it. You're hoping the numbers "work out."

But hope isn't a financial strategy. It's a feeling. And feelings are fickle, especially when they're fueled by fear.

Most lawyers don't avoid financial planning because they're lazy or careless. They avoid it because of fear–fear of finding out they're in worse shape than they thought, fear of feeling stupid in front of a financial professional, fear of facing the mountain of complexity that lives inside their spreadsheets and bank accounts.

But what I learned in that first year–the hardest year of my business life–is that you don't need a financial degree to lead a law firm. You need clarity. You need a stake in the ground. You need a single, unflinching truth to orient your decisions around. You need your **One Number**.

Your One Number is your monthly financial lifeline. It is the minimum amount of revenue your business must bring in every single month to survive–not thrive, not grow–*just survive*. It's your base camp. Your threshold. Your "I'm not dipping into savings, going into debt, or skipping payroll" number.

And here's why it's powerful: **once you know your One Number, everything else starts to make sense.**

You stop overanalyzing. You stop catastrophizing. You stop hiding from your bank account and start showing up with purpose.

You also stop making emotional decisions about money. No more panic-hiring because you "feel" busy. No more cutting your paycheck just because a big invoice hasn't cleared. No more hoarding cash while under-investing in systems, people, or growth. You make decisions from a place of clarity, not crisis.

And if you're anything like I was back then–scrambling between courtrooms, sending invoices from the passenger seat of your car, skipping lunch because the printer broke again–you don't have time for an Excel workbook with a dozen tabs. You need something simple. Fast. Grounding.

That's the brilliance of the One Number exercise. It doesn't require a CFO or a dashboard. It just requires brutal honesty.

What do I pay in rent?

What do I owe in payroll, subscriptions, case expenses, and taxes?

What do I *need* to pay myself to not live in constant anxiety?

Add it up. Round up. And commit to that number like your business depends on it. Because it does.

You'll refine it later. You'll build the dashboard and analyze the trends and color-code the cash flow report. But if you don't start with the One Number, all that other data becomes overwhelming noise.

You don't need to master finance overnight. You just need to *know the one number* that lets you sleep at night.

And if that's all you can hold onto while you build–then that's enough.

Because clarity always precedes power. And your One Number is the first clear step toward becoming the kind of business owner who leads with purpose, not panic.

CASE STUDY

ELLA FINDS HER NUMBER – AND HER POWER

Ella Murillo was no stranger to hard work. A fiery, fast-talking Latina from Brooklyn, she had clawed her way through law school while raising two kids as a single mom, working nights at a diner and weekends as a paralegal. When she passed the bar, she opened her own practice almost immediately–not out of some grand entrepreneurial vision, but because she couldn't stomach the idea of working 80 hours a week to line someone else's pockets. She figured, If I'm going to be broke and tired, I'd rather do it on my own terms.

Running on Hustle, Not on Numbers

At first, her firm–Murillo Legal Solutions–was scrappy and small, but full of hustle. She focused on immigration and family law, two practice areas that she cared deeply about and that kept her calendar full. She priced competitively, worked fast, and never said no to a client in crisis. Her phone never stopped ringing. Her inbox was chaos. And her brain? Constantly on fire.

On paper, things looked fine. Better than fine, even. Revenue was creeping toward $500,000 annually. Her caseload was full. She had one full-time paralegal and a receptionist who worked remotely. But behind the scenes, Ella was drowning.

Every month felt like Russian roulette with the bank account. Some weeks, she'd be flush with cash–settlement checks came in, retainers landed, court fees got reimbursed. Other weeks, she'd scramble to cover payroll, max out a credit card to pay the office lease, and "borrow" from her kids' savings account just to make ends meet.

She had no idea what anything cost. She didn't know her monthly burn. She couldn't tell you whether she was profitable. She just knew she was tired, wired, and perpetually behind.

Her turning point came during tax season. Her accountant emailed her a list of missing documents, flagged a $12,000 tax liability she hadn't planned for, and asked her–casually–what her monthly operating costs were.

Ella froze.

She guessed. Badly. "Maybe... $20,000? I think?"

Facing the Truth

Her accountant's silence was deafening. Then came the email back, with charts and attachments and balance sheets and a sentence that stabbed like a dagger: "It looks closer to $32,000 a month when you include payroll, your lease, insurance, software, and the amount you've been transferring to yourself."

Ella panicked.

That weekend, she joined a Law Firm Mentor virtual workshop about finances. She didn't tell anyone she was there. She kept her camera off. But she was listening.

And then she heard the phrase: "your One Number."

Her ears perked up.

The facilitator explained that the One Number is not your revenue goal, not your dream income, and not your budget–it's the minimum monthly number *your firm needs to bring in to stay alive, without debt, without skipping payments, and without leaving you personally hanging.*

Something about the simplicity–the finality–of that idea broke through Ella's fog.

From Overwhelmed to Empowered

When her assigned LFM coach followed up after the session and asked if she wanted help calculating it, Ella swallowed her pride and said yes.

Their first session was awkward. Ella deflected with humor. "I went to law school, not Wharton," she joked. But her coach was patient, warm, and firm.

They started with expenses. Rent. Payroll. Subscriptions. Dues. Case costs. Marketing. Estimated taxes. Minimum debt payments. Then came the hardest question: "How much do you need to pay yourself, non-negotiably, to feel stable?"

Ella choked out a number. $6,000.

It wasn't lavish. It was what she needed to cover her mortgage, daycare, food, and the occasional massage so she didn't fall apart.

When they added it all up, Ella's One Number landed at **$34,700.**

Ella stared at the number like it had slapped her.

"That's more than I thought," she whispered.

"Yes," her coach said. "But it's less than the chaos you're living with now."

The first few weeks were hard. Knowing her number brought clarity–but also panic. Ella realized how often she'd made money decisions based on feelings, not facts. She'd taken on clients she didn't want because she felt broke. She'd delayed hiring a second paralegal because she feared overspending, even though her caseload was bursting. She'd underpaid herself out of guilt.

But as the number settled into her bones, something shifted. It became her anchor.

She put it on a Post-it and stuck it to her monitor. She started measuring her weekly revenue against it. She looked at her calendar and stopped booking low-fee consults that drained time but didn't move the needle.

Her marketing changed. She created a "Fast Track Divorce" package priced intentionally to meet her margin needs. She restructured payment plans. She cleaned out software subscriptions she didn't need. She asked her paralegal to renegotiate a vendor contract that was bleeding cash.

Within 60 days, Ella had her first month above *her One Number–without maxing out a credit card.*

By month four, she had her first-ever "cash cushion"–$12,000 that she didn't have to touch.

She gave herself a raise.

She finally hired that second paralegal.

And she did something even more radical: she stopped apologizing *for wanting to be financially safe.*

"I used to think not knowing made me innocent," she told her coach one day. "But it just made me powerless. Now? I feel like a grown-ass businesswoman."

Ella didn't suddenly become a financial wizard. She still had spreadsheets she didn't fully understand. She still felt a pang of panic when taxes came around. But she wasn't guessing anymore. She had a number. A direction. A barometer. A financial truth that she could return to when things got murky.

And in that clarity, she found peace.

Because sometimes, the difference between drowning and leading is just knowing exactly how much water you can handle.

Final Word: Your First Financial Anchor

Knowing your One Number doesn't solve every financial challenge in your business. But it gives you a stake in the ground, a place to stand. It replaces guesswork with grounding. Chaos with clarity. It is your first act of financial leadership–not as someone who's "good with money," but as someone finally willing to look at it.

When you know your One Number, everything else begins to calibrate around it. You sell with more urgency. You price with more confidence. You stop chasing "busy" and start chasing "enough."

But of course, surviving isn't the same as scaling.

Takeaway: Your One Number keeps you afloat. But if you want to grow–intentionally, sustainably, and strategically–you need to start seeing around financial corners. You need to think *ahead*, not just in the now. That's where forecasting comes in.

Because when you can see what's coming—before it hits your bank account—you stop reacting and start steering. And that's the difference between staying in business... and building a business that lasts.

Let's go there next.

FORECAST OR FLATLINE: THINKING BEYOND THE BANK ACCOUNT

There's a particular kind of high that comes from seeing a fat balance in your business account.

It's the dopamine hit of perceived security. You log in, see that nice round number, and breathe a little easier. The team is paid. Rent is covered. Your credit cards are current. You might even splurge—on a new desk, a team lunch, or that software tool you've been eyeing. Why not? You've earned it.

But here's the problem: *your bank balance is not your budget.*

It's not even a reliable indicator of what you *can* spend. It's just a snapshot of a moment in time—and a dangerously deceptive one at that.

Because here's what most law firm owners forget: money sitting in your account today might already be *spoken for*. Upcoming payroll. Quarterly taxes. A vendor contract renewal. Trial prep expenses. Marketing campaigns. Maybe even the retainer you took in last week that will be bled out by case expenses before the month ends.

Without a forecasting habit—without the ability to look ahead and map out what's *coming*—you are steering your business while staring into the rearview mirror.

And if you've ever spent freely in a flush month only to be gasping for air six weeks later, you've lived this reality. You didn't fail because you weren't making money. You failed because you didn't *forecast* what was next.

This section is about shifting your mindset from reactive to proactive. From "I hope this is enough" to "I know what's coming, and I'm ready."

Forecasting isn't about predicting the future perfectly. It's about preparing for it powerfully.

And that's how real business owners stay in control—no matter what's down the road.

When the Bank Balance Lies

It starts with a breath of relief. A deposit clears, the balance looks solid, and for a moment—just a moment—you feel like you're finally ahead. You exhale. The tightness in your chest eases. Maybe you even celebrate a little—upgrade a subscription, buy a shiny new chair, take the team to lunch, or pull a bonus from the business for yourself. And why not? There's money in the bank.

But fast forward three weeks. Suddenly its payroll week again. A retainer you expected didn't arrive. An annual insurance premium just hit your account. A team member needs a new laptop. You're juggling. Transferring. Calling the bank to ask about holds. Watching the balance drop like a rollercoaster in freefall. And that beautiful surplus you were basking in? Gone.

What happened?

Here's what: **you looked at your bank account instead of looking ahead.**

Lawyers, by nature, are trained to think in facts and precedent. We solve problems. We plan for trials. We build timelines, arguments, and backup plans for every scenario. But when it comes to money, many of us operate like the judge is already in chambers and we're still flipping through our file for talking points.

We react. We hope. We "check the account" like it's a magic eight ball that will tell us whether we're allowed to make a decision.

But the bank balance is a *lagging indicator*. It shows you what *has* happened—not what's coming. And if you run your law firm based on what your bank balance says today, without knowing what's due tomorrow, next week, or next month, you are setting yourself up for an entirely preventable financial crisis.

Here's the reality: money doesn't flow in evenly. Law firms—especially those built on contingency, flat fees, or seasonal spikes—are **inherently cyclical.** You'll have flush months where cash is pouring in like Niagara Falls, and then droughts where the faucet barely drips. If you don't anticipate that rhythm—if you don't plan for the ebb that follows the flow—you will flatline.

And it's not just about survival. It's about the *emotional chaos* that comes with financial unpredictability.

You start second-guessing every decision. You become reactive with your team, your spending, your pricing. One slow month turns into a tailspin of cutting corners, taking clients you don't want, burning out your staff, and spiraling into scarcity. Not because your business is broken, but because your **sightline** is.

You simply didn't see what was coming.

And let's be honest—most lawyers *don't* forecast because they don't know how. Or worse, they believe they don't *deserve* to.

"I'll start tracking once we're stable."

"Once we hit a million, I'll worry about projections."

"I'm not a finance person."

But here's the truth: **you don't forecast because you're stable—you forecast to become stable.**

Forecasting isn't about being a spreadsheet wizard or financial savant. It's about building a relationship with your money that's *intentional*, not accidental.

It's about asking:

What expenses are coming up in the next 30, 60, 90 days?

What income do I realistically expect—and when?

What contracts are expiring, what bonuses are due, what software will renew?

What slow seasons should I plan for, and how can I insulate myself in advance?

Without answers to these questions, even your best months are financial landmines. You may *look* like you're winning—nice revenue, positive reviews, a full caseload—but behind the scenes, your business is one late retainer away from a cash crunch.

And perhaps the most impactful part? Forecasting doesn't just protect your finances—it protects your focus.

When you have a forecast, you stop obsessing over every invoice. You stop reacting to every little dip. You start making strategic decisions based on data, not desperation.

You launch a marketing campaign because the forecast shows a slow quarter coming.

You hold off on hiring because the cash flow won't support it yet.

You *do* hire—confidently—because you see the revenue that's coming in the next 90 days.

You give your team bonuses without fear, because you've planned for them.

You stop flinching every time a vendor invoice hits. You stop over-celebrating short-term wins because you know what's still ahead. And most importantly, you stop living at the mercy of your current bank balance and start leading from vision.

Forecasting creates emotional regulation around money.

It's the cure to the financial whiplash that so many law firm owners have normalized. You know the feeling: feast, famine, relief, anxiety, rinse, repeat.

But it doesn't have to be that way.

When you learn to forecast—not perfectly, but consistently—you gain access to the calm that comes from foresight. You become the kind of leader who doesn't just ride the wave but anticipates the swell. Who doesn't just "figure it out" but prepares in advance.

Forecasting turns the future from a threat into a tool.

And when you can look 30, 60, 90 days ahead and know exactly where your business stands—*that* is when you stop reacting and start commanding.

Because freedom isn't found in the balance. It's found in the foresight.

CASE STUDY

DEVON'S FORECAST FIX – FROM FLUSH TO FOCUSED

Devon Harper had always been the kind of guy who could sell. *A natural storyteller with the charm of a TED Talk speaker and the instincts of a streetwise entrepreneur, he built his boutique criminal defense firm in Charlotte, North Carolina, almost entirely on charisma, confidence, and gut. His clients loved him. His courtroom presence was magnetic. Referrals poured in. His reputation was golden.*

And the money? It came in fast. Large retainers. Rush cases. Emergency filings. Devon was clearing multiple six figures by his second year in practice. He drove a matte-black Tesla, wore custom suits, and picked up the tab at industry happy hours without blinking. He was that *guy–the one everyone assumed was killing it.*

But what no one saw was what happened after *the champagne stopped flowing.*

When Abundance is An Illusion

Devon was living in what he called "the illusion of abundance." His bank account looked full, so he spent like it. Hired a second associate on a handshake deal. Upgraded his office lease to a fancy downtown space. Bought a branded podcast mic (and never recorded a single episode). Enrolled in an online mastermind for "seven-figure law firm owners," even though he was still figuring out payroll.

He justified it all with the same line: I can always make more.

And for a while, he could. Until he couldn't.

The first time it caught up with him, it was subtle. A client's retainer bounced. Then another. A few big cases wrapped up earlier than expected, which meant less monthly revenue from payment plans. He dipped into savings. Then into the firm credit card. But the scariest part? He didn't see *it coming.*

Because Devon didn't forecast.

At all.

He logged into his bank account daily—sometimes hourly. That was his entire "financial system." If the number looked high, he felt relaxed. If it looked low, he canceled something. He was running a multi-six-figure business like a college student hoping there'd be enough left in checking for Uber Eats and laundry.

You've Got to Face It to Fix It

When he joined Law Firm Mentor, it wasn't because of a big crash. It was because he felt something—tightness. Like the floor beneath him wasn't stable anymore. Like he was growing, but not getting stronger. *And when he had to transfer $8,000 from his personal savings account to cover office rent, he finally admitted:* This doesn't feel right.

During his first coaching session, we asked him to list his recurring expenses for the next 60 days.

Devon froze.

"I mean... I could probably pull that up in QuickBooks?" he offered weakly.

"Great," we said. "Pull it up."

Cue the scrambling. The screen sharing. The digital rummaging. What followed was an hour of embarrassment and excuses—and the gut-punch realization that he had $18,000 in upcoming obligations he hadn't accounted for at all.

The real kicker? He'd just dropped $4,200 on new branding photos and a retreat in Miami.

He stared at the numbers like they'd betrayed him. "I thought I had money," he said.

"You did," we replied. "But you didn't plan for what's coming. So now you're paying the penalty for not having a forecast."

That's when it clicked.

Devon didn't have a revenue problem. He had a sightline *problem.*

We started small. Nothing fancy. No massive dashboards or five-tab spreadsheets. Just a 30-day cash flow forecast*—a simple Google Sheet with three columns:*

1. ***Expected Revenue***
2. ***Known Expenses***
3. ***Cash Balance by Week***

Each Friday, Devon committed to spending 30 minutes forecasting the next four weeks. He filled in known revenue (retainers, payment plans, court-appointed fees), added in hard expenses (rent, salaries, software, taxes), and calculated what was left.

The first time he saw the forecasted dip—three weeks out—his jaw clenched. "I wouldn't have seen that coming until it was too late," he said quietly.

Exactly.

That month, instead of spending freely, he held back. He cut two unnecessary subscriptions. Pushed a marketing campaign back by 30 days. And—most importantly—he hustled strategically to bring in two new retainers that covered the gap.

No panic. No payday loan. No missed payroll.

For the first time, Devon was steering, *not swerving.*

Over time, Law Firm Mentor helped him extend the forecast to 60, then 90 days. He started using it to make hiring decisions. To plan vacations. To assess when he could safely invest in advertising. He still had months that dipped—but never unexpectedly.

And that changed everything.

*His stress levels dropped. His team started receiving bonuses consistently. He finally launched his podcast—*after *forecasting what it would cost and how long it would take to see ROI.*

He even set aside a "quiet month reserve"—a cushion that allowed him to take two weeks off in December without grinding in guilt.

When we asked him what had changed, Devon said something we'll never forget:

"I used to look at my bank account and think, That's what I have. *Now I look at my forecast and say,* This is what I can do."

*Devon didn't become frugal. He didn't lose his swagger. He became something far more powerful–**focused.***

And that focus was only possible because he finally saw the road ahead, instead of driving blindfolded through traffic, praying for green lights.

Final Word: See It Before You Spend It

Forecasting isn't about getting every number perfect–it's about seeing enough of what's coming to make smart, grounded decisions before the chaos hits. It's about removing the emotional rollercoaster from your money management and replacing it with rhythm, reason, and readiness.

When you start forecasting regularly, you stop being blindsided by bills, panic-hiring, and surprise dips in cash flow. You become someone who leads–not just in the courtroom, but in the financial engine room of your business.

And yet, even the best forecasts can't save you if you're constantly plugging gaps with fast cash.

Takeaway: Because when money gets tight, many law firm owners reach for the thing that feels easy: **debt**. A credit card here. A line of credit there. A business loan that promises relief but delivers suffocation.

In the next section, we're going to tackle the myth of "easy money"–and how it quietly kills your freedom, your profitability, and your peace of mind.

Let's talk about how to stop financing chaos and start funding sustainability.

The Debt Trap: How "Easy Money" Keeps You Broke

When money gets tight, and the pressure starts to build, debt looks like a lifeline. It's fast. It's simple. It's a few clicks, a signed doc, and boom–money in the account. A credit card balance increase here, a line of credit there, maybe even a merchant cash advance that promises instant approval and same-day funding. What's the harm, right? You'll just pay it off when that big case settles... when that new associate starts producing... when that marketing campaign kicks in.

But here's the brutal truth: **most law firm owners don't use debt to grow–they use it to survive.** And every time they do, they sink a little deeper into a cycle of dependency that robs their business of power, flexibility, and profitability.

Debt is seductive because it solves today's pain. You're behind on payroll? Swipe. Tax bill due? Transfer. Need to buy time while you figure out your next move? Loan.

But what happens tomorrow? When the revenue slows? When the card is maxed? When that "quick fix" turns into $1,000 in interest fees and sleepless nights?

This section isn't about demonizing debt. It's about understanding it for what it is: **a tool with a very sharp edge.**

If you've been using borrowed money to patch over deeper operational issues, if your line of credit feels more like your emergency fund, if you're financing decisions you can't afford to make–you're not investing. You're mortgaging your future to survive your present.

Let's talk about how to stop bleeding from the inside out–and how to rebuild a business that funds itself from strength, not scarcity.

When Survival Comes with Interest

Debt doesn't feel dangerous at first.

In fact, it often feels like the solution. A relief. A moment of exhale when the pressure is crushing your chest and the accounts payable are looming like storm clouds. One quick application, a signature, and suddenly–*poof*–you've bought yourself a little time.

It's seductive like that.

For law firm owners especially, debt often masquerades as strategy. It's packaged in pretty language: "investing in growth," "accessing working capital," "bridging the gap." And sometimes, that's true. But far more often, debt is a Band-Aid on a bullet wound–applied in panic, fueled by exhaustion, and burdened with unspoken shame.

Because let's be honest: most law firm owners who are deep in debt didn't get there because they were reckless. They got there because they were overwhelmed. Because they were doing the work of three people. Because revenue was inconsistent, and clients were late paying, and someone on the team quit unexpectedly. Because the tax bill hit harder than expected, or the marketing agency bled cash without results. Because they had no systems, no cash flow forecast, and no safety net.

So they did what felt like the only option.

They borrowed.

First, it was a business credit card. Then a second one. Then a line of credit from a local bank. Then maybe a "working capital loan" from a flashy online lender that promised 24-hour turnaround and no credit check. Before long, it snowballed. What was once a short-term fix became a long-term trap.

You start robbing Peter to pay Paul. Transferring balances. Making minimum payments. Watching interest accrue like mold in a dark corner of your financial life. You feel it every time you log into your banking dashboard. That subtle nausea. That quiet panic.

And worst of all–you start normalizing it.

You start treating debt like part of doing business. Like an acceptable cost of entrepreneurship. Like the price of chasing success.

But it's not.

Debt isn't inherently evil. But **misused debt is a silent killer of profitability**. Every dollar you borrow at high interest digs into your margins. Every loan payment becomes a fixed cost that limits your freedom. And when the business grows, the debt often grows with it–because the operational issues that led to borrowing never got fixed. They just got buried under borrowed money.

It's a trap that doesn't look like a trap.

You might be bringing in $500K, even $1M a year in revenue–but if $250K is going toward paying off loans, interest, and emergency decisions from two years ago, **you're not running a business. You're digging out of a grave.**

And here's the cruel irony: the more debt you accumulate, the harder it becomes to fix the root issues. Why? Because debt shrinks your options. It kills your cash flow. It makes hiring feel impossible. It turns bold, strategic choices into pipe dreams.

You can't build a visionary firm when you're paralyzed by debt payments. You can't invest in a strong team, in marketing that works, in your own damn peace of mind–because every month, you're trying to figure out how to make it all stretch just far enough.

But the emotional toll? That's the real cost.

You stop sleeping well.

You dread your accountant's calls.

You feel a twinge of panic every time you swipe your card.

You stop trusting your own instincts.

You start to resent your business–and yourself.

And yet, the cycle continues.

Because when the pressure spikes again, and you need just one more cushion–what do you do?

You borrow again.

And now the problem isn't just money. It's identity.

You start to believe you're "bad with money." That this is just "how business is." That you're surviving by the skin of your teeth, and always will be. That you're faking success.

But here's the truth:

You don't have a money problem. You have a **misalignment problem**. You're funding systems that don't work with dollars you don't have. You're patching holes instead of fixing the foundation. You're choosing short-term relief over long-term sovereignty.

And you're not alone.

So many brilliant, high-achieving lawyers are buried in the same trap—strapped with debt not because they're bad at business, but because they've never been taught how to lead financially. Because no one told them that "scaling" without cash reserves, forecasting, and strategy is just chaos at a higher level.

And the worst part?

Debt keeps you quiet.

You don't talk about it. You hide it. You think you're the only one.

But you're not.

At Law Firm Mentor, we've seen debt destroy law firms that looked amazing from the outside. We've also seen debt *transformed*—when firm owners make the courageous choice to stop financing their dysfunction and start building a business that can fund itself.

That starts with awareness. With looking at every dollar you owe—and asking yourself: *Was this debt a strategic investment... or a panic button I pressed because I didn't have a better plan?*

Because you deserve better than survival.

You deserve solvency. Sustainability. Strategy. And freedom.

But none of that is possible if debt is calling the shots.

CASE STUDY

NATALIE'S DESCENT INTO DEBT – AND HER RISE FROM THE ASHES

When Natalie joined Law Firm Mentor, she was a rising star.

She'd launched her criminal defense firm in New Jersey with fire in her belly and a chip on her shoulder. She was whip-smart, no-nonsense, and had the rare gift of connecting with clients who felt *the system had already counted them out. When she came to LFM, she was doing around $200K a year–not bad for a solo–but she knew she was capable of more. Much more.*

And she was right.

Within two years, Natalie had crossed the $500K mark. Her systems were tight. Her consultations converted like clockwork. Her firm was growing, her name was spreading, and her confidence was sky-high. She even began mentoring other lawyers in her network. She was building not just a firm, but a movement.

Then came Jules.

When Success Turns to Survival

From the moment she took his case–a possession with intent to distribute charge with prior convictions–she knew something was off. Her gut told her not to do it. The vibe was wrong. The file reeked of drama. But Jules had the money. And Natalie, flush with success and craving just one more "big" case to elevate her reputation, said yes.

At first, things looked promising. The assigned prosecutor was someone Natalie vaguely knew–a decent guy from the same neighborhood Jules grew up in, and they'd begun working out a favorable plea. It was looking like a win.

Until the prosecutor got promoted and reassigned.

The case landed on the desk of someone new–someone who, by all appearances, had it out *for Jules. The plea evaporated. The tone changed. The new prosecutor demanded some demonstration of remorse before even thinking about a deal. Jules, stubborn and prideful, refused. He mocked the suggestion.*

The case went to trial. Natalie fought like hell.

But they lost.

Jules was convicted.

Still, he was allowed to remain out on bail pending sentencing. And that's when Natalie's life began to unravel.

First, there was the 1-star review.

Then another. And another. Soon, dozens. Jules had activated a network of friends, family, ex-girlfriends, internet trolls—anyone he could find to leave scathing, false reviews on every platform Natalie's firm was listed. Within weeks, she went from 40+ five-star reviews and a pristine 4.8 rating... to a grotesque swarm of 1-stars. Her rating plummeted to a 3.0.

Then came the photos.

Somehow, Jules' uncle—who happened to be friends with one of Natalie's ex-boyfriends—got his hands on old, private, compromising images of her. And like clockwork, they began to surface. On burner accounts. In the comment sections of her firm's social posts. On obscure internet forums. Every time her team got one image taken down, another would appear.

Natalie began dreading court. She stopped taking jail visits altogether after one visit where inmates leered and catcalled her, making crude references to images they'd seen. Even the guards, trying to be kind, would shoo the prisoners into silence and then make their own uncomfortable advances.

Natalie spiraled.

Drowning in Doubt and Debt

She fell into a deep depression and withdrew from criminal defense altogether. She had a handful of prior cases in family law and real estate, so she began trying to pivot—desperately—and rebuild a practice around something, anything, *that didn't carry the trauma of what she'd just endured.*

But that transition was harder than she ever imagined.

She no longer knew how to sell herself. She didn't feel credible outside of criminal law. Her posture during consultations was rigid, defensive, uncertain. She was technically proficient, but emotionally vacant. Worse—she was broke.

The cases stopped coming. The phone stopped ringing. And with no reliable revenue stream, Natalie turned to debt.

First, a business credit card. Then another. A personal loan. A line of credit. She used borrowed money to cover payroll for her paralegal and part-time assistant. To pay rent on an office she no longer had the heart to walk into. To cover groceries. Gas. A retreat she hoped would help her "bounce back."

But the bounce never came.

The more she borrowed, the more she tightened. Her consultations began to reek of desperation. Prospects could smell the panic on her. She'd stammer through pricing conversations, offer discounts before objections were even raised, and follow up with apology-laced emails asking for "just a few minutes to talk again." Her close rate tanked.

Natalie was imploding. The pressure of performance, debt, shame, and fear had fused into one giant knot in her chest that no coach, no pep talk, and no spreadsheet could untangle.

Until we stopped talking about money–and started talking about power.

Natalie came to one of our LFM intensives, her eyes tired and her voice hollow. When we sat down to talk through her situation, she couldn't even bring herself to say the total amount of debt she'd accumulated.

"It's bad," she whispered. "I don't even want to know."

But we insisted.

Together, we listed out every line of credit, every card, every payment due.

$147,000.

It felt like a punch to the gut.

But here's what we told her: You can't heal what you won't face. And you are not your debt.

Then we got to work.

Reclaiming Power. And Profit

We helped her identify every unnecessary expense she could cut or renegotiate. We mapped out a realistic cash flow forecast–not a fantasy, but a grounded picture of what she could produce in 90 days if *she focused. We helped her design a high-value offer in real estate law that built on her existing skill set. We rebuilt her consultation script–this time, not with "please hire me" energy, but with poise and power.*

It wasn't easy.

Natalie had to work through PTSD-level responses every time a new consult came in. She had to rebuild confidence on the fly. But we held her hand, and she held the line.

And slowly... she began to rise.

The phone started ringing again. She got her first retained client in a new practice area. She began posting online–not to sell, but to share what she knew, *what she stood for. She blocked every burner account. Changed her phone number. Refused to shrink.*

Within 6 months, Natalie had paid off over $30,000 in debt.

Within a year, she was profitable again.

She'll never forget what Jules took from her. But now, she measures herself not by that trauma–but by the woman who rebuilt anyway.

"I don't ever want to be in that place again," she told us. "And now I know... I never have to be."

Final Word: You Don't Owe Your Way to Wealth

Debt may feel like the easy button, but when misused, it becomes a silent, strangling force in your business. It eats away at your profit, clouds your judgment, and steals your power–quietly, month after month.

Natalie's story reminds us that desperation makes every decision heavier, and that borrowing your way through burnout only extends the chaos. But it also shows us something else: with the right

> support, the right systems, and a fierce commitment to facing the truth, *even the most devastating financial spiral can become a comeback story.*

Takeaway: The way out of the debt trap isn't more money—it's **better decisions** about the money you already have.

And those decisions are made not just in crisis, but in planning. Because the difference between firms that grow with grace and firms that collapse under pressure often comes down to one thing: **budgeting.**

Not the restrictive, joyless kind. But the bold, strategic kind that lets you say yes to the right risks, and no to the ones that cost too much.

In the next section, we'll show you how to budget like a business owner—not a bookkeeper. Let's talk about building a financial plan that makes space for your vision *and* protects your peace.

Budget Like a Boss: Planning for Profit and Possibility

For most law firm owners, the word *budget* triggers a visceral response—usually a blend of boredom, anxiety, and low-grade rebellion.

It feels like a trap. A punishment. A grown-up version of being told you can't go out and play until you clean your room.

Budgeting is seen as restrictive, rigid, even oppressive. Something built for accountants and financial advisors—not visionary entrepreneurs. After all, you didn't leave your firm or hang your own shingle just to spend your days counting pennies and coloring inside the lines.

But here's what most lawyers get wrong about budgeting: it's not about restriction.

It's about power.

A budget isn't a cage. It's a blueprint. It's a map of your values, your goals, and your future—all translated into numbers. It tells you what's safe to spend, when it's time to pull back, and when you can boldly say yes to a big investment without flinching.

Without a budget, every financial decision becomes a guessing game. You launch marketing campaigns without knowing if you can fund the follow-up. You hire based on feelings instead of forecasts. You tell yourself, "I'll figure it out," even as your bank account begs for structure.

But when you budget like a boss, you take command.

You create a living, breathing system that flexes with your business—but always keeps you grounded. You learn how to make room for the unexpected, plan for the bold, and protect your peace of mind while pursuing growth.

Let's reframe budgeting from a burden to a power tool—and show you how to use it like the CEO you're becoming.

When There's No Plan for the Money

Let's be real: most law firm owners don't have a budget.

They might have a sense of what rent costs. Maybe a rough number in their head for payroll. A gut feeling about what's "too much" for marketing or software. But a real, written, line-by-line budget that actually reflects what they want to build in their business? That's rare.

And it's not because they're lazy. It's because most lawyers were never taught how to treat their business like a business. We were trained to practice law—not to allocate capital, plan expenditures, or weigh opportunity costs. So we default to reacting, improvising, and hoping the money works itself out.

But here's the truth: **if you don't tell your money where to go, it will disappear without telling you where it went.**

Without a budget, your business becomes a financial free-for-all. You spend based on emotion. You buy tools because your friend swears by them. You hire because you're overwhelmed, not because the numbers say it's time. You swipe the card and say "it's fine" until it's not.

And even when revenue is high—even when the top line looks amazing—you still feel broke. Still feel stressed. Still feel like every decision is a shot in the dark.

Because it is.

That's the emotional toll of budgetless business. It's not just about overspending. It's about **never feeling safe**, even when you're doing well. It's about making money but having no peace. It's about feeling guilty every time you *do* spend—because you don't know if you should. It's about freezing when an opportunity comes, because you don't know if you can afford to say yes.

And so many law firm owners don't budget because they believe one of three lies:

Lie #1: Budgeting is restrictive.

They think of a budget as a straitjacket. Something that tells them "no" every time they want to take a risk or follow a hunch. They believe that being an entrepreneur means staying flexible—and budgeting feels like the opposite of flexibility.

Lie #2: Budgeting is unnecessary at my level.

They tell themselves, "I'm not a big firm. I don't need all that structure. I just need to bring in more." They think a budget is something you build *after* you're financially stable—not the thing that *gets* you there.

Lie #3: Budgeting is boring.

They'd rather do anything else than sit down with a spreadsheet. It feels tedious, stressful, and disconnected from the high-stakes, high-energy world of law. They want to spend time solving client problems, not categorizing expenses.

But here's the truth: **a budget is not a box—it's a battlefield map**.

It tells you how to deploy your resources. It protects your priorities. It guides your strategy. And it's not static—it evolves with your business.

The most successful firm owners don't use their budget to say "no" to everything. They use it to say "yes" *with confidence.*

Yes, I can afford to hire that associate—and here's how I'll fund the salary for 90 days before they produce.

Yes, I can sign that lease—and here's how much additional revenue I'll need to cover the increased overhead.

Yes, I can invest in that retreat, that course, that consultant—because I know my numbers, and I've built the room.

Budgeting isn't about minimizing. It's about maximizing—**intentionally**.

But that kind of power requires a shift. You have to stop seeing money as something to survive, and start treating it as something to direct. You have to zoom out from the frantic day-to-day of billing and filing and managing your team, and look at the *whole machine.*

And here's where most law firm owners really get stuck: **they don't know how to budget as entrepreneurs.**

They think budgeting means locking in numbers and never deviating. But entrepreneurial budgeting is different. It's dynamic. It creates lanes, not walls. It sets targets while making space for pivots.

Because let's face it: business is unpredictable. Sometimes you get a windfall. Sometimes you take a hit. Sometimes you need to seize an opportunity *now*, even if it wasn't in the original plan.

That's why your budget must be alive.

It should reflect where you are and where you're going. It should be reviewed regularly—not just annually. And it should leave space for possibility. Space to take a risk. To test a new strategy. To *build.*

A good entrepreneurial budget doesn't just tell you what you can't do—it shows you **what's possible, and what it will take to get there**.

And when you budget like that, you stop living in fear of the next big decision.

You stop hiring with a knot in your stomach.

You stop wondering whether you can afford to scale.

You know. You lead. You act.

Because budgeting isn't about control for control's sake.

It's about peace.

It's about power.

It's about building a business that doesn't just serve others—but also serves **you**.

CASE STUDY

TAMEKA'S BUDGET BREAKTHROUGH

Tameka Barnes was, in a word, brilliant.

A razor-sharp litigator with a booming family law practice in metro Atlanta, she commanded respect in the courtroom and warmth in the consultation room. Her presence was regal. Her voice steady. Her client roster impressive. She could close six-figure months with seemingly little effort. Her team adored her, her peers envied her, and to the outside world, Tameka was the picture of success.

But behind closed doors, she was constantly spinning.

The Chaos Hidden Behind the Numbers

Despite generating over $800K in annual revenue, she always felt cash-poor. She'd make a big hire—then panic about payroll. She'd invest in coaching, software, a rebrand—then freeze when the AMEX bill hit. She'd celebrate a record-breaking month, then wake up sweating at 3 a.m., wondering if the business was about to implode.

Tameka laughed when her LFM coach gently asked during a quarterly check-in, "Do you have a budget you're working from each month?" .

"A budget? No. I'm not there *yet. I'm still building. I need to stay flexible."*

That was her go-to line. Budgeting is for when I'm stable.

What she didn't realize is that her resistance to budgeting was the very thing keeping her from that stability.

Tameka operated her business the way a lot of high-performing lawyers do: intuitively. She "felt out" when it was time to hire. She used the bank balance to gauge whether she could invest in something. She celebrated windfalls with raises and retreats and hired help–but didn't run the numbers first. If money came in, she assumed it was available to spend.

It worked–until it didn't.

The breaking point came in Q4 of her third year in business. She had just wrapped a massive month: $92,000 in collected revenue. She rewarded her team with bonuses. Paid off a chunk of credit card debt. Enrolled in a high-end mastermind program. And finally pulled the trigger on a long-overdue office renovation.

Then–like a switch flipped–everything slowed.

Two major cases settled earlier than expected, and one of her top referrers took a leave of absence. Consults dried up. A new hire took longer than expected to ramp up. A trial she'd banked on got continued.

Cash flow cratered. Expenses didn't.

By December 15, she was staring down a $21,000 payroll, $9,000 in rent, and less than $13,000 in her operating account.

The Breakdown Before the Breakthrough

Tameka called her LFM coach in tears.

"I don't understand. I just had my best quarter ever. Where the hell did the money go?"

Together, they unpacked it. Bonuses. Non-refundable coaching deposits. An expensive renovation. A spike in vendor costs. A dip in receivables. And absolutely no *plan tying any of it together.*

Tameka had been running a business on instinct and adrenaline–and now, she was out of both.

It was time to stop flying blind.

Her coach didn't shame her. Didn't lecture her. She sat down with Tameka and said, "Let's build a budget. Not one to trap you—but one that lets you breathe."

And that's when everything started to change.

They created a working monthly budget. Not a spreadsheet with 42 tabs. Just a simple document that mapped out:

- *Fixed expenses (rent, salaries, subscriptions)*
- *Variable expenses (marketing, travel, professional development)*
- *Her target take-home pay*
- *A minimum net profit goal*
- *A monthly cushion target*

At first, it felt like handcuffs. "I don't want to be told what I can't *spend," Tameka grumbled.*

But her coach reframed it: "This budget isn't here to limit you. It's here to give you permission*—to say yes when it counts, and no when it protects you."*

They used the budget to assess every decision moving forward. Could she afford to hire a new intake specialist? Not yet—but the forecast said she could by March. Could she attend a legal tech conference? Yes, with a modest hotel instead of the resort she'd originally booked. Could she give her team raises? Absolutely—after hitting two consecutive months of forecasted profit.

The fog began to lift.

Tameka no longer flinched when reviewing her accounts. She stopped overspending in high months and starving in slow ones. She built a 90-day reserve. She started tracking profit—not just revenue.

But the biggest shift wasn't just financial. It was emotional.

"I used to feel like every decision was a guess," she told us. "Now, I feel like a grown-ass business owner."

The budget gave her boundaries. And in those boundaries, she found freedom.

She even began to innovate again. With a clear budget in place, she carved out funds for a podcast she'd been dreaming of launching. She finally invested in a fractional marketing director—something she'd avoided because it "felt too risky." And she took a real vacation for the first time in years, knowing her business would still be solvent when she returned.

Tameka didn't become rigid. She became resourced.

She still adjusted her budget monthly, using real data. She built in a "Flex Fund" to try new ideas. She used it to reward high performance and buffer low quarters. And she used it to decide not only what to do—but what not to do.

That clarity changed everything.

Tameka now teaches her team about budgeting in their quarterly meetings. Not because they handle the books—but because she wants them to understand how powerfully intentional money can be.

And every time she's tempted to spend impulsively—on a new hire, a shiny piece of software, a marketing gimmick—she goes back to her numbers.

She's not guessing anymore. She's guiding.

Because now, Tameka doesn't just make money.

She knows what to do with it.

Final Word: Boundaries Build Freedom

A budget isn't about saying no to growth. It's about saying yes—with confidence, clarity, and strategy that protects your future.

Tameka didn't lose her edge by budgeting—she found her footing. When you stop winging it and start planning for your firm's real needs, you stop making emotional decisions and start making intentional *ones. You gain the power to invest, to hire, to scale—but without burning down everything you've built in the process.*

> *And as your numbers become more predictable, so do your obligations—including one of the biggest (and most emotionally charged):* ***your taxes.***

Takeaway: Because budgeting isn't just about what you spend. It's about preparing for what you owe.

And too many law firm owners learn the hard way what happens when tax payments are an afterthought. No plan, no savings, no strategy—just panic when the IRS comes knocking with a bill you can't pay and penalties that make your stomach drop.

In the next section, we'll break down how to avoid tax-time chaos and build a proactive system that keeps you ahead of the curve—and out of hot water.

Let's talk about keeping what you earn, without letting taxes take you down.

TAXED AND TRIGGERED: FACING THE IRS WITHOUT FEAR

Nothing ruins a good revenue month like a surprise tax bill.

One minute you're celebrating a record-breaking quarter, and the next, your accountant delivers the punchline: *You owe five figures—and it's due next week.* The dopamine of success turns into a gut punch of panic. You scramble to pull together cash, dip into savings, or worse—ignore it and hope it goes away.

Sound familiar?

You're not alone.

Taxes are one of the most triggering, stress-inducing, avoidance-generating parts of entrepreneurship—and especially for law firm owners, who are often making good money *without a clear system* for how to track, plan, or pay what they owe.

So, what happens?

They file extensions year after year, avoiding the truth.

They ghost their accountant.

They tell themselves they'll deal with it later, when things are more stable.

They wait until April to realize they haven't set aside enough—and then borrow to pay what should have been budgeted all along.

And the shame spiral begins.

But here's the truth: tax chaos isn't just bad math. It's a **leadership issue.**

This section is about shifting from triggered to prepared. From dread to discipline. You'll learn how to plan for taxes proactively, how to avoid end-of-year surprises, and how to create a rhythm of payment that supports your peace of mind instead of destroying it.

Because when you own your tax strategy, you take back your power—and your profit.

Let's clean up the mess, stop the avoidance cycle, and finally face the IRS with your head held high.

When Taxes Become a Time Bomb

There's a unique kind of nausea that hits when you open an email from your accountant and see a number you weren't prepared for.

You skim the subject line—*"2024 Final Tax Liability Summary"*—and already your mouth goes dry. You open the message, hoping for a number with three digits, maybe low four. But there it is, glaring back at you:

$27,436 due. Immediately.

You stare. Blink. Re-read. Maybe it's a mistake. Maybe they're off. But no—the math is right. It's *you* who's been wrong.

You never planned for this. You didn't set anything aside. You didn't pay quarterly estimates. You didn't know how much you owed, and worse—you didn't want to know.

Because taxes trigger something deeper than dollars.

They bring up fear. Shame. Guilt. Confusion. For some law firm owners, they even bring up trauma–old stories of scarcity, financial instability, IRS horror stories from parents, or years of tax neglect from "figuring it out later."

So instead of facing it, they freeze. They go dark. They stop replying to their CPA. They file extensions, then forget to file at all. They avoid bookkeeping. They skip logging into QuickBooks. They treat tax planning like a seasonal emergency instead of a monthly responsibility.

And then they wonder why tax season feels like an ambush.

Here's the truth most lawyers won't say out loud: *They're terrified of the IRS.*

Not because they've done anything criminal–but because they've been *emotionally inconsistent* with money. They make six figures, even seven, and still feel like they're winging it. They don't understand how tax brackets really work. They confuse cash flow with profit. They don't know how much to set aside, or when. They worry they're doing it wrong–and so, they do nothing at all.

And that's when things go sideways.

They file late.

They miss estimated payments.

They rack up interest and penalties.

They sign up for IRS payment plans they can't afford.

They get hit with liens.

They drag the shame around like a financial ball and chain.

And worse? They build their entire business around avoiding the next tax crisis–cutting back when they should invest, staying small when they're ready to grow, keeping more work on their own plate because "if I hire, I'll owe even more."

But none of that is necessary.

The problem isn't the taxes themselves–it's the *avoidance* of taxes.

Because when you avoid planning, you lose your power. You let the IRS dictate your financial future instead of taking ownership of it. And that makes you reactive. Defensive. Emotionally vulnerable to every unexpected bill and bookkeeping blind spot.

But here's the most heartbreaking part: most law firm owners are *paying more than they should*, just because they didn't plan early enough to take advantage of available strategies.

They miss deductions.

They don't optimize their entity structure.

They don't set up retirement contributions.

They don't shift income strategically.

They don't work with their accountant–they just pay them to file and pray for a small number.

And year after year, the cycle continues.

But what if it didn't have to?

What if taxes became just another line item in your monthly budget–not a monster hiding in the closet?

What if your business was structured to minimize what you owe *legally and proactively*–instead of catching up after the fact?

What if you had a system for setting aside funds each month, so you never had to pull from payroll, savings, or your own peace of mind again?

Because that's what tax planning actually is.

It's not filing on time.

It's not asking your CPA "how bad is it this year?"

It's not seeing taxes as a necessary evil.

It's leadership.

It's choosing to stay in relationship with your numbers all year long–not just in March or April.

It's creating a rhythm where money is set aside each month or week, automatically and without fanfare. Where estimates are paid on time. Where your CPA becomes a strategic partner, not a last-minute cleanup crew.

And it's knowing your *real* tax liability–not guessing, not hoping, not rounding down in your head.

Because there's no version of financial mastery that includes tax chaos.

You can scale. You can earn. You can build an empire. But if the IRS is dragging behind you like a shadow of unpaid bills and mounting penalties, your business will always be walking with a limp.

You didn't start your firm to live in fear. And you don't need to.

You just need a plan.

A rhythm.

A system.

A commitment to pay what you owe—not because the IRS said so, but because your future self deserves the peace that comes from leading this part of your business like the CEO you are.

CASE STUDY

STEVEN'S BREAKING POINT

Steven Price never saw himself as the "money guy."

Growing up in a cramped duplex in Newark with three siblings and a single mom working two jobs, money wasn't something to be managed—it was something to chase, to stretch, to pray over. They never talked about taxes, budgets, or investing. The goal was always the same: survive the month.

So when Steven graduated law school, landed a job at a mid-sized firm, and started pulling in a steady paycheck, it felt like he'd made it. He could pay his bills. Take his wife, Mia, out for dinner. Send his mom a little something "just because." And when he finally launched his own criminal defense practice at age 35, it felt like the ultimate upgrade.

He'd made it.

Except... no one taught him what to do next.

The Weight of Providing

His business grew quickly. Steven was charming, a powerful speaker in court, and deeply respected in his community. He built a solid reputation among other Black professionals in the area, handling cases with passion and personal investment. Within two years of opening his firm, he was bringing in $400K in annual revenue.

And yet, somehow, he always felt broke.

But he didn't show it. He kept the firm moving. Made payroll. Paid the rent on his office space. Took Mia and their new baby boy on a beach vacation the summer after their son was born. He wanted to be the man. *The provider. The partner who could say, "You've worked hard enough. Let me carry us now."*

Because Mia had always made more.

She was a corporate project manager. Sharp, composed, disciplined. When Steven was still slogging through doc review at his old firm, she was already making six figures and planning their future. She always said it didn't matter who made more. But after their son was born—and she had to return to work six weeks later to cover the bills—something shifted.

She didn't complain. Not directly. But Steven could feel it.

In the silence when she packed her breast pump and laptop every morning. In the tired glances across the dinner table. In the way she double-checked the account before approving daycare payments.

So Steven made a decision. He would never let her carry that burden alone again.

When Avoidance becomes the Enemy

He worked harder. Said yes to every client. Took court-appointed cases at 80% of what he used to charge just to keep cash coming in. He cut corners on his own salary. Sacrificed sleep. Delayed joy. And, slowly but surely, he stopped paying his taxes.

Not because he forgot.

Because he chose not to.

Every quarter, he'd look at the numbers, calculate the estimates–and decide to hold off "just one more month." He told himself it was noble. Responsible. That taking care of his family came first. That the IRS could wait.

He didn't tell Mia.

That first year, it was about $12,000. Manageable.

The second year, with interest and penalties, it grew to $31,000.

By year four, he owed over $78,000.

He didn't know the exact number. He couldn't bring himself to look. The unopened IRS envelopes sat in a drawer under client intake folders. His accountant had stopped chasing him. He hadn't filed a return in two years.

But the shame? That was constant.

He felt it in his chest every time someone mentioned "quarterlies." Every time a business podcast talked about "tax strategy." Every time Mia casually asked, "Have you finished the books for the year yet?"

He was drowning in a secret.

And eventually, it caught up to him.

The IRS filed a federal tax lien.

He found out when a title company called. He was in the process of refinancing their home to help cover the cost of expanding his office. "We can't proceed with the closing," the agent said. "There's a lien on the property."

Steven's blood ran cold.

That night, he told Mia everything. The missed payments. The ballooning debt. The years of silent panic. The knot in his stomach that hadn't loosened in months.

She didn't yell.

She cried.

And that–more than the lien, more than the debt–is what broke him.

Accountability as Strength

The next day, he called his LFM coach and finally said the words he'd been avoiding:

"I need help. I can't do this alone anymore."

And that's where his real journey began.

*We started by facing the numbers–*all of them. *Together with his CPA, Steven tallied every unpaid tax bill, every interest charge, every penalty. The final number was staggering: $84,327.*

He wanted to throw up.

But we didn't stop there. We mapped out a 12-month recovery plan. We restructured his chart of accounts to ensure monthly tax savings. We created a dedicated business savings account labeled "Tax Hold"–and set up an automatic transfer of 20% of all revenue every Friday.

Every Friday. Without fail.

We connected him with a tax resolution specialist to negotiate a payment plan with the IRS. We coached him on how to communicate with Mia regularly about finances–not with guilt, but with ownership. We helped him revise his pricing model so his profit margin could support his life and *his obligations.*

The first few months were hard.

Every time the IRS payment hit his account, Steven flinched. But eventually, the trigger lost its grip. As his accounts became more organized, so did his mind. As the shame lifted, so did the pressure on his marriage.

Within a year, he was caught up on filings. His back taxes were down by half. He paid estimated quarterly taxes–on time, with confidence–for the first time in his life.

But more than that?

Steven stopped avoiding.

He started leading.

"Every Friday when that tax money transfers," he told us, "I don't feel fear anymore. I feel like I'm protecting my peace."

Because for Steven, paying taxes was no longer a punishment.

It was an act of fatherhood. Of partnership. Of sovereignty.

And this time, he wasn't choosing between his family and the IRS.

He was building a business strong enough to honor both.

Final Word: Peace Is in the Planning

Taxes aren't the enemy. Avoidance is.

The longer you delay facing what you owe, the more you pay–not just in penalties, but in peace, in power, in the emotional capacity to lead. Steven's story isn't rare–it's real. And it's a reminder that silence around money doesn't protect you. It poisons you.

The good news? You don't need to be perfect. You just need to be present.

Budget monthly. Forecast quarterly. Plan proactively. Pay regularly. Lead financially.

Takeaway: Because when you take control of your money–from your One Number to your tax strategy–you stop surviving your business and start *steering* it.

You're no longer just making money.

You're managing it like a master.

And that, more than anything else, is what turns financial chaos into financial freedom.

Let's keep going.

FINANCIAL CLARITY TEST

The financial concepts discussed in this chapter are paired with the Financial Clarity Test in **Appendix A.** This test will help you determine how you operate your firm's finances, with brief guidance on how to interpret your results. Before moving on, you may find it helpful to assess how financial assumptions and anxiety may be currently impacting your firm. In addition, expanded, interactive versions of all our decision-support tools are available online, accessible via links and QR codes included in the Appendix.

CHAPTER 10

PEOPLE POWER

MASTERING THE CHALLENGE OF HUMAN CAPITAL

If time is your most precious asset, your team is the machine that protects it–or pulverizes it.

The difference between a law firm owner drowning in minutiae and one who spends their time thinking, leading, and scaling isn't talent. It's **people**. The right hires. In the right roles. Doing the right work. With the right systems. That's where freedom lives.

But for most lawyers, team-building is a painful, confusing, and emotionally loaded process. We were trained to practice law, not manage humans. And yet, building a strong, high-functioning team is *the* lever that multiplies your impact, your income, and–most critically–your time.

In this chapter, we're going to dig deep into the five biggest people problems that plague law firm owners and steal their hours, energy, and sanity:

1. **Hiring Right:** How to stop hiring out of panic and start recruiting with purpose and clarity.
2. **Optimizing Employee Performance:** How to align expectations, measure outcomes, and build a team that actually performs.

3. **Delegation Dysfunction:** Why you're still doing everything yourself—and how to stop.
4. **Managing the Managers:** How to develop internal leaders so you're not the only one driving the bus.
5. **Culture that Carries:** How to build a values-based culture that holds even when you're not in the room.

You're not here to run a people circus. You're here to lead a people-powered machine.

Problem 1: Hiring Right – The Path to Efficiency

Most law firm owners don't hire when they *should*—they hire when they're drowning.

You're buried under a mountain of work, stretched to your limits, fantasizing about someone—*anyone*—who can take just one thing off your plate. And in that moment of panic, you do what most lawyers do: you write a vague job ad, maybe grab a template from ChatGPT, post it to Indeed, and pray for a miracle.

That's how chaos starts.

You bring someone on without knowing exactly what they're supposed to do, how you'll measure their success, or whether they're even the *right* person for the role. But now they're on payroll. They've got an email address, a key to your office, and access to client files. And suddenly, your already chaotic day is being eaten alive by questions, rework, and uncertainty.

The reality is, hiring is not a savior move. It's a *strategic decision* that, when done wrong, creates more mess than it solves.

Hiring should be intentional. Systematic. Rooted in clarity.

You should know who you need, why you need them, what "winning" looks like in the role, and whether your business is structurally ready to absorb them.

In this section, we're going to pull the curtain back on what it *really* takes to hire right. Not just to get a butt in the seat, but to build a team that fuels your growth instead of feeding your burnout.

Let's dig in.

Hiring When You're Drowning: The Hidden Cost of Desperation

There is a special kind of exhaustion that comes from carrying everything in your law firm.

It's not just the physical fatigue of long hours or the cognitive fatigue of complex legal analysis. It's the *emotional* weight–the constant tug-of-war between wanting help and fearing what that help might cost you.

So what do most lawyers do?

They wait. They hustle. They push through. Until the wheels are falling off the bus–and *then* they hire.

They hire when they're drowning.

And that, right there, is the first mistake.

Hiring in a panic means you're not hiring strategically. You're hiring reactively. Desperately. You're scanning resumes like a lifeline. You're not thinking about alignment, training, or how the hire will actually integrate into your systems–because let's be honest, *you don't have systems*. You just have need.

You know you're doing this when:

- You post a job ad without really knowing what the role needs.
- You repurpose someone else's job description or ask AI to write one–without verifying if it fits *your* firm.
- You hire someone with a great personality or impressive resume, without evaluating actual performance or alignment.
- You onboard them with vague instructions and blind hope that they'll "figure it out."

Sound familiar?

What happens next is entirely predictable: the new hire underperforms. Or they work hard but in the wrong direction. Or they require so much hand-holding that it's *more* work just to have them around. And instead of helping you climb out of the chaos, they're now standing next to you, needing a life jacket too.

This is where resentment kicks in.

You start thinking:

Why can't they just do their job?

Why do I have to explain everything?

Why does it feel easier to just do it myself?

And the truth is, they *can't* do the job well—not because they're incompetent, but because you never clearly defined what "good" even looks like. You didn't have a scorecard. You didn't create a training plan. You didn't hire with performance outcomes in mind.

You hired a person to solve a pain point—not to build a solution.

Let's go deeper.

Most law firm owners don't just struggle with hiring because of logistics. They struggle because they don't feel equipped to lead. They've never been taught how to manage people, set expectations, or build the infrastructure that supports high performance. They feel inadequate, so they outsource the process to instinct, urgency, or whatever HR advice they last heard in a webinar.

And underneath it all?

They're scared.

Scared of making the wrong decision. Scared of wasting money. Scared of being responsible for someone else's livelihood. Scared of confrontation if the hire doesn't work out. Scared of the vulnerability that comes with growth.

So they default to hoping instead of planning.

They hire and cross their fingers. They onboard with a quick walkthrough and a Dropbox link. They avoid giving feedback because they don't want to seem like a micromanager. They avoid creating systems because "I don't have time to document all that." They convince themselves they're being flexible—when really, they're just being avoidant.

But here's the brutal truth: **hope is not a hiring strategy**.

When you hire from a place of reaction instead of readiness, you don't just waste time—you compound chaos. You create more noise. You erode your confidence. And over time, you start to believe a very dangerous lie:

That no one will ever be good enough.

You start thinking, "I just need to suck it up and keep doing it myself." You stop hiring. Or you keep hiring badly. Either way, your firm remains stuck—dependent on your presence, your brain, and your hands.

That is *not* leadership. That's martyrdom in a business suit.

So let's be clear about what "hiring right" actually means.

It doesn't mean perfection. It doesn't mean you'll never make a misstep. It doesn't mean you need a full HR department or an MBA in people ops.

It means you:

- **Hire before you're drowning**—when you can afford to be thoughtful, not desperate.
- **Get clear on what the role actually needs to produce**—not just what tasks it includes.
- **Define success through a scorecard**—clear metrics, behavioral expectations, and timelines.
- **Create an onboarding plan that trains the person into the role**—rather than expecting them to magically assimilate.
- **Align hiring decisions with your firm's values, work style, and long-term goals**—not just your current pain.

Hiring right is a process of clarity, not charisma.

It requires discipline. Vision. A willingness to lead before the perfect person shows up.

But when you do this right?

You stop reacting. You stop hiring people who disappoint you. You stop hating Mondays.

You hire people who free you–not burden you. People who run the machine–not wait for instructions. People who align with your mission, amplify your brand, and help you *finally* get back your time.

Because that's what the right hire really does: they give you space to breathe.

Let's stop throwing lifelines and start building ships.

That's why at Law Firm Mentor, we teach clients to stop making hiring decisions based on panic or personality–and instead, evaluate every candidate (and even current team members) through the lens of **Attitude, Aptitude, and Cultural Fit.**

These three dimensions form the backbone of our **Culture Scorecard**–a deceptively simple yet ruthlessly effective tool that breaks performance into three categories:

- **Attitude** - Do they take initiative? Are they pleasant to work with? Do they try to make your life easier–or harder?
- **Aptitude** - Can they *actually* do the job? Are they accurate, resourceful, able to handle complex cases, make sound judgments, and produce results with minimal supervision?
- **Cultural Fit** - Do they align with your values? Are they compassionate? Inclusive? Motivated by achievement? Can they bring levity to the office without crossing a line?

This is not just about warm fuzzies.

Your firm's success depends on every person in it rowing in the same direction. A "C" player in any of these categories is going to drain your energy and stall your growth. The Scorecard gives you a clear, objective way to evaluate not only *whether* someone is the right fit, but *why* they are or aren't–and what to do about it.

Because hiring shouldn't be a guessing game. It should be an act of strategic leadership.

When you use the Scorecard as a filter—alongside a clear role definition, metrics, and onboarding—you don't just hire faster. You hire smarter. You hire intentionally. You hire in a way that protects your time instead of stealing it.

And when you do that?

You stop feeling like the business is sitting on your back.

You start building a team that can carry the weight *with* you.

CASE STUDY

THE HIRING SPIRAL – AND THE EXIT RAMP

When Joanna Lopez launched her estate planning firm outside of Austin, she had one goal: freedom.

She had spent twelve years working in BigLaw, trapped in the churn of back-to-back client calls, outdated partner politics, and long nights rewriting memos for partners who never remembered her name. Starting her own practice felt like the key to unlocking a life she could actually live.

At first, it was glorious. Working from home. Handpicking her clients. Making more in six months than she had in her first full year at the firm. But as the client load grew, so did the stress.

Every intake call landed directly on her calendar. She was the one creating the estate plans, printing the documents, binding the binders, answering client questions, invoicing, and even dropping off trust packets at the post office.

She was exhausted. And she was behind.

Her husband, watching her spiral night after night, finally said what she'd been trying not to admit: "You need help."

Hiring in a Panic

So, she did what most solo lawyers do in a panic–she went to Indeed, copy-pasted a generic job description for a "Legal Assistant," and fired it into the void.

The applications flooded in.

Some were clearly unqualified. Some looked promising. She skimmed for grammar and friendliness. She did three Zoom interviews, hired the one who seemed "smart and eager," and exhaled.

Until the first week.

The assistant, Leah, was pleasant. On time. Willing. But by the third time she forgot to check voicemails–or worse, didn't flag a time-sensitive one–Joanna's stress flared.

Tasks were completed halfway. Formatting was sloppy. The assistant kept asking, "Is this how you want it?" and Joanna found herself redoing nearly everything. She couldn't tell if it was a training issue, an attitude issue, or something else entirely.

But by month three, she realized she was doing more, *not less.*

So she did what most lawyers do when a hire doesn't work out–she kept her. Told herself to be patient. She hated confrontation. She didn't want to be unkind. She figured, "maybe this is just what it's like to have a team."

From Hope to Hard Truths

But the resentment brewed. The client experience slipped. Joanna's fuse shortened, her joy faded, and soon the dream firm she had worked so hard to build began to feel like a burden again.

That's when she found Law Firm Mentor.

At first, she joined for help with marketing and systems. But in her very first coaching call, the topic shifted.

Her coach asked, "How's your team?"

Joanna hesitated. "They're... okay. I mean, it's just one person. She's trying."

The coach pressed: "Trying isn't the standard. Performing is."

That hit hard.

Together, they walked through her assistant's tasks. Where was the bottleneck? Where were things falling apart? Where was Joanna still stepping in?

Then came the real shift: they pulled out the **Culture Scorecard.**

Joanna had never evaluated anyone like this before. She'd looked at resumes. She'd done annual reviews in her old job. But this? This was precise. Unapologetic. Three categories: **Attitude**, **Aptitude**, *and* **Cultural Fit**.

She scored Leah honestly:

- ***Attitude?*** *A 3 out of 5. Willing, but often passive. Avoided initiative. Needed repeated nudges.*
- ***Aptitude?*** *A 2 out of 5. She couldn't handle formatting, tech platforms, or follow-up without supervision.*
- **Cultural Fit?** *Also 2 out of 5. Clients weren't wowed. She didn't understand the sensitivity needed for families making end-of-life decisions.*

Joanna's heart sank. She realized she had hired out of hope, not strategy. She had onboarded vaguely. She hadn't clearly defined what success looked like. And she had never built a pipeline of candidates–just picked the first one who seemed "nice."

*With her coach's help, she made a bold decision: she would terminate Leah's employment, kindly but firmly. And she would hire again–***this time with intention.**

They rewrote the job description to reflect the actual *needs of the business. They created a scorecard* before *applications opened. They designed an onboarding plan with daily expectations and weekly milestones. And they posted the job broadly–but screened ruthlessly.*

In the new hiring round, Joanna used behavior-based interview questions. She gave a short test assignment. And most importantly, she used the Culture Scorecard *before making the offer.*

She found her unicorn: Shana.

Shana scored high across the board. She was upbeat, systems-oriented, and professional–but also warm and emotionally attuned to clients. She loved to organize. She had worked in a medical office and knew how to handle sensitive paperwork with discretion. And in her first month, she asked, "Can I redesign our intake flow to save you some time?"

Joanna cried.

Within 90 days of hiring Shana, client satisfaction was up. Tasks were handled before Joanna asked. And for the first time in a year, Joanna took a weekend off–*phone off, email off–and didn't feel like the business would implode.*

Hiring "right" didn't just save time. It restored her peace. It reminded her that she didn't have to do everything. That she could lead *without micromanaging. That she could hire for freedom, not friction.*

And it all started with a scorecard.

Final Word: Hire for Freedom, Not Friction

Hiring isn't about filling a seat–it's about building capacity.

When you take the time to define what you need, evaluate candidates through the lens of performance and cultural alignment, and bring people into your firm with clarity and structure, you don't just lighten your load–you expand your leadership.

Joanna didn't need someone with a perfect resume. She needed someone who could execute, grow, and fit. And with tools like the Culture Scorecard and strategic hiring systems, she made it happen.

But here's the truth: ***a great hire is just the beginning.***

Takeaway: Even the best team member will falter without structure, feedback, and a culture of accountability. And that's where most law firm owners drop the ball–not in hiring, but in *managing what they hired for.*

So in the next section, we're going to tackle exactly that: how to optimize your employees' performance once they're in the seat, so your business doesn't just *add people*, it *multiplies results*.

Let's turn potential into performance.

Problem 2: Optimizing Employee Performance

Most law firm owners misdiagnose performance problems. We blame "bad hires," "weak work ethic," or "kids these days," when the truth is more uncomfortable: people aren't failing–our **systems** are. High-caliber employees can't deliver high-caliber results inside a fog of chaos. When roles are fuzzy, goals keep shifting, and feedback arrives only when something catches fire, even talented staff will slow down, play small, or tap out. That's not incompetence; that's survival.

Chaos shows up as misaligned targets ("bill more hours" with no definition of how), accountability that's optional ("we'll circle back"), and leadership that changes tone depending on the day, the docket, or the owner's stress level. Phones ring a beat too long, deadlines cut too close, and files boomerang because no one is sure what "done" actually means. The owner steps in as heroic fixer, which trains the team to wait for rescue. Output becomes personality-dependent. Morale dips. Potential wastes away.

Optimizing performance isn't about squeezing harder; it's about **engineering clarity and cadence**. Clarity means documented outcomes, crystal-clear roles, and visible scorecards that tell the truth every week. Cadence means a steady rhythm–weekly one-to-ones, quick huddles, and structured feedback–so course corrections happen early, not after the grievance, the complaint, or the client meltdown. Layer on **coaching and consequences** (both positive and corrective), and you transform effort into results.

In other words: people don't rise to the level of your pep talks; they operate at the level of your systems. This chapter will show you how to replace reactive supervision with a repeatable performance engine–one that turns scattered effort into measurable progress, reduces your "hero time," and makes excellence normal instead of exceptional.

The Pain of Underperforming Teams

Every law firm owner has lived some version of this nightmare: the phone rings, and instead of a cheerful, competent voice answering on the first ring, it drones through three... four... five... before someone finally picks up, frazzled, unsure of what to say. A client is put on hold indefinitely, shuffled between desks like a hot potato. Deadlines slide by quietly, unnoticed until they are suddenly, catastrophically urgent. Associates grumble about missing documents, paralegals whisper about "who dropped the ball this time," and you–the owner–sit at your desk thinking, *Why does no one here seem to care as much as I do?*

This is the silent chaos of under-optimized performance. It's not always the dramatic blow-up of an outright bad employee–the thief, the liar, the saboteur. No, it's quieter than that. It's the employee who does "just enough," the associate who drafts halfway, leaving you to finish the thought, the receptionist who greets clients warmly but constantly botches intake details. They are not incompetent, and they're not malicious, but their work creates a drag–a constant, low-level friction that slows everything down.

Inefficiency is the first symptom. Files don't move through the pipeline smoothly. What should take a day stretches into three, then into a week. That inefficiency feeds mistakes: missing signatures, misfiled documents, deadlines entered incorrectly into the case management system. Each small slip might be forgivable in isolation, but together they create an avalanche of rework. The attorney ends up reviewing the same file twice, the paralegal re-drafts the same letter, and you–the owner–spend your weekends "catching up" on what should have been handled without your intervention.

Then comes the morale problem. Underperforming staff create resentment–not just in you, but across the team. High performers look around and see their peers rewarded with the same paycheck despite delivering half the effort. They burn out faster, because they're constantly compensating for others' gaps. They start to ask themselves, *Why should I work so hard if no one else does?* And when your best people begin to disengage, the culture decays. Soon, everyone operates at "minimum necessary" levels, and the energy in your office feels heavy, stagnant, lifeless.

This disengagement is particularly brutal in law firms, because the work is exacting by nature. Legal practice requires precision. A missing comma in a contract, an incorrect date in a motion, an overlooked fact in discovery–these small cracks can become gaping chasms when adversaries exploit them or when judges lose patience. You, as the owner, know this instinctively, which is why you carry the stress like a weight in your chest. You can't afford these mistakes, but you also can't keep working yourself to the bone as the backstop for every flaw.

It's not just the errors themselves–it's the **mental load** of always being on guard. Owners in this state describe feeling like they have a second job: monitoring everyone else's job. They wake up at 2 a.m. in a cold sweat wondering if the motion deadline was calendared correctly. They scan outgoing mail themselves to be "extra sure." They proofread emails before they go to clients, not because they want to, but because they no longer trust their own staff to get it right. This kind of double-work is soul-crushing. It's like paying twice for the same product–once in salary, and again in your own time and sanity.

The resentment grows deeper still because of the story owners tell themselves: *I'm the only one who cares about this business.* That phrase is repeated like a mantra in firms across the country. It's said with bitterness, with exhaustion, with resignation. It fuels a vicious cycle: the owner cares more, so the owner does more, so the team does less, which proves again that the owner is the only one who cares. The business becomes a hamster wheel of frustration.

And here's the cruelest twist: often, it isn't even the employees' fault. Without **clarity of expectations, feedback loops, and accountability systems**, people default to doing what feels easiest or safest. They aren't willfully underperforming–they're operating blind, waiting for correction, hoping they don't step on a landmine. Without systems, it's impossible to know whether someone is truly a poor performer or simply under-directed. As a result, law firm owners live in a gray fog of uncertainty: is this person actually incapable, or am I failing to lead them well?

That uncertainty breeds indecision. Many owners tolerate mediocrity for far too long because they can't prove, even to themselves, where the failure lies. They fear firing someone only to discover the next person is just as bad. They fear the downtime of retraining, the disruption to workflow, the potential unemployment claim or awkward office gossip. So they keep the "C-minus" employee in place, rationalizing, *At least I know what I have.*

This is why **systems matter so much**. When you have documented scorecards, weekly check-ins, and transparent metrics, performance is no longer a guessing game. The moment someone misses the mark, it's visible. The team member knows it, you know it, and the system itself proves it. And here's where the power lies: when the system is strong, you can finally distinguish between someone who simply needs coaching and someone who truly doesn't belong. With superior systems, you can say with confidence, *This isn't us–it's you.* That clarity is liberating. It frees you from the guilt of wondering whether you gave the employee "enough chances." It also signals to the rest of your team that excellence is the standard, not the exception.

But until that clarity exists, chaos reigns. Deadlines continue to slip. Clients complain about lack of communication. You spend your evenings fixing typos in briefs while your family eats dinner without you. The dream of owning a firm that runs smoothly feels distant, maybe even impossible. You start to question your judgment, your leadership, even your sanity.

This is the raw, unvarnished cost of failing to optimize employee performance. It isn't just a few sloppy mistakes or a little inefficiency—it's the erosion of your confidence, the burnout of your best people, and the slow death of a culture where excellence was once possible. Left unchecked, this problem metastasizes until you're not running a law firm at all—you're babysitting adults, spinning plates, and praying nothing comes down too loudly.

CASE STUDY

MELISSA'S TURNING POINT

Melissa was a divorce attorney in Dallas who had built her firm on grit and reputation. By her mid-thirties, she was known in her market as a fierce litigator who never backed down in the courtroom. Clients loved her passion and trusted her judgment. Word of mouth referrals kept her calendar full. What Melissa hadn't counted on, however, was that success would bring a flood of cases she could no longer handle alone.

From Growth to Overwhelm

She did what every ambitious lawyer does: she hired. First one paralegal, then a receptionist, then another attorney to cover hearings while she prepped for trials. Soon, her office was buzzing with activity—phones ringing, clients coming in and out, staff huddled around conference tables. From the outside, it looked like a thriving law firm. But inside, Melissa was suffocating.

The cracks showed in little ways at first. A client called to ask why no one had returned her voicemail from three days ago. A paralegal filed a motion with the wrong cause number, which embarrassed Melissa in front of the judge. An associate handed her a draft that was barely more than bullet points, expecting her to fill in the substance. Every week, Melissa found herself correcting mistakes, rewriting documents, and stepping in to soothe angry clients. The more staff she hired, the more her to-do list seemed to multiply.

She grew resentful. Why do I pay salaries only to do the work myself anyway? *At night, she lay in bed staring at the ceiling, the phrase running on repeat in her mind:* I am the only one who cares about this business.

When Leadership Becomes the Bottleneck

When Melissa first came to Law Firm Mentor, she was defensive. She described her staff as "mediocre at best," convinced the problem was them, not her. She confessed that she'd already replaced her receptionist twice in six months and was ready to fire her associate. "I just don't think people want to work anymore," she said flatly.

We gently pushed back. What if, we suggested, the problem wasn't only the people, but the absence of a system that told them what excellence looked like and measured whether they were achieving it? Melissa bristled. "I shouldn't have to babysit grown adults," she snapped. "If they can't figure out how to do their jobs, they shouldn't be here."

Her resistance was classic: she equated "system" with micromanagement. But in reality, Melissa was already micromanaging—hovering, redoing, and checking every detail. The difference was that her micromanagement was reactive, draining, and endless. A system, we explained, would shift the responsibility back onto her staff by giving them clarity, structure, and measurable accountability.

Melissa wasn't convinced. She decided to "try it her way" first. She created a list of tasks for each role and told her staff to check them off daily. Within two weeks, the lists were abandoned, left half-filled or scribbled on the edges of case files. She tried holding a team meeting to "set expectations," but it turned into an airing of grievances. Everyone talked in circles, and nothing changed. Her frustration deepened.

Finally, she admitted defeat. "Fine," she said in her coaching session, her voice heavy with exhaustion. "Show me how to do this right."

We started small: a weekly scorecard. Melissa worked with us to identify the most critical metrics for each role–number of calls answered live, percentage of completed intakes, motions filed on time, billable hours logged. At first, the process felt clunky. Her paralegal balked, saying she wasn't a "numbers person." Her associate rolled his eyes. Melissa herself was skeptical: "I don't want to spend half my week updating spreadsheets."

But within a month, something remarkable happened. The scorecards made invisible problems visible. Melissa could see at a glance who was keeping up and who was slipping. The data told the truth that her gut had always suspected. The receptionist, who she thought was "fine," was answering only 60% of calls live. The paralegal who claimed to be "overwhelmed" was actually spending hours every week redoing work because she never asked for clarification upfront. The associate, who always defended his light workload, had the lowest billables on the team by far.

For the first time, Melissa had evidence. She didn't need to wonder whether her staff was performing. She could point to the numbers and say, Here is where you're excelling, and here is where you're falling short.

We layered in weekly accountability meetings. At first, Melissa dreaded them. She expected whining, excuses, and more wasted time. But the opposite occurred. With clear scorecards, the meetings were efficient. Each person reported their metrics, owned their results, and received coaching on how to improve. Melissa discovered she didn't have to lecture; the numbers did it for her. The culture began to shift from finger-pointing to problem-solving.

Still, there were bumps. Her associate pushed back, arguing that "quality matters more than quantity." Melissa wanted to cave–after all, his legal writing was strong–but the scorecard showed that his low productivity was dragging the firm down. With coaching, Melissa held the line. "We need both," she said firmly. "Excellence in work product and efficiency in output." Within two months, his billables doubled, and he admitted the structure was helping him stay focused.

Her paralegal, on the other hand, continued to struggle. Despite coaching, her error rate remained high. Melissa no longer agonized over whether she was being "too harsh." The system had spoken. With confidence, she let the paralegal go, explaining, "It's not us–it's you." To her surprise, the rest of the team felt relieved. The removal of a chronic underperformer lifted morale.

Melissa hired a replacement, this time with a clear scorecard from day one. The new paralegal thrived in the structure, quickly becoming one of the firm's most reliable team members. Clients noticed. They began complimenting the professionalism of her staff, not just Melissa herself. For the first time, Melissa felt like she wasn't the lone soldier holding the line.

Her emotional journey was palpable. She went from skepticism to grudging acceptance, from exhaustion to empowerment. She discovered the freedom that comes when performance is systematized: she no longer had to hover, redo, or silently seethe. Instead, she could coach, lead, and ultimately trust her team.

The ripple effects were profound. Melissa's revenue increased because cases moved faster and clients were happier. Her stress levels plummeted. She began taking Friday afternoons off, confident that her team could handle the workload without her constant oversight. She no longer muttered, "I'm the only one who cares." Instead, she found herself saying, with pride, "My team is killing it."

What Melissa learned–and what every law firm owner must accept–is that optimizing performance isn't about hiring unicorns.

> *It's about building a system that allows ordinary, capable people to deliver extraordinary results. And when someone can't rise to that system? You know without a shadow of a doubt: the problem isn't you; it's them.*
>
> ### *Final Word: When Blame Feels Easier than Accountability*
>
> *Optimizing employee performance is not about wringing more sweat out of your people or resigning yourself to endless micromanagement. It's about building a system where expectations are undeniable, accountability is consistent, and results are transparent. When the systems are strong, the owner no longer has to carry the business on their back. The team rises, not because you pushed harder, but because the path to excellence is paved clearly before them. And if someone refuses to walk that path? The data speaks for itself. You can part ways decisively, with no guilt, because you know it's* them, not you.

Takeaway: The real payoff isn't just in improved productivity–it's in restored trust. You trust your team. They trust each other. And together, you create an environment where high performance is the norm, not the exception.

But optimizing output is only half the equation. Once you've built a team that performs, the next challenge is keeping them engaged, committed, and loyal. In the following section, we'll explore the problem of retention–why great employees leave, how chaos accelerates turnover, and what it really takes to create a firm where talented people want to stay and grow.

Problem 3: Retention: Why It Is and Is Not Your Fault

Few things sting more than losing a team member you've invested in. You spend months, even years, training them, mentoring them, pouring your time, money, and energy into their growth–only to watch them walk out the door, often without so much as an honest conversation about why. The gut reaction is almost always self-blame: *What did I do wrong? Am I a bad boss? Am I not good enough?*

But here's the reality: retention is more complicated than that. According to the U.S. Bureau of Labor Statistics (BLS), those who work in legal occupations experience a median tenure of 5.8 years in 2020, dropping to 4.7 years in 2022.[1] Movement is baked into the profession. The work is grueling. Client demands are relentless. Society views lawyers with suspicion and derision, and those messages seep into our bones. It's easy for lawyers to believe the problem is their environment: *If I just worked at a better firm, I'd be happy.*

In other words: sometimes it really isn't you. But–sometimes it is. And if your firm lacks systems, clear expectations, growth paths, and culture, then retention chaos is a monster of your own making.

The Retention Problem

Let's start with the hard truth: you could do *everything* right for the *right* employees, and still be totally wrong for the *wrong* ones.

Some lawyers leave purely for money. It's not even that they're underpaid–it's that they lack the wherewithal to engage in meaningful conversations with their bosses. Rather than asking for a raise, they quietly field offers from competitors. And, let's get real. Many lawyers are not meeting expectations where they are, so the moment another firm dangles a bigger paycheck, they're gone.

Others leave because their egos are hungry. Many people enter this profession to fight for others because they did not feel empowered in their own lives. That's noble–but it also means they require constant ego support. And nothing strokes the ego quite like being courted by another law firm.

Then there's the allure of what many law firm owners simply cannot offer: more prestige, more money, more status, more opportunity.

1 https://www.bls.gov/news.release/archives/tenure_09222022.pdf

A younger attorney may fantasize about the glimmer of a national platform or the sheen of a downtown high-rise office. No matter how strong your leadership, you can't outshine the siren song of "bigger and better." Sometimes the misalignment is subtler. A lawyer may think she craves a lighter lifestyle—fewer hours, more work-life balance—only to discover she actually feels most accomplished under pressure, logging long hours and taking on heavy demands. She leaves, convinced she's chasing peace, and then realizes she misses the grind.

All of this is to say: it's not always you. Sometimes people move because of their own unmet needs, their own lack of communication, their own restless search for validation or status. And it's worth remembering that even the most abusive, least supportive, most hostile firms out there—the ones with legendary reputations for "kiss the ring" culture—are often the *largest*. How? They convince young lawyers that they should be grateful to suffer, that the prestige alone is worth the misery. Lawyers conditioned in that environment don't have the self-esteem to leave. The only factor that matters is the perception of superiority: "I must be good because I work at Such-and-Such LLP." So, yes, they stay. Not because the leadership is good, but because they've been groomed to believe survival equals success.

So if someone leaves you, take heart. Sometimes their departure has nothing to do with your competency, your generosity, or your leadership. Sometimes it's simply about them.

But here's the flip side—and it's a big one. Sometimes, it *is* you.

Retention chaos happens when law firm owners fail to build the systems their people need to thrive. Employees stay when they have clarity, consistency, and a sense of growth. They leave when the environment feels disorganized, expectations are vague, and leadership wavers between micromanagement and benign neglect. Without a system for leading, managing, and organizing people's activity consistent with firm goals, your employees are left to guess. And guesswork breeds disengagement.

Picture the scene: one associate thinks "success" means racking up billable hours at any cost, while another thinks "success" means client satisfaction, even if that means writing off time. A paralegal files documents the way she did at her last job, while another paralegal does it differently, and neither way matches your preferred process. Staff float around like free agents, each following their own instincts. Deadlines are missed. Work is duplicated. Fingers point in every direction.

Without structure, your best people get frustrated and leave, while your worst people linger like barnacles. You wake up one day realizing the talent drain wasn't inevitable–it was the natural result of your firm's lack of systems. And the irony? It's usually the strongest, most capable employees who leave first, because they know they can succeed elsewhere.

Retention systems aren't just about perks or paychecks. They're about creating an environment where people know what's expected, have tools to meet those expectations, and see a pathway to grow their careers. That means documented standards. That means scorecards and accountability meetings. That means opportunities for skill development, coaching, and recognition. When you fail to provide those things, you're not just "losing" people–they're *escaping* a workplace that felt chaotic and unsustainable.

So yes, it's not always your fault when someone walks out the door. But sometimes, it is. And the good news is that this side of the coin–the part that *is* your fault–is entirely within your power to change. By systematizing the way you lead, manage, and grow your people, you not only retain more of the right employees–you build a culture that repels the wrong ones before they even get through the door.

CASE STUDY

JONATHAN'S STRUGGLE WITH RETENTION

Jonathan was a well-regarded intellectual property lawyer in Miami, Florida. He had built a boutique firm focused on trademarks, copyrights, and patents, representing a mix of scrappy startups and mid-sized companies protecting their brands. By most outward measures, he was thriving. His client base was expanding, his reputation was growing, and his revenues had doubled in the past three years.

But inside the firm, Jonathan was exhausted. He'd hired bright young attorneys and paralegals, invested in their training, and offered competitive salaries. Yet the turnover was relentless. Every time he felt like he had finally built a reliable team, someone would resign.

At first, Jonathan told himself it wasn't his fault. His star associate announced she was leaving for a national firm in New York, and the opportunity was, in her words, "just too prestigious to pass up." Jonathan couldn't blame her. How could his boutique in Miami compete with the lure of a Manhattan skyline office and the promise of Fortune 500 clients? Deep down, he knew he was too small to match the salary packages and status symbols that came with a giant platform. All he could do was swallow the sting and tell himself, This one was never mine to keep.

Then there was the paralegal who left for a competitor down the street for an extra $5,000 a year. She hadn't asked Jonathan for a raise, and he would have gladly given her one if she had. But instead, she entertained the first offer that came her way, and by the time Jonathan found out, it was too late.

Another attorney left after just eighteen months, telling Jonathan she wanted a "better work-life balance." But a few months later, he spotted her LinkedIn update: she'd joined a high-demand patent litigation firm notorious for 70-hour weeks. Clearly, she didn't actually want fewer hours–she wanted a different kind of validation. Jonathan shook his head. "That one's on her, not me."

For a while, Jonathan comforted himself with that narrative. It's not me. It's them. People chase money. They chase ego. They chase prestige. And he wasn't wrong–sometimes that was exactly the reason.

But then came the departure that forced him to face the mirror.

The Departure He Couldn't Ignore

Carlos was a paralegal Jonathan had hired straight out of a paralegal certificate program. Jonathan trained him from scratch. Carlos was meticulous, hardworking, and eager to learn. Clients adored his responsiveness. Associates relied on his research. Jonathan often told people Carlos was "the glue that held the office together." So when Carlos walked into his office one morning with a resignation letter, Jonathan was stunned.

"I'm not unhappy here," Carlos said carefully. "But I don't really know what my future looks like. I don't know what growth means at this firm. I don't have a clear sense of how I can build a career, not just a job. Another firm offered me a pathway to become a case manager in two years. They have training programs, defined expectations, and benchmarks. I feel like I can build something there."

That was the gut punch. Jonathan realized that for all the times he had blamed the revolving door on money, ego, or prestige, he had failed to see his own blind spot: his firm had no system for people.

He had no written career paths. No documented standards. No performance scorecards. Reviews happened only when something went wrong. Associates never knew whether they were on track or falling short until Jonathan exploded in frustration over a missed deadline. Paralegals weren't sure how their work tied into the firm's larger goals. Everyone was just...winging it.

Turning Chaos Into Structure

Carlos's departure forced Jonathan to confront the uncomfortable truth: sometimes it is *you. Retention chaos isn't just about who leaves; it's about why they feel compelled to leave. And in this case, Jonathan had failed to give his team the clarity and growth they craved.*

When Jonathan came to Law Firm Mentor, he was skeptical. He believed systems were for giant firms, not boutiques like his. But he was also desperate. So he started where we told him to: with structure.

First, he built **scorecards** *for every role. Associates were measured not only on billable hours, but also on turnaround times, client satisfaction scores, and contributions to firm-wide projects. Paralegals tracked filings, error rates, and response times. Suddenly, expectations weren't fuzzy–they were crystal clear.*

Next, he instituted **quarterly reviews and career path conversations.** *Each team member could see the benchmarks for advancement: what skills they needed to develop, what performance targets to hit, and what opportunities would open up if they stayed. Jonathan resisted at first–he didn't want to overpromise–but he quickly realized that people weren't demanding guarantees, just clarity.*

Then came **weekly one-on-one meetings.** *Instead of waiting for problems to boil over, Jonathan created a cadence for feedback, coaching, and recognition. At first, it felt awkward. His associate, Maya, sat stiffly across from him, unsure what to say. But over time, the rhythm built trust. Maya admitted she wanted more courtroom experience, and Jonathan found ways to delegate motion hearings. Her confidence skyrocketed. She stopped browsing job boards.*

The cultural shift was dramatic. Turnover slowed. People felt invested, not expendable. Jonathan's team began to see his firm as a place where they could grow, not just collect a paycheck until the next recruiter called.

There were still departures, of course. One associate left for a national firm that offered a prestigious in-house secondment with a sports franchise. Another paralegal moved out of state to be closer to family. But Jonathan no longer internalized those exits as personal failures. He could say with confidence, "It's not me." And when someone underperformed despite the systems–when their scorecard glared red month after month–he no longer agonized. He knew it was them.

Jonathan's journey captures the nuance of retention. Some people will always leave for money, ego, or prestige. That's the nature of the profession. But others will leave if you fail to provide structure, standards, and a path forward. And that part–that's on you. Once Jonathan embraced that truth, he stopped seeing retention as a mystery and started treating it as a system.

Final Word: Creating the Foundation for Retention

Retention is never a simple equation. Sometimes, no matter how supportive you are, no matter how clearly you set expectations, and no matter how fairly you compensate, people will still leave. They'll chase prestige, ego strokes, or the illusion of greener pastures. That's not your fault, and it's not a reflection of your leadership. It's simply the reality of a profession where mobility is common and temptation is constant.

But sometimes, departures are *your fault. They stem from the absence of structure, growth opportunities, and systems that make people feel secure and invested in their work. That part–the chaos created by vague expectations, inconsistent leadership, and lack of career paths–is fully within your power to change. When you implement systems for performance, feedback, and development, you not only keep your best people longer, you also free yourself from second-guessing whether someone left because of you. You'll know.*

Takeaway: You can't control every factor, but you can control the environment your people experience every day. And when that environment is clear, consistent, and growth-oriented, you'll keep more of the right people–and lose fewer to chaos.

Next, we turn to a problem that is the flip side retention: **managing managers**. Because even the best people will fail to thrive–or worse, leave–if they're never trusted with responsibility. But once you trust them with responsibility, specifically responsibility for others, you cannot simply walk away and leave them to their own devices. And this is where the role of a law firm leader becomes an exponential challenge.

Problem 4: Managing the Managers – Building a Leadership Spine

Delegating responsibility is one thing. Delegating leadership is another. Far too many law firm owners make the critical mistake of elevating strong employees into management positions and then assuming the hard part is over. "She's great with clients–she'll make a good manager." "He's been here the longest–he can oversee the paralegals." With little more than a handshake and a new title, the owner steps aside, relieved to have "one less thing" on their plate.

But this isn't delegation–it's abdication. And abdication is destructive.

When managers are left to their own devices without direction, training, or accountability, chaos spreads like wildfire. All the problems we've already examined–bad hires, inconsistent performance, weak retention–become amplified under poor management. A bad manager doesn't just fail at their own job; they infect the performance of everyone beneath them. Morale dips. Communication breaks down. Standards crumble. And because the law firm owner assumes "the manager is handling it," these problems often fester until they explode.

This is why building a *leadership spine* is non-negotiable. Your managers are the vertebrae of your firm's structure. If they're weak, your firm slouches. If they're brittle, it snaps. But if they're strong, aligned, and supported, they hold the entire body of the business upright.

Managing managers is not about relinquishing control; it's about creating a system of oversight, mentorship, and accountability that ensures your leaders lead well. Without that spine, your firm cannot stand tall.

The Abdication Trap

Promoting someone into management feels like progress. For the law firm owner who's been drowning in details—fielding client complaints, answering staff questions, troubleshooting tech issues—it feels like sweet relief to finally say, "You're in charge now. Handle it." But that moment of relief is often the beginning of a new, bigger problem.

Too many owners confuse elevation with delegation. They give a capable paralegal the title of "office manager," or tap their most senior associate to "lead the litigation team," and then step back, believing they've lightened their load. But what they've actually done is hand the keys to the firm's engine room to someone who has never learned to drive.

This is not delegation; it's abdication. And abdication breeds chaos.

Here's how it shows up:

The office manager, once a stellar paralegal, suddenly spends her days in a fog of frustration. She knows how to manage cases but not how to manage people. She shies away from hard conversations with underperforming staff, so she ignores problems until they snowball. The receptionist grows lax with intake calls. Deadlines slip. Files are mishandled. Instead of raising the issues, the new "manager" either tries to fix everything herself—burning out—or does nothing, hoping it will all work out.

The senior associate, once the sharpest litigator on the team, now carries the added burden of overseeing younger attorneys. But without training or guidance, he confuses leadership with micromanagement. He nitpicks drafts, rewrites every motion, and barks at associates for being "sloppy." Morale plummets. Associates stop taking initiative because they know their work will just be torn apart. Resentment festers. Before long, the best young lawyer on the team is polishing her résumé.

And the owner? He sees the fallout too late. He thought these "managers" were handling it, but in reality, they were floundering. And because he stepped back completely, the damage spread unchecked. Clients complain. Turnover spikes. Revenue stagnates.

Every problem we've discussed so far—hiring, performance, retention—becomes exponentially worse when weak managers are left unsupported. A bad hire may slip through the cracks because no one is screening effectively. Underperforming employees may linger for months because the manager is conflict-averse. Talented staff leave because they're suffocating under poor leadership. And the culture? It crumbles. People no longer know who to follow, so they follow no one.

The insidious part is that this dysfunction often hides behind a veneer of "busyness." A bad manager can look like they're working hard—running meetings, sending emails, generating reports—while the actual output of their team nosedives. Owners mistake activity for effectiveness, and by the time they realize the truth, the damage is already done.

Why does this happen so often in law firms? Because lawyers are trained to practice law, not to lead leaders. We're comfortable telling a paralegal how to assemble a trial binder or showing an associate how to draft an affidavit. But teaching someone how to coach performance, give constructive feedback, or align their team with firmwide goals? That's a different skill set entirely. And most law firm owners never develop it.

So they do what feels easiest: they promote the "best worker" into management, then cross their fingers and hope it works out. But as the old saying goes, what got them here won't get them there.

The skills that make someone a stellar individual contributor rarely translate into management success without training, mentorship, and accountability.

And this is where the abdication trap becomes most destructive: by naming a manager the owner believes they've solved a problem, when in fact they've created a bigger one. Because when a manager fails, they don't just fail alone–they drag their entire team down with them.

It's like building a skyscraper without reinforcing the steel beams. The exterior looks impressive, but the structure has no spine. Eventually, the weight becomes too much, and the whole building starts to sag.

This is why "managing the managers" is non-negotiable. You cannot simply anoint leaders and walk away. You must actively build their capacity to lead. That means clear role definitions, leadership training, performance metrics, regular check-ins, and consistent feedback. It means setting the standard that managers are not free agents but stewards of the firm's vision, culture, and goals.

Without this leadership spine, your firm cannot stand tall. Managers will wobble, teams will drift, and chaos will seep into every corner of the business. You'll find yourself wondering why nothing seems to improve despite having managers in place. And the answer will be simple: because managers without oversight are not managers at all. They're placeholders. And placeholders can't carry a firm forward.

CASE STUDY

GRACE'S WAKE-UP CALL

Grace was a first-generation Asian-American attorney in Seattle, Washington, who built her boutique firm around employment law. She fought for clients who had been wrongfully terminated, discriminated against, or denied fair wages. Her advocacy was fierce, her reputation solid, and her docket full. By the time her firm reached its sixth year, Grace had grown from a solo to a team of twelve: five attorneys, four paralegals, and three support staff, including a receptionist and a two-person intake team.

From the outside, Grace's firm looked strong and steady. Inside, Grace was exhausted. She thought she had solved the bottleneck of being "the only leader" by promoting from within. Her longest-tenured paralegal, Denise, was given the title of "office manager." Her most senior associate, Victor, was named "team lead" for litigation. Grace congratulated herself for "building a management layer" so she could focus on strategy, client development, and trial work.

But what she had actually built was a leadership vacuum.

When "Managers" Aren't Actually Managing

At first, Grace felt a sense of relief. She finally had people to "handle things." When the receptionist struggled with tardiness, Grace sent the matter to Denise. When a client complained about delays, she asked Victor to "tighten up the attorneys." Grace told herself she was learning to be the CEO–finally pulling back from the weeds.

But Denise had no training in managing people. She was brilliant at drafting discovery responses and prepping for depositions, but she shrank from conflict. When one of the intake specialists routinely failed to capture complete caller information, Denise sighed and corrected it herself, late at night. She avoided direct conversations, hoping problems would fix themselves. Meanwhile, the errors piled up. Prospective clients had to repeat their stories because of incomplete intakes. Some grew frustrated and hired other firms.

Victor took the opposite approach. Empowered with his new "team lead" title, he began micromanaging associates to the point of suffocation. He rewrote every brief, nitpicked their wording choices, and publicly scolded paralegals for minor mistakes. His team lived in constant fear of his criticism. One young associate quietly took recruiter calls. Another stopped volunteering for new cases, convinced that no matter how hard she worked, Victor would tear it apart.

Grace, unaware of how bad things were, assumed her managers had it under control. That was the point, wasn't it? She had given them authority so she could step back. But soon, the warning signs were undeniable. Morale plummeted. The intake team lost one of its strongest members, who resigned in tears after telling Grace, "I love this work, but I don't feel supported. There's no consistency here." Client complaints rose. And for the first time in her career, Grace got the dreaded Google review that described her firm as "disorganized and unresponsive."

The breaking point came when Fredreick, one of her most trusted paralegals, turned in his notice. Fredreick had been with the firm nearly four years–he was loyal, efficient, and beloved by clients. Grace was stunned.

"I respect you deeply," Fredreick told her, "but I can't keep working in this environment. Victor's leadership style is crushing. Denise means well, but nothing really gets resolved. I don't see a future here unless things change."

That conversation gutted Grace. She realized the problem wasn't just Denise or Victor–it was her. She had abdicated leadership. She gave her managers titles without training, authority without accountability, and responsibility without oversight. She assumed leadership was an instinct instead of a skill, and her firm was paying the price.

You Can't Delegate What You Don't Define

When Grace came to Law Firm Mentor, she admitted through tears: "I thought I was empowering them. But really, I just walked away and left them to sink or swim. And they're sinking."

We helped Grace build her **leadership spine.**

First, we defined what management actually *meant in her firm. Denise wasn't just "office manager"–she was responsible for the systems that governed support staff and intake. That meant she needed tools, not just a title. With our guidance, Grace created job descriptions, decision-making guidelines, and performance score-cards. Denise now had benchmarks to measure intake accuracy, call capture rates, and administrative compliance.*

Next, Grace instituted **weekly leadership meetings** *with Denise and Victor. These weren't casual chats–they were structured sessions with agendas. Each manager reported on metrics: case deadlines met, client satisfaction surveys, staff performance issues, and opportunities for improvement. Grace coached them in real time on giving feedback, setting standards, and handling conflict.*

Denise struggled at first–her aversion to confrontation made her hesitant. But with role-playing and scripts, she began tackling issues head-on. Within weeks, she addressed the intake specialist's performance directly and saw immediate improvement. For the first time, Denise wasn't just fixing mistakes–she was preventing them.

Victor bristled more. He was used to unchecked authority. But when his team's turnover risk and client delays showed up in the metrics, Grace held him accountable. "Leadership isn't about control," she told him. "It's about results through others." With coaching, he learned to redirect his energy into mentoring instead of micromanaging. Slowly, his associates began to relax and grow, and morale rebounded.

The impact was transformative. Clients noticed faster responses. The intake team's accuracy improved. Associates began to take initiative again. Grace felt the difference in her own workload: instead of firefighting daily crises, she was leading leaders who were truly leading their teams.

Grace's story is the cautionary tale of what happens when law firm owners abdicate instead of manage. Promoting managers without training or oversight magnifies every problem–hiring, performance, retention–until the whole firm teeters. But when you build a leadership spine–clear definitions, structured accountability, and consistent mentorship–you stop wobbling and start standing tall.

> *Final Word: Building the Leadership Spine*
>
> *The hardest lesson for law firm owners to absorb is that promoting managers doesn't mean you can step away. Titles alone don't create leaders. If anything, handing out authority without training or accountability multiplies chaos. Weak managers don't just fail quietly–they poison entire teams, magnify dysfunction, and drive away your best people.*
>
> *The antidote is building a* leadership spine.

Takeaway: When you define roles clearly, provide ongoing coaching, and measure results through objective metrics, your managers stop being placeholders and start becoming multipliers. They carry the vision of your firm into the day-to-day, ensuring that culture, standards, and systems are consistently applied. That's when your firm shifts from wobbling under its own weight to standing tall with strength and resilience.

But managing managers is only one layer of the leadership challenge. The next level requires you, as the owner, to step fully into the role of visionary. Because once the spine is in place, you must decide what kind of body it will support. In the next section, we'll explore how law firm leaders can align vision and systems to ensure not just survival, but sustainable growth.

Problem 5: Culture That Carries – Keeping Your Standards When You're Not in the Room

You can hire brilliantly, optimize performance, retain the right people, and even manage your managers well. But there's still one more layer before your firm becomes truly self-sustaining: culture.

Culture isn't slogans on a wall or the words you say at the holiday party. It's the lived experience of your people every single day. It's how deadlines are handled, how clients are spoken to, how mistakes are corrected, how wins are celebrated.

Most importantly, it's what happens when you're not in the room.

That's the true test. Does your firm still operate at the standard you set even when you're in court, on vacation, or simply behind closed doors working strategy? Or does the quality slip the moment your back is turned?

The glue that holds culture together is vision. The law firm owner must be more than the boss—they must be the evangelist for what the firm is building, why it matters, and how every role contributes to it. This isn't about rah-rah pep talks. It's about relentlessly articulating your vision until it becomes the shared compass for every decision, from the managers down to the most junior support staff.

Culture that carries ensures your standards are lived out, not just spoken. It's the connective tissue between your people systems and your leadership. Without it, everything else you've built can unravel the moment you step away.

The Vision Vacuum

One of the most common blind spots for law firm owners is the reluctance to speak their vision out loud. Many harbor bold dreams: dominating a practice area in their state, becoming the go-to firm for high-net-worth divorces, scaling to multiple offices, or building the reputation that wins the most complex, high-stakes cases.

But those dreams stay locked in the owner's head. Why? Fear.

Lawyers, trained to hedge risk and avoid embarrassment, are terrified of declaring a future that isn't guaranteed. "What if I tell my team I want to dominate the market, and we fall flat? What if I promise we'll open three offices, and we never get past one? I'll look foolish. I'll lose credibility." So they keep their ambitions quiet, speaking only in safe, generic terms: "We want to serve our clients well. We want to grow. We want to be successful."

But here's the problem: generic goals don't inspire anyone. They don't magnetize people. They don't galvanize action. Without a clear north star, employees show up for a paycheck, not a purpose. They do the tasks in front of them but don't feel pulled toward anything larger. The energy becomes transactional. And when the culture is transactional, talent doesn't stick.

Vision is the glue that binds people together. When an owner boldly declares, "We are going to be the premier employment law firm in Seattle for executives in transition," that vision becomes a rallying cry. It shapes conversations in team meetings. It informs hiring decisions. It sets the bar for service. Suddenly, staff don't just have jobs—they have a role in building something bigger.

Speaking vision creates common language. It gives people shorthand for what matters most.

- If "premier" is the standard, then everything from the receptionist's phone greeting to the formatting of briefs gets measured against it.
- If "dominating the market" is the goal, then marketing, business development, and client service are all infused with urgency.
- People begin to see themselves as contributors to a shared mission, not isolated workers punching the clock.

Vision also acts as a filter. It magnetizes the right people—the ones who want to be part of a firm on the rise, who crave challenge, who want to push themselves. And it repels the wrong people—the ones who are content with mediocrity, who see their role as "just a job," who bristle at high standards. In that sense, vision isn't just a motivator; it's a recruitment and retention strategy.

When owners withhold their vision, they deny their teams this unifying force. Without it, culture drifts.

- Managers interpret priorities differently.
- Associates pursue individual agendas.
- Support staff work in silos.
- Everyone does their own version of "good work," but there's no shared definition of *great*.

The result is fragmentation—like a choir where each singer belts out their own tune instead of harmonizing.

This fragmentation shows up in subtle but devastating ways. A paralegal argues with an associate about deadlines because each is working toward a different standard. The intake team captures leads diligently, but the marketing team doesn't follow through because they aren't aligned on who the firm is trying to attract. Even client service suffers: one attorney emphasizes empathy while another emphasizes speed, leaving clients confused about what the firm really stands for.

And the owner? They end up frustrated, asking, "Why don't my people care as much as I do?" The truth is, they might care deeply—but without a vision, they don't know where to aim their energy.

Here's the paradox: the very thing owners fear—looking foolish if they fail—is what makes them human, relatable, and worth following. Teams don't need guarantees; they need direction. They need a leader who is willing to plant a flag and say, "This is where we're headed," even if the path is uncertain. Vision doesn't have to be a contract. It's a compass.

And that compass is what turns employees into a culture. It gives rise to inside jokes, rallying phrases, shared rituals. It creates the "feel" of a firm—the invisible but undeniable atmosphere clients notice the moment they walk through the door. It's what makes someone say, "I don't just work at a law firm. I'm part of *this* law firm."

Without vision, there is no glue. There are only individuals doing individual tasks. With vision, there is cohesion. Standards are upheld even when the owner isn't watching, because everyone knows what they're building and why it matters.

Failing to articulate vision is failing to supply the very ingredient that transforms a collection of employees into a team. It's what keeps your standards alive when you're not in the room. And without it, all the systems you've built—hiring, performance, retention, management—risk collapsing under the weight of indifference.

CASE STUDY

SOPHIA'S QUIET FIRM

Sophia was an accomplished trial lawyer in Denver who had built her family law practice from scratch. She was brilliant in the courtroom–sharp on her feet, fearless with cross-examinations, relentless in pursuit of her clients' goals. But inside her firm, she led with quiet restraint.

She had grown up with messages many women absorb: don't brag, don't make yourself the center of attention, don't talk too big about the future. Humility wasn't just encouraged; it was demanded. When she launched her firm, she told herself she would "let the work speak for itself." She thought clients would see her results, staff would naturally follow her example, and success would flow without her having to stand on a chair and declare her ambitions.

So Sophia kept her vision tucked away like a private journal. She dreamed of being the *premier family law firm in Colorado, dominating high-net-worth divorce and custody disputes, but she never said those words aloud to her team. What if it didn't happen? What if she failed? She feared they'd laugh behind her back, or worse, lose respect for her. She settled for safe statements: "We want to serve clients well. We want to grow steadily."*

Her team liked her. They respected her talent. But they didn't feel inspired.

When Vision Stays Silent

Without a north star, everyone operated on their own assumptions. Her associate attorneys pursued cases based on personal preference–one sought settlement-heavy matters while another chased high-conflict litigation. Paralegals developed their own filing systems, each convinced their way was best. Intake staff described the firm differently to prospects: one emphasized affordability, another emphasized aggressiveness, another emphasized compassion. Clients got mixed messages. Some praised the firm's sensitivity; others complained about its lack of backbone.

The real problem wasn't performance–it was **drift**. *People were working hard but not rowing in the same direction. There was no common language, no shared definition of success, no glue holding the culture together. And Sophia didn't see it clearly until she lost her best associate.*

That associate, Maya, was a rising star–talented, ambitious, and beloved by clients. When she resigned to join a larger firm, Sophia was devastated. "I want to be part of something bigger," Maya explained gently. "I'm not sure what we're building here. I know you care about clients, but I don't know where this firm is headed. At the new firm, it's clear: they want to dominate the Denver market. That excites me. I want to grow into that vision."

Sophia was gutted. She had that exact vision*–but she had never spoken it. She had let her fear of "bragging" keep her silent. And in her silence, she lost one of her best people.*

Learning to Lead Out Loud

When Sophia came to Law Firm Mentor, she admitted, "I feel like I've been hiding my own dreams from my team. I want us to dominate, but I don't want to look arrogant if we don't. I don't want to be the one making big promises I can't keep."

We told her the truth: **vision isn't about promises–it's about direction.** *People don't need guarantees; they need a compass. Without it, they drift. With it, they align.*

Sophia agreed to experiment. At her next team meeting, she did something she had never done before: she declared her vision. She told her staff, "I want us to be the premier family law firm in Colorado. I want our name to mean excellence in complex divorce. And every single one of you is part of building that reality."

The reaction startled her. No one rolled their eyes. No one whispered behind her back. Instead, her team leaned in. They asked questions. They wanted to know how their roles fit into the plan. They wanted benchmarks, goals, markers of progress. In that moment, Sophia realized the thing she had feared—looking foolish—was never the risk. The risk was silence.

From there, she began weaving vision into everything. She created a **vision statement** *that wasn't just framed on the wall but spoken weekly in team huddles. She tied staff evaluations to whether they embodied the firm's cultural values. She started telling prospective hires exactly what the firm was building—repelling the ones who wanted "just a job" and attracting the ones who wanted to be part of something bigger.*

Her culture transformed. Associates began collaborating instead of competing, because they saw themselves as building the same future. Paralegals standardized systems, because they understood consistency was part of being "premier." Intake staff began speaking the same language to every caller: high-value service for high-stakes clients. Clients noticed. Reviews shifted from "good lawyers" to "a first-class, professional firm."

And perhaps most importantly, Sophia herself transformed. She stopped hiding. She became the vocal proponent of her vision, the evangelist for where the firm was headed. Her humility didn't disappear—she still listened, credited her team, and remained grounded. But she no longer confused humility with silence.

The truth is, women in particular struggle with this more than men. Men are certainly socialized not to "brag" or "boast," but for women, humility often becomes part of identity. To speak boldly feels like breaking character. But leadership requires breaking that conditioning. Because if you don't speak vision, no one else will. And if no one else speaks it, your culture will drift until your best people leave for someone else's.

Sophia's firm today operates like a true team, guided by a shared north star. When she steps out of the room, her standards remain, because her people know not just what they're doing—but why they're doing it.

Final Word: Vision Becomes Reality

Culture is not what you hope people will do when you're gone—it's what you have taught, reinforced, and repeated until it becomes second nature. It's the north star your team steers by when you're in court, on vacation, or locked in strategy sessions. Without vision spoken aloud, your people are left to drift, each making up their own definition of "success." With vision, you give them purpose, language, and shared identity. That is the glue that keeps your standards alive when you're not in the room.

And here's the hard truth: if you don't speak your vision, no one else will. If you're afraid of looking foolish, your silence becomes the greater risk—the risk of losing your best people, of diluting your culture, of watching the firm you've built slowly fragment.

Takeaway: You must be the evangelist for your vision. Say it often, say it boldly, and weave it into the fabric of everything your firm does.

This brings us to our next chapter. Up to now, we've focused on people—hiring them, optimizing them, retaining them, managing them, and uniting them with vision. But Chapter 13 is about *you*—the law firm leader. Because once you've built a culture that carries, the question becomes: will you rise into the kind of leadership that sustains it?

CHAPTER 11

THE LEADERSHIP LEVER
CRUSHING CHAOS FROM THE TOP DOWN

Leadership. It's the word every law firm owner claims, but few truly embody. We love the *idea* of being a leader. We love the title. We might even like the sound of it when someone introduces us at a bar event or awards gala: "This is so-and-so, the managing partner of her own firm." It sounds impressive.

But here's the truth that stings: *most law firm owners are not leading.* They're managing. They're juggling. They're grinding. They're solving everyone else's problems while avoiding the one problem that only they can fix—their own failure to step into true leadership.

And make no mistake: leadership is not optional. At a certain point, no amount of hard work, no level of brilliance, no volume of cases will carry your firm forward without leadership. Your growth will stall. Your people will disengage. Your systems will rust. Because businesses don't rise to the level of their technical expertise—they rise (or fall) to the level of their leadership.

In the earlier chapters of this book, we focused on people. How to hire them. How to optimize their performance. How to retain the right ones. How to manage the managers. How to weave vision into culture so it sticks when you're not in the room. But here's the pivot: none of that works if you don't lead. You can put in place all the systems in the world, but if you're a weak leader, the systems will collapse under the weight of uncertainty and inconsistency. People don't follow processes—they follow leaders. And if the leader isn't leading, no process can save you.

The problem is that most lawyers were never trained for leadership. Law school taught you how to think like a lawyer, not lead like a CEO. The profession rewards perfectionism, risk-aversion, and individual heroics—all traits that make you a damn fine attorney and a terrible leader. Leadership requires different muscles: vision, authority, consistency, execution, and growth. Without those, you're not leading—you're babysitting adults with law degrees.

And this is where chaos creeps back in. Because when you fail to lead, the firm fills the vacuum with confusion. People invent their own priorities. Managers go rogue. Staff do just enough to stay under the radar. Culture fragments. Clients notice. And you, the owner, feel like you're carrying an entire firm on your back while everyone else rides shotgun.

So let's take a quick look at the five most common leadership failures that create chaos in law firms. We'll go into more detail on each further below.

1. **The Lone Wolf Leader – Why You Can't Carry It All**
   This is the owner who tries to be everything to everyone: rainmaker, trial lawyer, office manager, HR, billing, IT, therapist. They confuse busyness with leadership, believing that being the hardest worker equals being the best leader. Wrong. True leadership requires altitude. You must get in the helicopter and look down at the terrain, not dig trenches with the troops. And that requires shedding jobs—especially the jobs you're good at but shouldn't be doing. Without that decision, you'll never stop being a lawyer who happens to own a firm instead of a CEO who leads one.
2. **Fear of Authority – Confusing Popularity with Leadership**
   This is the owner who desperately wants to be liked. They soften standards, avoid tough conversations, and confuse

harmony with health. They'd rather tolerate mediocrity than risk someone being upset. But leadership isn't about being popular; it's about being respected. It's about setting clear expectations, enforcing them consistently, and being willing to be disliked in the short-term to build credibility in the long-term. Without authority, your firm becomes a democracy of dysfunction.

3. **Reactive Leadership – Running on Emotion, Not Systems**
   Some leaders aren't absent–they're erratic. They lead by mood, by crisis, by gut instinct. One day they're fired up about marketing, the next day they've abandoned it for a new idea. Staff whiplash sets in, and nobody knows which direction is up. Reactive leaders confuse energy with strategy. But real leadership requires rhythms, cadences, and systems that stabilize the firm regardless of whether the owner is in a good mood, a bad mood, or no mood at all.
4. **Vision Without Execution – Inspiring But Not Operationalizing**
   Other leaders are great at inspiring people but terrible at following through. They're the "idea generators" who paint grand pictures of the future but never break those ideas into measurable goals, KPIs, and accountability. The result? Staff nod and smile in meetings, but nothing changes. Inspiration without execution is malpractice in leadership. Vision is critical, but it must be operationalized into action or it's just hot air.
5. **Leadership Isolation – Failing to Grow Yourself as You Grow the Firm**
   Finally, there's the leader who stalls out personally. They've built a decent firm, but they stop investing in their own growth. They don't read, they don't train, they don't seek mentors or coaches. They tell themselves, "I don't have time." But here's the law of leadership: your firm cannot outgrow you. If you plateau, so will your business. True leadership

means committing to your own evolution as relentlessly as you expect your people to commit to theirs.

These are the five fractures in the leadership spine. Left unaddressed, they will collapse your firm into chaos no matter how well you hire, manage, or systematize. But the good news is this: every one of these problems can be solved if you're willing to do the work. Leadership isn't a title; it's a discipline. It's not about perfection; it's about consistency. It's not about charisma; it's about clarity.

And here's the kicker: leadership is a choice. You must decide to stop playing small, stop hiding behind the lawyering, stop drowning in the daily grind, and step fully into the role of CEO. It will feel uncomfortable. It will trigger every instinct to retreat in your risk-averse, perfectionist brain. But the only way out of chaos is through leadership.

So buckle up. In the pages ahead, we'll dissect each of these five problems. You'll see how they show up in your firm, why they create chaos, and how to crush them. You'll meet law firm owners who stumbled in each of these areas—sometimes spectacularly—and turned it around by embracing true leadership. And you'll learn the tools, systems, and mindsets to stop merely managing a practice and start leading a business.

Because in the end, leadership is the ultimate lever. When you pull it, everything else moves.

Problem 1: The Lone Wolf Leader – Why You Can't Carry It All

Law firm owners are notorious for juggling too many jobs. Trial lawyer. Rainmaker. Office manager. IT troubleshooter. HR department. Billing clerk. The list is endless, and for a time, it feels like a badge of honor. After all, this firm is your creation—shouldn't you be the one holding it all together?

But here's the truth: the more hats you wear, the less effective you are as a leader. The less effective you are, the more chaos breeds.

Leadership requires altitude. It's about climbing into the helicopter, hovering above the terrain, and seeing the full landscape–where the firm is headed, what obstacles are ahead, and how to steer the team forward. You can't do that if you're buried in client files, chasing down invoices, or fixing the copier. Every job you cling to erodes your ability to lead: You can't see opportunities, anticipate threats, or chart the next direction. You're too busy reacting to what's right in front of you. And the longer you stay buried in "jobs" that aren't CEO work, the more your firm stagnates.

Some owners argue, "But I don't have the staff yet...someone has to do it, and I'm the best at it." That mindset is the trap. If you don't decide today that you will stop being responsible for tasks that are not CEO tasks, you always will be. Leadership is not an accident; it's a deliberate choice. It starts with a decision and is reinforced by a firm commitment to embody the role of CEO, not just a lawyer who happens to own a law firm.

And here's the kicker: growing slowly isn't safer–it's riskier. Lawyers are highly risk-averse by nature. The profession attracts people who crave certainty and control. When growth gets tough, slow growth gives them more time to second-guess, more opportunities to quit, and more excuses to justify retreat. Growing quickly in the early stages forces momentum. It builds proof faster, calms fear sooner, and cements commitment before doubt can derail you.

Leadership isn't about doing more–it's about doing less, with greater focus. The lone wolf must step back, or the pack will never move forward.

The Lone Wolf Trap

There's a reason so many law firm owners end up exhausted, burned out, and secretly resentful: they're trying to carry it all themselves. They pride themselves on being the hero–after all, it's how they built the firm in the first place. But here's the truth: being the hero is exactly what keeps you from being the leader.

Why do so many lawyers fall into this trap? Part of it is training. The profession attracts people who are risk-averse, detail-oriented, and perfectionistic. These qualities make you an excellent attorney and a terrible leader. As lawyers, we're rewarded for carrying the case ourselves, for knowing every fact and precedent, for being the smartest person in the room. But those same instincts cripple you as a business owner. A law firm is not a law school exam. You don't get extra credit for doing it alone.

Another part of the trap is fear. Lawyers tell themselves: "But I don't have the staff yet. Someone has to do it, and I'm the best at it." That excuse feels noble, but it's deadly. Because if you don't decide—today—that you will not remain responsible for tasks that aren't CEO tasks, you always will be. There will always be "not enough staff." There will always be a reason why you "just need to jump in this one time." There will always be a justification for staying the Lone Wolf. Leadership is not a status you stumble into; it is a deliberate choice you embody.

And make no mistake: the cost of staying in Lone Wolf mode is enormous. The firm revolves around you. Clients insist on speaking only with you. Staff stop taking initiative because they know you'll step in anyway. Growth slows to a crawl because there is only so much of you to go around. You think you're carrying the firm forward, but in reality, you've become the bottleneck strangling it.

The chaos of Lone Wolf leadership is obvious to everyone but the Lone Wolf. Staff see it in the late nights you spend "catching up." Clients see it when their emails sit unanswered because you're in trial, and no one else is empowered to respond. Family sees it in your absence at dinner, weekend after weekend. And you feel it every time you collapse at your desk, wondering why you're working so hard and still not moving forward.

Here's the irony: most Lone Wolves tell themselves they're sacrificing now so they can lead later. But "later" never comes. Without a decision, without a commitment, you'll keep doing all the jobs forever.

You'll keep being the lawyer who happens to own a firm, not the CEO who leads one. Leadership doesn't just happen when you're "ready." Readiness is an illusion. Leadership begins the moment you decide to stop carrying it all and start building something bigger than yourself.

This is why at Law Firm Mentor, we argue that it's actually *safer* to grow faster, not slower. Most lawyers assume the opposite: "If I grow cautiously, I'll stay in control and minimize risk." But remember who you are: a risk-averse professional in a risk-averse profession. When growth gets messy—and it always does—your instinct will be to retreat. To stop hiring. To stop delegating. To shrink back into what feels comfortable: being the Lone Wolf who does it all. And if you're growing slowly, you'll give yourself too much time to overthink, too many opportunities to justify quitting, too many reasons to decide "this isn't worth it."

Fast growth, on the other hand, forces momentum. It pushes you past hesitation into commitment. The sooner you step out of the day-to-day and into the role of CEO, the sooner you get proof that it works. And that proof builds confidence. Nothing quells fear like results. If you want to grow at all, you'll do yourself the greatest service by growing as quickly as possible in the early stages—before doubt convinces you to give up.

CASE STUDY

DANIEL'S BREAKING POINT

Daniel was a litigation attorney in Chicago who had built his reputation on being relentless in the courtroom. His clients loved him because he never seemed to stop working—he was the one answering late-night emails, drafting motions at dawn, and showing up at every single hearing no matter how minor. For years, that intensity was his calling card. It was also his prison.

The Myth of the Indispensable Owner

When Daniel launched his firm, he prided himself on doing it all. He handled every case, drafted every pleading, reviewed every invoice, and signed off on every client intake. When something broke in the office printer, he fixed it. When staff had a conflict, he mediated it. When payroll glitched, he called the bank. He was the hero, the fixer, the Lone Wolf leader.

At first, it felt exhilarating. He wore his exhaustion like a badge of honor, boasting to colleagues about how hard he worked. But slowly, the cracks showed.

His associate attorneys stopped taking ownership. They knew Daniel would swoop in to rewrite their motions anyway, so they submitted drafts that were "good enough." Paralegals hesitated to make decisions without his approval, so simple tasks bottlenecked. Even his receptionist defaulted to asking Daniel whether to schedule new consults, afraid of doing it "wrong." Instead of freeing him, his team chained him tighter to the grind.

The cost bled into his personal life. Daniel's wife grew tired of empty seats at dinner and weekends hijacked by case prep. "You don't run a firm," she told him one night, exasperated. "You are *the firm. And it's killing you."*

Still, Daniel resisted. His identity was wrapped up in being the indispensable one. When his business coach suggested he start cutting back on his caseload, Daniel bristled. "I can't just walk away from clients. I'm the best litigator we have." He convinced himself his involvement was for their benefit. In reality, it was his inability to let go.

Then came the breaking point.

Daniel took on a high-profile corporate litigation case that consumed every ounce of his time. For six months, he was buried–late nights, early mornings, weekends at the office. During that time, the rest of the firm withered. Intake numbers dropped by nearly half. A paralegal left for another firm, citing "too much chaos." Billing fell behind. By the time Daniel returned to breathe after the trial, his revenue had flatlined. His "big win" in court had cost him dearly at home and in business.

Finally, he admitted the truth: the firm wasn't growing because he refused to stop being the Lone Wolf.

Letting Go to Grow

When Daniel came to Law Firm Mentor, he was desperate. "I don't know how to be anything but the lawyer," he confessed. "I know how to win cases, not how to be a CEO."

The first step was the hardest: deciding to reduce his caseload. He resisted, fearing revenue would tank. But the opposite happened. With fewer cases on his desk, Daniel finally had the altitude to lead. He instituted weekly leadership meetings, developed clear KPIs for each role, and began holding his managers accountable instead of jumping in to fix everything himself. He replaced himself in client intake by hiring a dedicated intake specialist, and for the first time, prospective clients weren't waiting days for a call back.

As Daniel stepped back from the day-to-day, he discovered what true leadership meant: focus. He stopped spreading himself thin across ten jobs and concentrated on one–being the CEO. He didn't abandon lawyering entirely, but he reserved his time for the cases that mattered most to the firm's growth, while empowering others to handle the rest.

The transformation was startling. Associates began producing higher-quality work because they knew Daniel wouldn't swoop in to redo it. Paralegals stepped into real ownership of processes. Managers grew confident under his guidance. Within a year, revenue doubled–not because Daniel worked harder, but because he finally stopped carrying it all.

And personally? Daniel rediscovered his life. He ate dinner with his family again. He took weekends off. He stopped defining his worth by how many fires he put out and started defining it by how well his team functioned without him.

Looking back, Daniel admitted something he had once refused to see: "The firm wasn't growing because I wouldn't let it. I kept telling myself I had no choice, but really, I was choosing to be the Lone Wolf. Once I chose to be the CEO instead, everything changed."

Daniel's story is every Lone Wolf's story. The belief that "no one can do it as well as I can" keeps owners trapped in exhaustion and chaos. The truth is, leadership isn't about being the best at every job. It's about creating the focus, systems, and vision that allow others to thrive. Until you decide to stop carrying it all, you'll never lead.

Final Word: From Lone Wolf to Leader

The Lone Wolf mindset is seductive. It flatters your ego, reinforces your competence, and convinces you that no one else could possibly do it better. But it is also the ceiling on your growth. The truth is stark: you cannot be the rainmaker, the litigator, the office manager, the bookkeeper, and the visionary all at once. The more you cling to every role, the more you suffocate your firm.

Leadership begins with a decision–a firm commitment to stop being the lawyer who owns a firm and start being the CEO who leads one. That means shedding jobs, even the ones you love. It means climbing into the helicopter, zooming out from the daily grind, and only zooming in when a problem requires your precision.

Will it feel risky? Absolutely. But slow growth is the riskiest of all because it gives fear too much time to take over. The sooner you step into true leadership, the sooner your firm can accelerate, stabilize, and prove to you that it can thrive without you doing it all.

Takeaway: Leadership is not about being indispensable–it's about building something that can stand without you. And until you choose to let go of the Lone Wolf role, you will never know how high your firm can soar.

The Lone Wolf problem keeps owners trapped in doing the wrong work. But even when they finally step back, many find themselves trapped again, by something deeper: the fear of leading. That brings us to our next problem.

Problem 2: Fear of Authority – Confusing Popularity with Leadership

Most law firm owners secretly crave an easy office: everyone getting along, no raised voices, no uncomfortable conversations. Staff show up on time, do their jobs well, and respect one another. Managing feels effortless, and the business owner can finally exhale. It's a beautiful fantasy. Unfortunately, it is just that–a fantasy.

People are complicated. Put them together in a workplace, and there will be friction. Not necessarily chaos, but friction. Different personalities, different communication styles, different expectations–all rubbing against one another. And friction is healthy. It sharpens ideas, pushes people to grow, and strengthens culture when it's managed well. But many owners can't stomach it.

Instead, they fall into a trap: using their teams to meet their own emotional needs. The need to be liked. The need to be appreciated. The need to feel indispensable. Instead of leading with authority, they chase validation. They avoid difficult conversations because they don't want to risk being disliked. They soften standards because they'd rather be seen as "nice" than demanding. They let problematic behaviors slide because they fear confrontation.

On the surface, it looks like harmony. But beneath, it breeds dysfunction. Mediocrity takes root. High performers lose respect for the leader. Standards erode. And the very peace the owner longs for slips further out of reach.

Leadership is not about popularity. It's about clarity, consistency, and the willingness to be disliked in the short term to build respect in the long term. When authority is traded for approval, chaos is inevitable.

The Approval Trap

Too many law firm owners confuse popularity with leadership. They want to be liked. They want their team to see them as kind, approachable, even "cool." They crave validation—smiles, approval, the sense that they're the good boss everyone loves working for. And because they chase that approval, they avoid the very actions that define leadership: setting standards, holding people accountable, and confronting problems directly.

But people are people. They come with egos, insecurities, quirks, blind spots, and different ways of communicating. Put them together in the pressure cooker of a law firm—tight deadlines, emotional clients, financial pressures—and friction is guaranteed.

Friction isn't the problem, though. Chaos is. And chaos happens when the leader refuses to lead.

Here's how it shows up:

- **Avoiding tough conversations**. An associate is chronically late with briefs, but instead of addressing it head-on, the owner sighs, picks up the slack, and tells themselves, *She's under a lot of pressure—I don't want to pile on.*
- **Softened standards**. A paralegal's work is riddled with typos, but the owner tells themselves, *At least she's loyal. She tries hard.* Meanwhile, high performers resent carrying the weight.
- **Tolerating toxic behavior**. A rainmaker attorney bullies junior staff, but the owner looks the other way because, *He brings in too much business to rock the boat.*

Each decision feels like a way to keep the peace, but it's really a way to protect the owner's ego. They're avoiding the discomfort of being disliked, even temporarily.

And the cost? Immense.

First, standards erode. Once your team sees that expectations aren't enforced, they loosen their grip on excellence. The associate who used to stay late to polish a motion now shrugs: *"Why bother? No one else cares."* Mediocrity becomes the norm, not the exception.

Second, respect collapses. Staff may smile at you and say you're a "great boss," but privately, they lose faith. They know you won't hold people accountable. They know they can get away with cutting corners. High performers, in particular, feel betrayed. They work hard, follow the rules, and deliver results, only to watch others coast without consequence. Eventually, they leave—not because of too much authority, but because of too little.

Third, the culture rots. Without clarity and accountability, the firm becomes a playground for personalities. Cliques form. Gossip spreads. Passive-aggressive emails replace direct conversations. Instead of one unified team, you have factions competing for favor. And because you—the leader—won't step in with authority, those factions harden.

This dysfunction often stems from something deeper: leaders using their teams to meet emotional needs that should be met elsewhere. The need to be liked. The need to be needed. The need to feel important. Instead of seeing staff as professionals to be led, owners treat them as a source of validation. They want their team to soothe their insecurities, boost their self-esteem, and stroke their egos.

But your team is not your therapist, your spouse, or your friend group. They are employees. Their role is to fulfill the mission of the firm—not to prop up your identity. When leaders blur that line, they trade authority for approval, and the firm pays the price.

What makes this trap so seductive is that, on the surface, it feels like harmony. People smile at you. They say you're easy to work for. The office feels "pleasant." But underneath, the work suffers. Deadlines slip. Quality dips. Growth stalls. And eventually, the smiles fade, replaced by quiet disengagement or outright departure.

Here's the hard truth: leadership is not about being liked. It's about being clear, consistent, and respected. Respect often requires short-term discomfort—calling out the missed deadline, correcting the subpar work, confronting the toxic behavior. It means risking eye rolls, awkward silences, or even tears. But without that discomfort, there can be no growth.

And growth is what your people actually want. High performers crave accountability. They want to know where the bar is and how to reach it. They want to be stretched, challenged, and developed. They may not like you in the moment when you push them, but they will respect you. And respect, not popularity, is the foundation of loyalty.

The owner who fears authority doesn't just fail to lead–they actively create chaos. By avoiding confrontation, they force staff to navigate dysfunction themselves. By softening standards, they breed mediocrity. By tolerating toxicity, they send the message that results matter more than culture. And by seeking approval, they undermine their own authority.

So if you're chasing popularity, know this: your people don't need a friend. They need a leader. And until you stop confusing the two, chaos will follow you like a shadow.

CASE STUDY

MONICA'S NEED TO BE LIKED

Monica had always been the "nice one." As a child, she was the peacemaker in her family–the one who smoothed arguments, made everyone laugh, and tried to keep harmony at all costs. That tendency followed her into adulthood. After years in a corporate law firm, she left to start her own practice in estate planning. Part of her motivation was practical–she wanted more autonomy–but part of it was deeply personal. Monica hated conflict. The adversarial system of justice, with its depositions, objections, and constant battles, drained her. Estate planning felt safer: collaborative, client-focused, and far removed from courtroom combat.

"Being Nice" As a Leadership Strategy

When she launched her firm in Phoenix, she assumed her natural warmth would make her a great leader. "If my team likes me," she thought, "they'll be motivated to work hard for me."

At first, it seemed to work. Her staff adored her. They praised her generosity and kindness. The office had a family-like feel. People brought in baked goods. Birthdays were celebrated. On the surface, everything looked healthy.

But underneath, the cracks were widening.

One associate was consistently late with drafting trusts and estate documents. Monica knew the delays were hurting client relationships, but she hated confrontation. Instead of addressing it directly, she stayed late at night fixing the work herself. "She's young," Monica rationalized. "I don't want to discourage her."

A paralegal had a habit of gossiping about clients in the breakroom. Other staff complained, but Monica laughed it off. "That's just her personality," she said. "She doesn't mean any harm."

Even her receptionist was inconsistent in greeting clients warmly. Some days she was bubbly; other days she was curt. When a client left a Google review complaining about the "coldness" of the office, Monica brushed it aside. "She's going through a tough time," she told herself.

Each time Monica avoided addressing these issues, she felt a pang of guilt–but also relief. No one got upset with her. No one rolled their eyes or accused her of being "mean." She stayed the "nice boss."

But the consequences were piling up.

Deadlines slipped. Client satisfaction dipped. High performers grew resentful. One associate, frustrated at constantly carrying the slack, left for another firm. "I just want to work somewhere with higher standards," she told Monica bluntly. That stung.

Then came the real blow. Her lead paralegal, Otto, resigned after seven years. "I love you, Monica," he said carefully, "but I don't respect how you lead. You let problems fester. You avoid hard conversations. It makes it harder for people like me, who want to do things right. I can't keep working in a place where standards are optional."

That conversation rocked Monica to her core. She realized her need to be liked was costing her the very respect she craved. People smiled at her, but they didn't trust her to lead. They saw her kindness as weakness, her tolerance as indifference. She wasn't creating harmony–she was enabling dysfunction.

Stepping Into Authority

When Monica came to Law Firm Mentor, she admitted her fear: "I don't want my team to hate me. I don't want them to see me as a tyrant."

We told her the truth: leadership is not about being liked–it's about being respected. *Respect doesn't come from avoiding conflict; it comes from consistency, clarity, and fairness.*

At first, Monica struggled. Her instinct to soften was strong. But she started small. In her next team meeting, she addressed the gossip issue head-on. "This stops today," she said firmly. "We are professionals. Gossip has no place here." The room went silent. She waited for the backlash. None came.

Next, she sat down with the associate who was chronically late on estate planning documents. Instead of quietly fixing the errors, she laid out clear expectations and deadlines. The associate bristled, but Monica held her ground. "If this continues, we'll have to discuss whether this is the right fit," she said–words she never imagined herself saying.

Slowly, something shifted. Staff began taking her more seriously. High performers breathed easier, knowing the bar was finally being enforced. Even the receptionist, after being coached directly, improved her client greetings. For the first time, Monica realized authority wasn't the opposite of kindness–it was the structure that allowed kindness to flourish without chaos.

Within a year, the culture of her firm transformed. Turnover decreased. Client satisfaction rose. Productivity improved. And while Monica wasn't always "liked" in the moment–sometimes her tough conversations made people uncomfortable–she noticed something powerful: she was respected. Staff sought her guidance. Associates asked for her feedback. People trusted her leadership.

Looking back, Monica admitted: "I thought avoiding conflict would keep the peace, but all it did was create resentment and mediocrity. The moment I stopped chasing approval and started enforcing standards, my team grew stronger–and so did I."

Monica's story is a warning and an encouragement. Avoiding authority feels safe, but it is deadly to a firm's culture. When you trade leadership for popularity, you lose both. When you embrace authority–fairly, consistently, unapologetically–you create the respect that fuels true loyalty.

Final Word: The Results of Real Leadership

The need to be liked is a powerful trap. It whispers that harmony is safer than conflict, that silence is kinder than correction, and that popularity is proof of leadership. But the truth is the opposite. When you avoid authority, you don't protect peace–you poison it. Standards erode, dysfunction festers, and high performers walk away.

Takeaway: Leadership and authority are not about being everyone's friend. They are about being clear, fair, and consistent–even when it makes you unpopular in the moment. Respect is born in those hard conversations, in the courage to say what needs to be said, and in the willingness to risk short-term discomfort for long-term strength.

But authority isn't the only place leaders stumble. Even owners who embrace their authority often lead reactively running on mood, crisis, and impulse instead of rhythm and systems. In the next section, we'll explore the chaos of reactive leadership and why stability, not spontaneity, is the hallmark of a strong law firm leader.

Problem 3: Reactive Leadership – Running on Emotion, Not Systems

Law firm owners often expect their employees to mirror their own work ethic, sacrifice, and passion. After all, *you* built this firm with sweat and sleepless nights. *You* answer client calls at midnight, skip family dinners, and push through weekends. Shouldn't your team feel the same sense of urgency?

Here's the hard truth: no, they shouldn't. Your employees are not you. They are not owners. They will never reap the rewards–or shoulder the risks–of ownership. Their relationship with the firm is transactional: they work, you pay. Period. Some will go above and beyond, but most won't. And resenting them for that only exposes your own immaturity as a leader.

Yet too many owners fall into the trap of reactive leadership. They get triggered when staff don't volunteer to come in early or stay late. They point fingers at employees when a client complains about service. They fume when procedures aren't followed, as though it's proof of betrayal rather than a signal of weak systems. Instead of calmly diagnosing problems and adjusting systems, they lash out–reacting with blame, anger, or self-pity.

The result? Chaos. Staff feel whiplashed, never knowing what mood the boss will bring that day. Standards become inconsistent because enforcement depends on emotion, not structure. And the firm lives in a cycle of crisis management instead of steady growth.

Leadership isn't about demanding employees feel like owners. It's about building systems that work whether they care like you do or not. Until you accept that reality, your leadership will remain reactive, and your firm will remain chaotic.

The Trap of Emotional Leadership

No one works harder for your law firm than you do. That's the truth. You're the one who stayed up until 2 a.m. preparing for trial. You're the one who took the terrifying leap to leave a paycheck behind and build something from scratch. You're the one who carries the sleepless nights when payroll is tight or a key client threatens to walk. It's natural, then, to expect that same level of intensity and ownership from your team.

But here's the problem: they aren't you. They never will be.

Your employees don't have equity in the business. They don't have their name on the door. They don't face the same risks if revenue dips or a malpractice claim lands. Some may care deeply about the mission. Some may invest emotionally in the clients. But no employee—no matter how loyal—will ever feel the same sense of urgency you do. And that's not a flaw. That's reality.

Unfortunately, too many law firm owners can't accept this truth. They confuse employment with ownership. They expect staff to behave like mini-versions of themselves—staying late, sacrificing weekends, volunteering to take on extra work without complaint. When staff don't, the owner feels slighted, even betrayed.

That's when reactive leadership takes over.

Reactive leaders operate from emotion, not systems. They get triggered by normal human behavior and respond with blame, frustration, or even rage.

- When staff leave at 5 p.m. instead of staying late, the owner fumes: *Don't they care? Don't they see how much needs to be done?*
- When a client complains, the owner points the finger at staff: *If you'd just followed through, this never would have happened.*
- When procedures aren't followed, the owner interprets it as disrespect: *Why do I even bother setting rules if no one listens to me?*

In each case, the reaction is emotional, not strategic. Instead of asking, "What system failed?" or "What training is missing?" or "How can I reinforce accountability?" the owner personalizes the failure. They make it about loyalty, effort, or moral character.

The consequences are brutal.

First, the culture becomes unstable. Employees never know which version of the boss they're going to get—the calm professional or the angry finger-pointer. This unpredictability breeds anxiety. People stop taking initiative because they're afraid of triggering the boss's wrath. Instead of solving problems, they hide them.

Second, standards become inconsistent. In a reactive environment, rules aren't enforced systematically—they're enforced emotionally. The same mistake might be ignored one day and punished the next, depending on the owner's mood. Staff quickly learn that consistency doesn't matter; what matters is staying off the boss's radar.

Third, growth stalls. A firm run on emotions is always in crisis mode. Energy is spent putting out fires, smoothing over flare-ups, and managing the boss's moods instead of building scalable systems. Reactive leadership keeps the firm small because no one can plan or execute long-term strategy while living in constant reactivity.

And let's not forget the toll on the owner. Living in reactive mode is exhausting. Every misstep feels personal. Every problem feels like betrayal. The owner becomes resentful, muttering about how "no one cares as much as I do" and secretly fantasizing about firing the whole team and starting over. But here's the harsh truth: the problem isn't the staff—it's the leader.

The real work of leadership is building structures that function regardless of how much an employee "cares." Procedures that are so clear, training that is so thorough, and accountability that is so consistent that the work gets done even when staff are simply showing up for the paycheck. High performers will still shine. Low performers will be exposed quickly. And you, the leader, won't have to run your firm on adrenaline and disappointment.

Reactive leadership is, at its core, emotional immaturity. It's the refusal to accept the reality of employment. It's holding staff to an impossible standard—that they should feel what you feel, care as much as you care, sacrifice as much as you sacrifice. And when they inevitably fall short, you lash out instead of leading.

Until you break this cycle, chaos is guaranteed. Because moods don't scale. Anger doesn't create accountability. Blame doesn't build systems. And resentment doesn't lead.

True leadership is calm, consistent, and rooted in structure. It doesn't require staff to be you. It requires you to stop expecting them to be.

CASE STUDY

ANTHONY'S FIRE IN THE COURTROOM, CHAOS IN THE OFFICE

Anthony was a civil litigator in New Jersey with a reputation that made opposing counsel groan when they saw his name on a case. He was aggressive, relentless, and razor-sharp on his feet. Judges respected him, juries leaned in when he spoke, and clients adored his take-no-prisoners approach. His "big-D energy" was exactly what you wanted if your business was on the line in a lawsuit.

The courtroom was where Anthony thrived. But back at the office, that same energy was tearing his firm apart.

The Energy That Won Cases But Broke Culture

Anthony had grown his practice to twelve employees: three associates, four paralegals, an intake team, and support staff. On paper, he had everything he needed to scale. But in reality, he was the bottleneck. Every problem seemed to ignite his temper.

When an associate left at 5 p.m. sharp while Anthony was still grinding through depositions, he seethed. "Unbelievable. Do they even care about this firm?" He muttered under his breath all evening, stewing over how no one worked as hard as he did.

When a client complained about poor communication, Anthony immediately blasted his staff in a team meeting. "This is unacceptable. You're making me look bad!" His voice echoed through the office, leaving people red-faced and silent.

When paralegals missed steps in the filing process, Anthony took it personally. "Why do I even bother creating procedures if no one follows them?" he snapped, slamming files on his desk.

To Anthony, every misstep was evidence that his team was lazy, careless, or disloyal. He expected them to match his intensity, his hours, and his obsession with perfection. But they weren't owners–they were employees. And the more he demanded they act like him, the more they withdrew.

The turnover started quietly. His best paralegal resigned, citing "stress." An intake specialist followed, telling HR she "never knew what kind of mood Anthony would be in." The associates stayed, but their energy plummeted. They stopped taking risks, stopped innovating, stopped volunteering for challenging cases. Why bother? They knew if they slipped up, Anthony would explode.

Anthony told himself he just had a "bad team." He grumbled to colleagues that "no one wants to work anymore" and fantasized about firing everyone and starting over. What he couldn't see was that his reactivity was the real problem. His staff weren't failing because they didn't care–they were failing because he hadn't built systems strong enough to function without his constant emotional policing.

Replacing Passion With Process

When Anthony came to Law Firm Mentor, he was burned out and bitter. "I don't understand," he vented. "I'm giving everything to this firm. I'm in here nights and weekends. And my people clock out at five like it's just a job."

We told him the truth: it is just a job for them. *They aren't you. They aren't owners. They don't reap the rewards or shoulder the risks of ownership. Their relationship with you is transactional: they work, you pay. Expecting them to bleed for the firm the way you do is like expecting your clients to volunteer their weekends to help you prepare for trial. It's not rational.*

What Anthony needed wasn't more passion from his team–it was more structure from him. He had to stop leading with moods and start leading with systems.

So he began with **clarity.** *Instead of vague expectations like "work harder" or "care more," Anthony's coach had him create role scorecards with measurable KPIs: deadlines met, billable hours, client communication turnaround. Now performance wasn't a guessing game–it was quantifiable.*

Next, Anthony work with his coach to implement **cadence.** *Weekly one-on-ones replaced explosive team meetings. Associates knew exactly when feedback would come, and Anthony learned to deliver it calmly, without theatrics. Paralegals had structured check-ins to review compliance with filing procedures. Problems were addressed before they spiraled into crises.*

Finally, Anthony worked on his **mindset.** *With consistent feedback and support from his coach, he stopped expecting employees to act like owners. He reminded himself daily: They are not me. They shouldn't be me. My job is to lead them, not expect them to be like me.*

It wasn't easy. His instinct to lash out never disappeared entirely. But with systems in place, his triggers had less room to fire. When a client complained, Anthony no longer exploded. He reviewed the communication scorecards, identified the weak spot, and adjusted training. When an associate left at five, Anthony didn't stew–he looked at whether the day's work was complete. If it was, there was no problem. If it wasn't, he addressed it in their next meeting.

Within six months, the difference was dramatic. Turnover slowed. Morale improved. Associates began taking initiative again because they trusted they wouldn't be ambushed by Anthony's temper. Clients noticed more consistent communication. And Anthony himself felt lighter, less angry, less alone.

Looking back, Anthony admitted: "I thought my fire was what made me a good leader. But in the office, it just burned people out. Once I stopped expecting everyone to be me and started building systems to support them, everything changed. My people didn't have to care as much as I did–they just had to know exactly what was expected and be held accountable for it."

Anthony still brings his big-dog energy to the courtroom, where it belongs. But in the office, he learned that leadership isn't about passion–it's about structure. And when he stopped running his firm on emotion, the chaos finally quieted down.

Final Word: Redefining What It Means to Lead

Passion in the courtroom can win cases. But passion in the office–when it shows up as reactivity–only creates chaos. Employees will never care as much as you do, and they shouldn't. They aren't owners. They aren't paid to shoulder your risks or mirror your sacrifices. Expecting them to act like you is not leadership–it's emotional immaturity.

The truth is simple: moods don't scale, but systems do. When you replace emotional outbursts with clear expectations, structured cadences, and consistent accountability, your team no longer has to guess at your standards. They know what matters, how it will be measured, and what happens when they fall short. That's what creates stability. That's what builds trust.

Takeaway: Reactive leadership is exhausting—for you and for everyone around you. Calm, system-driven leadership is sustainable. When you stop running on emotion and start leading on structure, the chaos subsides, and your firm finally has the foundation to grow.

But clarity and consistency aren't enough if your vision never leaves the clouds. Next, we'll tackle the problem of leaders who inspire with words but fail to operationalize them: vision without execution.

Problem 4: Vision Without Execution – Inspiring But Not Operationalizing

Every law firm owner has said it at some point: *I have a big vision for my firm.* And often, that's true. Owners imagine dominating their local market, becoming the go-to name in their practice area, or scaling to multiple offices. Some dream of creating a legacy firm that outlives them. Vision is exciting. It's energizing. It makes people lean in.

But vision without execution is just a pep talk.

Too many leaders stop at the inspiring speech. They tell their team, "We're going to be the top family law firm in the state" or "We're going to double revenue this year." Everyone nods, maybe even claps. Then they go back to their desks and carry on exactly as before—because no one translated that lofty vision into concrete actions, measurable goals, or daily habits.

That's the dysfunction of leadership without follow-through. You can inspire people once or twice with passion alone. But if they never see progress, if they never know what's expected of them to make the vision real, the inspiration turns hollow. Staff nod politely while secretly thinking, *Here we go again.*

And the damage runs deeper than wasted words. Vision without execution erodes trust. Employees stop believing you when you say, "We're going to the next level." They disengage, because no one wants to row a boat when the captain doesn't pick up the oars.

Leadership requires both: the spark of vision and the grind of execution. Without that combination, you're not leading—you're performing. And performance doesn't build a firm.

The Hollow Echo of Vision Without Execution

Vision is the spark that ignites a law firm's potential. It's the bold declaration of what could be: becoming the most respected criminal defense practice in the city, building a statewide estate planning powerhouse, or scaling a boutique litigation firm into a national player. Vision makes people sit up straighter. It gives employees something to believe in. It gets them excited.

But vision without execution is just noise. It inspires in the moment, then evaporates into disappointment when nothing changes.

Too many law firm owners love casting vision but hate grinding it into reality. They stand in front of their teams and announce lofty goals: "We're going to triple revenue this year!" or "We're going to expand into three new markets!" or "We're going to be the premier firm for high-net-worth divorce." Staff clap politely, maybe even feel a flicker of excitement, but within a week, nothing is different. No new systems are in place. No KPIs are set. No accountability structures exist. The vision was declared, but not operationalized.

And here's the danger: people remember. When vision is repeated but never acted on, it stops inspiring and starts eroding trust. Employees begin to roll their eyes when the owner announces a new initiative. They whisper, "Just wait, this will fizzle out like the last one." The very thing that was supposed to motivate them now creates cynicism.

Lawyers, in particular, are prone to this dysfunction. Our profession rewards rhetoric—persuasive arguments, big-picture thinking, compelling stories. It's easy for owners to believe that saying something passionately is the same as making it happen. But leadership isn't litigation. A great closing argument may sway a jury, but it won't grow a firm.

Vision without execution creates chaos in subtle but devastating ways.

- **Staff drift.** Without concrete action steps, each employee interprets the vision differently. One associate thinks "dominate the market" means filing more aggressive pleadings. A paralegal thinks it means producing sleeker documents. The intake team thinks it means answering calls faster. Everyone works hard, but not in the same direction.
- **Inconsistent priorities.** Because the vision was never broken down into measurable objectives, managers set their own agendas. One focuses on marketing, another on client service, another on technology. Without alignment, the firm pulls in different directions.
- **Erosion of respect.** When owners repeatedly declare big goals and then fail to follow through, staff quietly lose faith. They stop believing the owner's words. Even worse, they stop believing their efforts matter, because nothing seems to add up to the promised future.

Employees want to believe in vision. They want to be part of something bigger than themselves. But they also want proof. They need to see the bridge between today's reality and tomorrow's possibility. That bridge is built with execution: clearly defined goals, step-by-step plans, consistent accountability.

Think about it this way: if you told a client, "We'll win your case," but never filed a motion, never showed up to hearings, never deposed a witness, what would happen? They'd fire you, and rightly so. That's what vision without execution feels like to your team: a promise without performance.

And the damage isn't limited to morale. Vision without execution kills momentum. Every time you declare a goal and fail to operationalize it, you train your team to discount you. So when you finally set a goal you *do* intend to pursue seriously, you're met with skepticism instead of energy.

This dysfunction also feeds the chaos cycle. Instead of laying out structured steps, the owner relies on bursts of inspiration. One week, they push everyone to focus on marketing. The next week, they've forgotten about marketing and want to overhaul client service. The following week, it's all about hiring. Staff are left dizzy, chasing the owner's latest idea of the moment. Without execution systems, vision turns into whiplash.

The irony is that many owners avoid operationalizing vision because of fear. Declaring vision feels exhilarating. It's abstract, it's inspiring, and it carries no immediate accountability. But translating vision into specific goals? That feels risky. It means defining what success looks like–and exposing yourself to failure if you don't hit it. So owners keep it vague. They prefer the rush of inspiration to the vulnerability of execution.

But leadership requires courage. And the real courage isn't in dreaming–it's in doing. It's in saying, "We're going to increase revenue by 20% this year," and then breaking that down into monthly goals, assigning responsibilities, and holding people accountable. It's in saying, "We're going to dominate high-net-worth divorce," and then setting specific marketing campaigns, training staff on client experience, and measuring every step along the way.

Vision without execution is malpractice in leadership. It creates chaos by breeding cynicism, eroding trust, and scattering energy. Execution doesn't make vision smaller; it makes vision real. Without it, you're not leading–you're just performing for an audience that has stopped clapping.

CASE STUDY

MARIO'S FLUFF PROBLEM

Mario was magnetic. The kind of lawyer who could walk into a room and instantly command attention. He had the charisma, the booming voice, and the natural ability to inspire confidence. Clients trusted him immediately. Judges respected his sharp arguments. His peers admired his energy.

So when Mario opened his own business litigation firm in Atlanta, no one doubted he'd be successful. He had the vision—and he loved talking about it.

Words Without Substance

At quarterly staff meetings, Mario delivered stirring speeches about the future. "We are going to be the *premier firm for complex business disputes in Georgia," he proclaimed. "We'll expand into two more offices within five years. We're going to double our revenue in eighteen months." His staff clapped, nodded, and left the room buzzing with energy.*

For a few days.

Because after the speeches ended, nothing changed.

There were no new marketing campaigns. No new case management systems. No clear targets for billable hours or client acquisition. Mario went back to trial prep, and everyone else went back to their desks, unsure what the big goals actually meant for their daily work.

At first, the staff gave him grace. He was busy. He was juggling cases. They assumed the strategy would follow the speeches. But as months rolled into years, they noticed a pattern. Big talk, little action. Lofty vision, no execution.

Behind closed doors, whispers began. "Mario's a nice guy, but it's all fluff." Associates rolled their eyes at his pep talks. Paralegals joked that the quarterly meetings were "story hour." Intake staff shrugged when he announced new goals, muttering, "We'll see how long this one lasts."

The culture shifted. Cynicism set in. People stopped taking his vision seriously.

One associate, a rising star named Stephanie, finally left. In her exit interview, she was blunt: "I came here because I believed in Mario's vision. But it's all words. There's no strategy, no plan. I want to work somewhere that actually follows through."

That was the gut punch. Mario realized his gift for inspiration was now his liability. His people liked him, but they didn't trust him. They admired his energy but discounted his leadership. He had become the boss everyone thought was a "great guy" but ultimately ineffective.

From Words to Action

When Mario came to Law Firm Mentor, he admitted, "I don't get it. I tell them where we're going, and they don't follow. What else am I supposed to do?"

We told him the truth: Vision without execution is betrayal. *It excites people in the moment, then disappoints them when nothing happens. Over time, it kills trust.*

Mario didn't need to stop casting vision—he needed to operationalize it.

So we had him start small. Instead of declaring, "We're going to double revenue," he set a concrete goal: "We will increase revenue by 20% this year." Then he broke it down into quarterly, monthly, and weekly benchmarks. Intake was tasked with increasing consult conversions by 10%. Associates were given specific billable hour goals. Marketing was assigned three measurable campaigns tied to lead generation.

Next, Mario instituted accountability rhythms. Weekly leadership meetings tracked progress on KPIs. Monthly staff check-ins reviewed wins and gaps. Quarterly meetings still included his speeches–but now, they were followed by slide decks with charts, numbers, and assigned action items. Inspiration plus execution.

At first, his team was skeptical. They'd heard it all before. But when they saw the goals broken down and tracked consistently, they leaned in. They started connecting their daily tasks to the firm's vision. Intake saw how every consult scheduled impacted revenue goals. Paralegals realized how accurate filings affected client retention. Associates began competing–not to survive Mario's speeches–but to hit their KPIs and celebrate wins in the next meeting.

Within a year, Mario's firm didn't just meet its 20% revenue goal–it exceeded it. More importantly, his people stopped rolling their eyes. They believed again. His vision had substance because it was tied to execution.

Looking back, Mario admitted: "I thought my charisma was enough. That if I painted the picture, people would naturally rise to it. But I see now–it wasn't their job to translate vision into action. It was mine. Once I gave them structure, they stopped thinking of me as fluff and started trusting me as a leader."

Mario didn't stop giving speeches–he still loved them, and his staff still appreciated his energy. But now, the speeches were paired with strategy, tactics, and follow-through. Inspiration wasn't the end of the story; it was the beginning. And that made all the difference.

Final Word: From Vision to Execution

Vision is powerful, but only when it's backed by action. Without execution, vision is little more than performance art–an inspiring show in the moment that quickly turns into disappointment. Mario's story illustrates the risk: when leaders talk big but fail to follow through, they don't just waste words. They erode trust. They breed cynicism. They turn their greatest strength–charisma–into their greatest weakness.

Takeaway: Leadership demands more. It demands that you translate inspiration into structure, ideas into metrics, and dreams into daily action. That's what creates alignment. That's what sustains culture. And that's what convinces your people to believe—not because you said it, but because they can see it happening.

But execution isn't the final hurdle. Even owners who operationalize vision often hit another wall: themselves. They stop learning, stop evolving, and stop investing in their own growth. The firm grows, but the leader doesn't—and the ceiling crashes down.

In the next section, we'll tackle the last great dysfunction of leadership: isolation. Because no matter how strong your systems, your authority, or your vision, your firm can only grow as far as you do.

Problem 5: Leadership Isolation – Failing to Grow Yourself as You Grow the Firm

Here's the hard truth: your business will only grow to the extent that you do.

Lawyers love chasing growth in familiar ways. They take CLEs on trial practice. They read books on marketing hacks. They hire SEO consultants. They obsess over the next shiny tool that might bring in more clients. And while all of those things have value, none of them replace the one investment that truly moves the needle: growing *yourself*.

Your growth is not optional. You are your firm's ceiling. No matter how talented your associates, how skilled your paralegals, how brilliant your marketing team, your firm cannot outpace the limitations of its leader. If you avoid uncomfortable conversations, your culture will stagnate. If you cling to control, your managers will never rise. If you refuse to invest in your mindset, your fear will keep your firm small.

And this is where many lawyers stumble. They think of growth as knowledge acquisition—better briefs, sharper arguments, new certifications. But technical mastery doesn't make you a better leader. It just makes you a more skilled technician. True business growth comes from growing the owner: developing emotional resilience, expanding your capacity to lead, learning how to make hard decisions, and facing your blind spots.

People will come and go—associates, paralegals, COOs, office managers, even rainmakers. But you? You're the constant. You are your firm's greatest investment. And when you stop growing, your business does too.

The Ceiling You Don't See

Every law firm owner wants their business to grow. More revenue. More clients. More prestige. More stability. And yet, many hit a wall. They work harder, hire more people, pour money into marketing, but nothing seems to push them past a certain level. They assume it's a staffing issue, a cash flow issue, or a market issue. In reality, it's often a *leadership issue.*

Here's the uncomfortable truth: your firm will never outgrow you.

That's because businesses don't grow in a vacuum. They grow through the people who lead them. And while your team can carry some of the weight, the culture, direction, and strategy of the firm are always limited by your own capacity as the owner. If you can't delegate, your managers stay small. If you avoid conflict, your standards slip. If you resist making investments in leadership development, your firm plateaus.

The problem is that most lawyers misunderstand what growth actually looks like. They assume growth means learning more about *lawyering.* They sign up for CLEs on evidence, sharpen their trial advocacy skills, or chase certifications in mediation. They learn marketing tricks or social media tactics. They master technical skills. And while those things have value, they don't create real business growth. At best, they make you a better technician. They don't make you a better leader.

True growth looks different. It's about mindset, not motions. It's about developing emotional resilience when clients lash out or staff disappoint. It's about learning to make decisions under uncertainty instead of paralyzing yourself with "analysis." It's about facing the fears you've buried–the fear of failure, of rejection, of not being good enough–and refusing to let them dictate your choices.

When you neglect this kind of growth, you create isolation. You keep doing the things you know, staying in your comfort zone, and hoping it will carry the business forward. You avoid coaches, masterminds, or mentors because you don't want to feel vulnerable. You tell yourself you don't have time to read, study, or reflect. You put your head down and grind, convinced that sheer effort will make up for the gap.

It won't.

Without investing in yourself, you become the bottleneck. Your staff can only rise as high as you allow. They can only stretch into opportunities that you create. And if you stay stuck in old patterns, you drag them down with you. High performers will eventually leave for firms where the leader is growing. Mediocre staff will stay, happy to coast. And your firm, no matter how much you spend on external "fixes," will stall.

This is where the spiral begins. An owner who feels stuck often doubles down on tactics. More marketing. More hires. More micromanaging. But without personal growth, those efforts fail. And each failure reinforces the belief that growth is impossible. The owner becomes isolated–not just from their team, but from their own potential.

The irony is that most lawyers see themselves as lifelong learners. They pride themselves on mastering knowledge. But knowledge isn't enough. You don't need another skill at drafting briefs. You need the courage to fire the toxic associate who poisons your culture. You don't need another book on SEO. You need the resilience to keep investing in marketing when the ROI isn't immediate. You don't need another course on negotiation. You need the confidence to negotiate with yourself–to push past the comfort of staying small.

And here's the kicker: you are your greatest investment. Employees will come and go. Paralegals will leave. Associates will be poached. COOs will retire. Marketing managers will move on. But you? You are the one constant. You will be here until the end. If you stop growing, your firm stops growing. If you stretch, expand, and evolve, your firm does too.

Your growth isn't optional. It's the foundation for everything else. Without it, every system eventually buckles, every hire eventually leaves, and every dream eventually stalls. The ceiling isn't out there—it's you. And the only way to raise it is to grow.

CASE STUDY

CAMILLE'S CEILING

Camille was a powerhouse. A Black woman litigator in Washington, D.C., she had carved out a thriving boutique firm representing small businesses in commercial disputes. She was respected in the courtroom, admired in her community, and a mentor to younger attorneys of color. By most measures, she had "made it."

But behind the accolades, Camille was stuck.

The Ceiling She Couldn't Break

Her firm had plateaued at $2.5 million in annual revenue. For three years straight, she hovered at the same level. Some years, she added a few more clients, but then a key associate would leave and revenue dipped back down. She worked harder, put in longer hours, doubled down on marketing, and invested in staff training. Nothing broke the ceiling.

The frustration gnawed at her. "I know we're capable of more," she told herself. "But maybe this is just our limit."

In truth, Camille had built her firm on grit and brilliance. She was the rainmaker, the strategist, the one who inspired confidence in clients. But she hadn't built herself into a CEO. And that was the invisible ceiling pressing down on her business.

Camille believed she was growing. She took CLEs, earned certifications, and read every new book on digital marketing. She even completed an online course on leadership for women lawyers. But none of it shifted her results. Why? Because all of that "growth" was knowledge acquisition. It made her a sharper attorney, maybe even a savvier marketer–but it didn't make her a stronger leader.

Her blind spot was herself.

Camille avoided tough conversations with underperformers, convincing herself that loyalty outweighed results. She micromanaged key associates because she couldn't stand the thought of losing control. She said she wanted to scale but secretly feared taking on the risk of debt or expansion. Every fear she refused to face kept her firm locked in place.

Becoming the CEO Her Firm Needed

When Camille joined Law Firm Mentor, she was candid but skeptical. "I don't need another class," she told us bluntly. "I need a breakthrough."

The first thing we told her: your firm will not grow until you do.

At first, she bristled. She thought she had *been growing. But as we unpacked her patterns, she saw the truth. She was investing in knowledge, not in herself. She was sharpening the saw without ever felling the tree.*

The real growth Camille needed was profoundly uncomfortable. It wasn't about reading another business book or attending another seminar. It was about working on herself–confronting old wounds, rewiring entrenched beliefs, and stepping into a new identity as a true CEO.

For Camille, one of the hardest challenges was her fear of abandonment. Every time she considered having a difficult conversation with an underperforming team member, she felt a familiar knot in her stomach. She worried that if she pushed too hard, the person would quit–and their departure would feel like a rejection of her, *not just the job. That wound ran deep, reaching back to childhood experiences of being left behind or overlooked. So instead of holding people accountable, she softened, avoided, or simply took on the work herself. Working on herself meant facing that wound, recognizing that someone leaving her firm was not a replay of abandonment, but a natural outcome when accountability revealed misalignment.*

She also had to tackle her deeply entrenched money beliefs. Growing up, money was scarce, and the message drilled into her was to hold on tightly, never spend unless absolutely necessary, and avoid risk at all costs. So when the time came to hire a COO–a role that would command a six-figure salary–her first instinct was panic. "What if it doesn't work? What if I can't afford it? What if I hire the wrong person and the whole firm collapses?" Working on herself meant challenging those scarcity patterns, reprogramming her mindset to see money as a tool for growth rather than something to hoard for safety. It meant choosing faith in her vision over fear of the unknown.

And perhaps most importantly, Camille had to embrace a new identity. For years, she saw herself as a lawyer who ran a firm. To break the ceiling, she had to see herself as a CEO who happened to practice law. That shift required peeling back layers of perfectionism, control, and fear–and stepping into a role that demanded vision, authority, and resilience. None of that growth came from a textbook. It came from stretching herself–emotionally, mentally, and spiritually–into someone who could lead at the next level.

It wasn't easy. Camille wrestled with fear and doubt. She told herself stories: "What if the COO fails?" "What if we grow too fast and collapse?" "What if I'm not cut out to run a bigger firm?" Each story was a mirror of her own insecurities, not the reality of her business. But with coaching, she began to see the patterns clearly. Every time she invested in her own growth–mentally, emotionally, strategically–the firm responded.

When she finally let go of micromanaging associates, they stepped up and produced at a higher level. When she replaced the toxic attorney, morale and retention improved overnight. When she hired the COO, operations stabilized and freed her to focus on strategy and rainmaking.

The revenue followed. Within eighteen months, Camille's firm broke the $3 million mark for the first time. Two years later, she was closing in on $4 million. But more importantly, Camille felt different. She no longer carried the firm on her back. She led with clarity and confidence, knowing her team could execute because she had invested in her own capacity to lead.

Reflecting on her journey, Camille put it simply: "I thought my problem was revenue. My real problem was me. I stopped growing, so my firm stopped growing. Once I invested in myself, everything else followed."

Camille's story is the story of countless lawyers who hit a ceiling and assume it's external. But the ceiling is almost always internal. You are your greatest investment. Staff will come and go. Systems will evolve. Markets will shift. But you will still be here. And if you don't grow, neither will your firm.

Final Word: The Hardest Work Is Inner Work

Camille's breakthrough illustrates the ultimate truth of leadership: your firm can never outgrow you. Systems matter. Staff matter. Strategy matters. But the real lever–the one that raises the ceiling or keeps it firmly in place–is you.

Growth is not optional. It is the price of admission for every next level of success. And it's not the kind of growth lawyers instinctively

> *chase—more knowledge, more certifications, more technical mastery. Those things may sharpen your legal skills, but they don't transform your business. What grows a firm is when the owner grows: when you confront the wounds that keep you conflict-avoidant, rewire the scarcity beliefs that paralyze you, and embrace the identity of CEO instead of just "lawyer who owns a firm."*

Takeaway: You are your greatest investment. Staff will come and go. Markets will rise and fall. But you will remain. If you grow, your business grows. If you stop, your business stalls.

And that brings us full circle: leadership is not about what you *know*, but who you *become*. In this chapter, we've shown you the fractures in leadership—and how to heal them. The next step is to dig deeper into what it truly means to embody leadership at scale. Because when you grow yourself, you crush chaos for good.

ROLE CLARITY & OWNERSHIP CHECKLIST

The leadership practices discussed in this chapter are paired with the Role Clarity & Ownership Checklist found in **Appendix A**. This checklist is designed to help you identify critical misalignments, with brief guidance on how to interpret your results. Before moving on, you may find it helpful to assess whether role clarity is showing up adversely in your firm. In addition, expanded, interactive versions of all our decision-support tools are available online, accessible via links and QR codes included in the Appendix.

CHAPTER 12

SYSTEMS
THE HEART AND ART OF CRUSHING CHAOS!

Every law firm owner has felt the squeeze: too many cases, too many clients, too many moving parts. The phones ring off the hook, deadlines loom, staff need direction, and somehow, you're expected to be both the rainmaker and the quality-control department. Without systems, it all collapses into chaos.

Systems are the heart of your business. They keep the lifeblood of work moving–ensuring deadlines are met, clients are updated, and bills go out on time. Without them, everything depends on memory, heroics, or luck. And luck is not a business strategy.

But systems are also the art of your business. They are the creative structures that let humans thrive inside your firm. A system isn't just a checklist–it's a philosophy. It says: here's how we do things consistently, here's how we ensure excellence, and here's how we make room for growth. Systems don't strip people of autonomy; they give them freedom. Freedom to trust that nothing essential will slip. Freedom to focus on high-value work instead of reinventing the wheel. Freedom to grow inside a structure that scales.

Here's the truth: the absence of systems isn't just messy–it's dangerous. It invites malpractice. It hemorrhages profit. It drives away your best employees and frustrates your clients. Yet systems that are rigid, outdated, or ignored create chaos just as quickly.

In this chapter, we'll explore the five ways systems break down—and how to transform them into the backbone of a firm that doesn't just run, but runs smoothly. Because when you master the heart and art of systems, chaos has no place left to hide.

The five ways systems breakdown are:

- Misaligned Priorities
- Leaking Profits
- Fragile Systems
- Rogue Operators
- Rigid Robots

Let's dig in.

Problem 1: Misaligned Priorities – When Everything Feels Urgent, Nothing Gets Done

Every law firm has "that day." The phones won't stop ringing, emails are piling up, and three clients suddenly "need to talk" right now. Meanwhile, there's a motion due at 5:00 p.m., payroll that has to be processed, and a paralegal out sick. Everyone is running, no one is breathing, and yet—when the dust settles—it feels like nothing truly important got done.

This is the danger of misaligned priorities: when the urgent consistently trumps the essential. A late discovery response might be salvageable with a groveling extension request, but a missed statute of limitations? That's malpractice. A frantic scramble to pacify a needy client might buy a few hours of peace, but neglecting proactive communication systems guarantees more fires tomorrow.

Law firm owners often make this worse without realizing it. They're wired to jump on the loudest fire, so they drag their teams with them from crisis to crisis. The problem is that "urgency" isn't the same as "importance." Without systems that sort, triage, and protect the highest and best use of time, the firm runs on adrenaline instead of strategy. And chaos becomes the culture.

The truth is simple: you can't get it all done. But you can get the right things done. Systems create the guardrails that ensure the essentials—the tasks that prevent grievances, malpractice, and client attrition—never slip through the cracks, even on the busiest day. Without them, the firm's survival depends on luck, and luck is a lousy business plan.

Drowning in the Urgent

Step into almost any law firm on a Monday morning, and you'll feel it. The phones are already ringing, emails stack up like bricks in the inbox, and a client has left three voicemails marked "urgent" before the staff even pour their first coffee. Somewhere, a motion is due this afternoon, a filing deadline has been overlooked, and a paralegal is frantically asking the attorney if they have "just five minutes" to review something before it goes out the door.

This is what it looks like when urgency becomes the firm's operating system. Everyone is sprinting, but no one is steering. The work gets done, but not the right work.

The problem is simple: when everything feels urgent, nothing gets prioritized. Staff spend hours putting out fires, while the truly essential tasks—the ones that prevent malpractice, bar complaints, or catastrophic client loss—sit unattended. The loudest voice gets the most attention, even if that voice belongs to the client who just "wants an update" instead of the court clerk demanding a properly filed response.

Lawyers are especially vulnerable to this trap because they're trained to be crisis managers. Law school doesn't teach systems—it teaches spotting issues, reacting fast, and marshaling arguments under pressure. That skill is useful in a courtroom. But when it runs unchecked inside a firm, it creates chaos.

Worse, owners often feed the cycle themselves. They burst into the office mid-morning with a new "top priority," pulling staff off what they were working on to chase the latest shiny problem. Or they micromanage, inserting themselves into low-level issues because they can't bear to let go. Every interruption screams urgency, and soon the entire team is conditioned to drop everything and respond instantly to whatever the boss says, regardless of actual importance.

This creates predictable fallout:

- **Deadline drift.** A response that could have been finalized days ago is now being polished in a panic minutes before filing. One mistake, one missed signature, one overlooked exhibit–and the risk of malpractice is real.
- **Client dissatisfaction.** Because staff are constantly firefighting, proactive client updates fall through the cracks. Clients only hear from the firm when they're already angry, which makes them angrier.
- **Burnout.** Employees who live in reaction mode never feel the satisfaction of finishing meaningful work. Instead, they limp home each night exhausted, wondering why they worked so hard and accomplished so little.

And for the owner? It's a special kind of torment. They look around the office and feel like they're the only one who cares. They see staff scrambling yet missing the essentials and conclude: *If I don't keep cracking the whip, this place will fall apart.* So they push harder, fuel more urgency, and inadvertently accelerate the cycle.

Here's the irony: law firm owners don't expect their doctors to treat them based on who yells the loudest in the waiting room. They wouldn't want their accountant ignoring tax deadlines to chase down every client question in real time. But inside their own firms, they allow urgency to dictate priorities, instead of building systems that protect what matters most.

The truth is unavoidable: you cannot get it all done. Law firms are endless machines of tasks, calls, filings, and client needs. But you *can* get the right things done—if you have systems that separate the essential from the optional. Systems that triage tasks, track deadlines, and reserve human energy for the highest and best use of time. Systems that prevent malpractice and client complaints, not just soothe temporary fires.

Without those systems, urgency rules the day. And when urgency rules, chaos wins.

CASE STUDY

LAURA'S FIRM OF FIRES

Laura was a family law attorney in Nashville who built her firm with passion, persistence, and sheer grit. She was known for her tenacity in court and her fierce advocacy for clients. But inside her office, the story was very different. Her firm ran on adrenaline, and the chaos was constant.

Living in Firefighting Mode

From the moment the doors opened each morning, Laura and her staff were in firefighting mode. Phones rang nonstop. Clients demanded updates. Court deadlines loomed. It seemed like every day was one long sprint toward 5:00 p.m., with no finish line in sight.

Laura's paralegals spent hours answering frantic client calls instead of preparing discovery. Associates stayed late drafting motions they should have finished days earlier because their days were hijacked by "urgent" interruptions. Even the receptionist was overwhelmed, trying to juggle intake, handle walk-ins, and placate angry spouses calling for their lawyers.

And Laura? She was the biggest firestarter of all.

She'd sweep into the office mid-morning, after a hearing, declaring some new crisis: "Drop everything–we need to get this motion filed today!" or "This client is threatening to leave–we need to call her right now!" *Staff scrambled to comply, even if it meant abandoning other critical work. Laura's sense of urgency became the firm's default setting.*

The result was predictable. Deadlines slipped. Typos made it into filings. Clients grew frustrated with inconsistent communication. And Laura herself was exhausted, convinced she was the only one who truly cared. "Why does it feel like I'm dragging everyone uphill with me?" she lamented.

The Problem Wasn't Her People

When Laura came to Law Firm Mentor, she framed her problem as a staffing issue. "I've hired good people, but they're not productive. They don't keep up. I feel like I'm carrying the whole firm on my back."

What Laura didn't realize was that her staff weren't failing–they were drowning. Without systems to prioritize the essentials, they spent their days reacting to whatever screamed the loudest. Worse, Laura modeled the same behavior, constantly pulling people off one task to chase another. It wasn't incompetence; it was chaos.

We started by teaching Laura to separate urgency from importance. Not everything needed to be done right now. *Some things–like statutes of limitation, court-imposed deadlines, and client retainers–were truly essential. Others–like a client's emotional need for an update or Laura's sudden brainstorm for a new marketing campaign–could wait.*

The key was systems.

First, we implemented a **triage calendar**. *Every task, deadline, and client deliverable was entered into a centralized case management system with clear deadlines and assigned ownership. Staff* *knew exactly what had to be completed each day, and they could see which tasks were mission-critical versus optional.*

Second, we created **communication protocols.** *Instead of paralegals fielding endless client calls, every client received scheduled updates. Calls were logged, and true emergencies were flagged for immediate response. This cut "fire drills" by more than half within two months.*

Third, Laura learned to **control herself.** *She committed to bringing new "urgent" ideas only to the weekly leadership meeting. If a thought struck her midweek, she wrote it down instead of derailing her team. That single discipline transformed her staff's productivity.*

At first, Laura resisted. She worried that slowing down to create systems would make her firm less responsive. But within weeks, she saw the opposite. With essentials prioritized, her team stopped scrambling and started performing. Motions were filed early. Clients praised the proactive updates. Even her associates, once hesitant and reactive, began taking ownership of cases because they weren't constantly yanked in different directions.

Within six months, Laura noticed a shift in herself. She no longer walked into the office dreading the chaos. She felt calmer, more confident, and more in control–not because she worked harder, but because her systems carried the weight.

Looking back, Laura admitted: "I thought my staff was the problem. But I was the one fueling the fires. Once I stopped reacting and built systems that protected the essentials, everything changed. I don't feel like I'm dragging people anymore. We're all moving in the same direction."

Final Word: The Results of Real Systems

Laura's story is proof of the painful truth: chaos doesn't come from bad employees or lazy staff. It comes from the absence of systems that protect the essentials. When urgency rules, nothing important gets done. When systems rule, everything essential gets done—and chaos has nowhere to hide.

Law firms that run on adrenaline may look busy, but beneath the surface they're fragile—deadlines slip, client trust erodes, and employees burn out. The problem isn't that you don't care enough or that your team isn't capable. The problem is that without systems, the essentials aren't protected.

Takeaway: Systems create the triage your firm needs. They separate the noise from the mission-critical. They guarantee that the work that matters most—the filings that protect your clients, the communication that builds trust, the processes that keep malpractice at bay—gets done first, every time. Systems transform firefighting into strategy, and scrambling into consistency.

But prioritization is only the beginning. Even if you know what matters most, your firm will bleed profits if the wrong people are doing the wrong work. In the next section, we'll look at how failing to match tasks with the right level of skill and cost turns even the hardest-working firms into money pits—and how systems can plug those leaks before they sink you.

Problem 2: The Profit Leak – When the Wrong People Do the Wrong Work

In too many law firms, people are working hard—but on the wrong things. Attorneys are drafting routine discovery that a paralegal could handle. Paralegals are processing invoices that should be done by admin staff. Receptionists are juggling intake calls when they should be focused on greeting clients. Everyone is busy, but no one is optimized.

On the surface, it may feel like teamwork—people "helping out" wherever there's a gap. But underneath, this practice is one of the biggest drains on profit in a law firm. Because every time someone performs work below their highest and best use, the firm loses money. Attorneys who should be strategizing at $500 an hour are typing tasks worth $200 an hour. Paralegals who should be pushing cases forward at $200 an hour are licking envelopes worth $25 an hour. The result? A hidden but massive leak in profitability.

And it's not just about money. When staff are forced into the wrong roles, quality suffers. Attorneys resent clerical work. Paralegals grow frustrated when they're underutilized. Admin staff feel overwhelmed when they're expected to handle complex legal issues. Misaligned work breeds burnout, turnover, and chaos.

The truth is simple: if you want your firm to grow, every person must consistently work at their highest and best use. That requires systems—clear role definitions, task allocation protocols, and accountability to ensure the right work is always being done by the right person, at the right rate. Otherwise, your firm isn't just losing money—it's bleeding it.

The Hidden Cost of Misaligned Work

At first glance, a law firm buzzing with activity looks successful. Attorneys are busy drafting, paralegals are glued to their computers, reception is juggling calls, and the admin staff are "helping" wherever needed. Everyone is working hard. But beneath that surface-level hustle is often a brutal truth: most of that work is misaligned, and the firm is quietly bleeding profit.

The problem begins when lawyers, paralegals, and staff step outside their lanes. Maybe the attorney doesn't trust the paralegal to draft the discovery, so she does it herself. Maybe the paralegal notices that billing is behind and spends half a day sending invoices. Maybe the receptionist gets pulled into intake because "someone has to take the call." Each decision feels harmless in the moment—even admirable. Everyone's just pitching in, right? But when misaligned work becomes the culture, it destroys efficiency and profit.

Let's make this concrete.

Suppose a lawyer bills at **$500 per hour**. That lawyer spends an hour drafting standard interrogatories–work that a paralegal, billing at **$200 per hour**, could have handled. On the surface, nothing looks wrong. The work got done. The client gets billed. But here's the math:

- If the lawyer bills for it at the paralegal's rate ($200/hour), the firm just lost **$300/hour** in opportunity cost–the difference between the lawyer's rate and the paralegal's. That's $300 of profit gone, simply because the wrong person did the work.
- If the lawyer decides not to bill for it at all, thinking, *"It wasn't worth my time to charge,"* the firm just lost **the full $200/hour** that the paralegal could have ethically billed. The lawyer worked for free, and the firm lost revenue.
- If the lawyer bills it at her own $500/hour rate, she cheats the client by overcharging **$300/hour** for work that should have been delegated. That's not only wrong–it's unethical.

Either way, the firm loses. One option cheats the firm, the other cheats the client. Neither is acceptable.

And this is just one hour. Multiply that by five hours a week, across ten attorneys, for a year, and the loss is staggering. Hundreds of thousands of dollars evaporate–not because the work wasn't done, but because the wrong person did it.

This same math plays out everywhere in the firm:

- A paralegal, at $200/hour, spends a morning stuffing envelopes and mailing discovery packets. That's work a $25/hour admin could have done. The firm just lost **$175/hour** in margin.
- A receptionist fields intake calls that should be handled by a trained intake specialist. Prospective clients slip through the cracks, leaving potentially tens of thousands in lost revenue on the table.
- An attorney insists on hand-holding clients through scheduling, instead of leaving it to a paralegal or client concierge. Not only

is it a poor use of attorney time, but it also dilutes the client's perception of the lawyer's role.

When the wrong people do the wrong work, the cost compounds:

1. **Financial loss.** Profit margins shrink because high-value labor is wasted on low-value tasks.
2. **Quality loss.** Work suffers because it's not being handled by the person best trained to do it. Attorneys rushing clerical tasks make mistakes. Paralegals pressed into attorney-level analysis miss legal nuance.
3. **Morale loss.** No one enjoys working outside their lane long term. Attorneys resent clerical busywork. Paralegals feel undervalued when they're stuck with admin tasks. Support staff feel overwhelmed when expected to perform legal functions beyond their training.

Over time, this dysfunction breeds resentment and burnout. High performers leave because they're tired of being underutilized or overburdened. Mediocre employees stick around, glad to blend into the chaos. And the owner, exhausted from plugging leaks and redoing work, concludes that "no one around here cares as much as I do."

But the truth is, this isn't a problem of caring. It's a problem of systems. Without systems that define roles, allocate tasks, and enforce accountability, people default to what's urgent rather than what's profitable. They "help out" in the wrong places. They freelance. They improvise. And the firm pays for it–literally.

Law firms love to say, "Everyone wears many hats." But in reality, when everyone wears many hats, no one wears theirs well. A profitable firm has one simple rule: the least expensive, most skilled person for each role handles the work. Period. Anything else is malpractice against your own business.

And here's the bottom line: profit leaks don't fix themselves. If you don't create systems that force the right work into the right hands, the firm will keep bleeding–quietly, invisibly, but fatally.

CASE STUDY

MARTIN'S $5M FIRM THAT LEAKED LIKE A SIEVE

Martin had built a name for himself in Charlotte, North Carolina. After fifteen years of grinding as a solo, he had grown his firm into a $5 million practice with ten attorneys, seven paralegals, and eight support staff. The firm covered family law, real estate transactions, and estate planning. On paper, Martin had achieved what most small-firm owners dream of: a thriving, multi-practice firm with a steady pipeline of clients.

But Martin couldn't shake a gnawing frustration. Despite the size and success of his firm, his margins were razor thin. Payroll was always a stressor. Bonuses were a stretch every year. He felt like he was constantly "feeding the beast" just to keep the lights on.

The Profit Leaks Hiding in Plain Sight

The truth was hiding in plain sight. His firm leaked profit at every level.

Attorneys billed at $450–500 per hour were routinely drafting standard interrogatories, assembling closing binders, and even filing deeds at the courthouse. Paralegals, at $200/hour, were running payroll, mailing documents, and chasing down overdue invoices. Support staff, instead of answering phones or managing intake, were constantly pulled into "helping" with legal drafting they weren't trained to do. Everyone was working. Everyone was *busy. But almost no one was consistently working at their highest and best use.*

The numbers were brutal.

Martin sat down with his COO (hired under pressure from his accountant) and reviewed time logs. What they discovered made him sick to his stomach.

*One of his top litigators, billing at **$500/hour,** had spent nearly **20 hours in a single month** drafting discovery requests and formatting exhibits–work that could have been handled by a paralegal at **$200/hour.** Do the math:*

- *20 hours × $500/hour = $10,000 of attorney time.*
- *20 hours × $200/hour = $4,000 of paralegal time.*

*Every one of those hours represented a **$300 loss.** In just one month, that single attorney had cost the firm **$6,000 in lost margin.** Over a year? $72,000–gone.*

And that was only one attorney. Multiply similar patterns across ten lawyers and seven paralegals, and Martin realized his firm was bleeding hundreds of thousands annually–not from lack of clients, but from misaligned work.

The ethical risk hit him just as hard. In some cases, his attorneys were billing paralegal-level work at attorney rates. That meant clients were overcharged for work that didn't require attorney expertise. One sharp client noticed, questioned an invoice, and threatened to file a grievance. The incident was quietly resolved, but it shook Martin. He realized his firm wasn't just inefficient–it was vulnerable.

At first, Martin tried to address it with pep talks: "Everyone needs to focus on their lane." But without systems, nothing changed. Attorneys still hoarded routine drafting, paralegals still filled in for admins, and the bleed continued.

When the Numbers Came into Focus

When Martin joined Law Firm Mentor, we showed him the math clearly: "Every time your attorneys do paralegal work, you're losing $300/hour. Every time your paralegals do admin work, you're losing $175/hour. And every time you bill clients attorney rates for paralegal-level tasks, you risk an ethics complaint. How long can you afford to pay this tax?"

That got his attention.

We helped Martin design a **role clarity system.** *Every position—attorney, paralegal, support—was documented with clear responsibilities and limits. Tasks were broken down by role, and case workflows were mapped so everyone knew exactly who did what, when. Attorneys were instructed:* if it can be done by a paralegal, it must be delegated. *Paralegals were trained to push clerical tasks down to support staff.*

Next, we built **task allocation systems**. *Matters were tracked in project management software, and tasks were assigned automatically by role. If an attorney tried to assign a paralegal task to themselves, the system flagged it. Intake staff were trained to handle the first wave of client communications, so attorneys weren't constantly interrupted.*

Finally, Martin enforced **accountability**. *Weekly scorecards tracked role alignment. Each month, the COO pulled reports showing how much attorney time was spent on paralegal or admin tasks. For the first time, Martin could see the leaks closing in real time.*

The results were dramatic. Within six months, attorney utilization skyrocketed. Associates were suddenly billing close to their full capacity at attorney rates, because their calendars were freed from paralegal work. Paralegals, no longer bogged down with clerical tasks, pushed more cases forward. Support staff, properly utilized, created smoother intake and happier clients.

The financials told the story. In the first year of alignment, Martin's margins increased by 18%. Payroll pressure eased, bonuses were funded without drama, and Martin was finally able to take distributions without guilt.

Looking back, Martin was blunt: "I thought I had a staffing problem. What I really had was a systems problem. My people weren't lazy–they were misused. Once I forced the work into the right lanes, my firm went from bleeding profit to building it."

Martin's story proves the point: law firms don't just lose money when clients don't pay. They lose it every time the wrong person does the wrong work. Without systems to enforce role alignment, even a thriving $5 million firm will quietly leak itself into exhaustion.

Final Word: The Payoff of Systems Alignment

Martin's story reveals what so many law firm owners miss: profit doesn't just vanish when clients don't pay. It leaks out quietly, every time the wrong person does the wrong work. An attorney spending an hour on paralegal tasks isn't "helping the team"–they're draining $300 of profit the firm will never recover. A paralegal licking envelopes instead of pushing cases forward isn't "pitching in"–they're costing the firm margin and morale.

And when lawyers bill clients attorney rates for paralegal-level work? That's not only bad business–it's unethical.

Takeaway: The solution is crystal clear: systems that force role alignment. Systems that ensure every task is handled at the highest and best use of time, skill, and cost. With those systems in place, attorneys can focus on strategy, paralegals can move cases forward, and support staff can keep the wheels turning. Everyone wins–the firm, the team, and the clients.

But even the best role-based systems can't be built once and left forever. As your firm grows, the very systems that serve you today will eventually break. In the next section, we'll explore why fragile systems sabotage scaling–and how to anticipate and evolve them before chaos returns.

Problem 3: Fragile Systems – Why What Worked Yesterday Breaks Tomorrow

One of the biggest lies law firm owners tell themselves is: *We already have a system for that.*

On its face, that sounds good–responsible, even. But systems aren't like stone monuments you build once and admire forever. They're more like bridges under constant traffic: they wear down, they buckle, and eventually, they fail if you don't reinforce them. What worked perfectly when your firm had three employees often collapses when you reach ten. A system that flowed smoothly with a handful of cases can grind to a halt with fifty.

This is the problem of fragile systems: they're not built to evolve.

Owners often confuse "having a process" with "having a durable process." They design intake around one receptionist. They build billing on one paralegal's spreadsheet. They track deadlines with sticky notes or a shared calendar. At first, it feels efficient. But as the firm grows, those fragile systems break under the weight of new people, new workflows, and higher client demands. And when they break, they don't just cause inconvenience–they cause chaos. Missed deadlines. Lost leads. Angry clients. Overworked staff.

The truth? Every system has an expiration date. The question isn't whether it will break, but when–and whether you'll be ready.

The Shelf Life of Systems

Every law firm owner feels a sense of accomplishment when they finally create a system. Maybe it's an intake process, a billing routine, or a checklist for discovery. For a while, it works beautifully. Calls get answered, invoices go out, cases move forward. The owner breathes a sigh of relief: *Finally, we've got this under control.*

But here's the truth few owners realize: every system has a shelf life.

Systems don't break all at once, like a glass shattering. They erode slowly, like a rope fraying strand by strand. The system that worked when you had two employees will strain at five, snap at ten, and become obsolete at twenty. And unless you anticipate that evolution, you'll find yourself blindsided by chaos all over again.

Take intake as an example. A solo attorney might create a "system" where the receptionist answers the phone, takes notes on a pad, and drops them on the attorney's desk. At that size, it works fine. But add a paralegal, then another attorney, then five new matters a week—and suddenly the sticky-note intake system collapses. Calls get lost. Clients don't get follow-ups. Prospects sign with competitors. What once felt "good enough" is now actively costing revenue.

Or consider billing. At three attorneys, tracking hours on a shared Excel sheet might function. At ten attorneys, that same spreadsheet becomes a nightmare—hours go unrecorded, invoices get delayed, and clients dispute charges because there's no centralized system. The process hasn't just outlived its usefulness; it's now a liability.

Fragile systems also depend too heavily on individuals. "Sally handles billing," "Tom manages deadlines," or "Maria is in charge of discovery checklists." The problem is, Sally eventually takes a vacation, Tom quits, or Maria gets sick. Suddenly, the system isn't a system at all—it's one person's memory. And when that person disappears, so does the process.

The chaos this creates is predictable and painful:

- **Missed deadlines.** Court notices slip through because the one person tracking them is overwhelmed.
- **Lost revenue.** Intake fails because sticky notes don't convert into signed retainers.
- **Burnout.** Staff run ragged trying to compensate for systems that don't scale.
- **Client frustration.** Promises fall through the cracks, and the firm's reputation suffers.

The deeper issue is mindset. Too many owners treat systems like one-time projects. They design something, check the box, and move on. They don't ask: "When will this break? What happens when we add five more cases, or three more staff, or another office?" They don't build systems with growth in mind.

And yet, growth is the very reason you need systems. Every time your firm expands—more clients, more staff, more revenue—your systems must expand too. Otherwise, they buckle.

Here's the irony: many owners cling to fragile systems because they seem to be "working." They tell themselves, *If it ain't broke, don't fix it.* But by the time a system looks visibly broken, the damage is already done. Deadlines have already been missed. Clients have already walked away. Staff are already burned out. The fix becomes ten times harder because you're repairing trust, not just process.

The strongest firms avoid this trap by treating systems as living organisms. They assume every system will eventually fail. They build in review points—quarterly checkups, annual overhauls—so they're proactively asking: *"Is this still serving us? Is it built for the next level, not just today?"* They don't just look for cracks after the collapse; they reinforce the bridge before traffic overwhelms it.

The truth is simple but sobering: fragile systems are not systems at all. They're temporary scaffolding. They'll hold for a while, maybe even longer than you expect, but they will always, inevitably, collapse under growth. The only question is whether you'll anticipate their expiration—or be buried in the rubble when they break.

CASE STUDY

PRIYA'S SYSTEMS THAT SNAPPED

Priya had always been proud of her efficiency. A family law attorney in Phoenix, she left her mid-sized firm to open her own shop, determined to run a lean, well-oiled operation. In the beginning, she did everything: answered phones, drafted pleadings, tracked deadlines on a color-coded calendar. As her caseload grew, she hired a paralegal, then a receptionist. She built systems as she went, and for a while, everything flowed smoothly.

When Growth Outpaces the System

By year three, Priya's firm had grown to four attorneys, three paralegals, and two support staff. On paper, things looked great. Revenue was over $2 million, referrals were strong, and clients praised her team. But underneath the surface, cracks were forming.

Her intake "system" was still a glorified sticky-note process. Calls came in through the receptionist, who scribbled details on slips of paper and left them on the attorneys' desks. Priya's paralegal tried to organize them into a spreadsheet, but it was easy for notes to get lost or delayed. As call volume grew, prospective clients fell through the cracks. By the time Priya realized it, they were losing an estimated ***10–15 new clients a month*** *simply because no one had followed up.*

Billing was another weak spot. In the early days, Priya tracked time in Excel. Each attorney kept their own tab, and once a month, her paralegal compiled them into invoices. With four attorneys, this became chaos. Hours were often entered late, some were missed entirely, and clients pushed back on vague invoices. In one quarter alone, Priya's firm wrote off nearly ***$75,000 in unbilled or disputed time****—not because the work wasn't done, but because the system couldn't handle the volume.*

And then, the breaking point came.

One of Priya's senior paralegals, Maria, went on maternity leave. Maria had been the unofficial keeper of the firm's deadlines, maintaining a massive Excel sheet that tracked filings, hearings, and discovery cutoffs. When she left, no one knew how to manage it. Within weeks, deadlines slipped. A motion in a custody case was filed late, and Priya had to beg the judge for mercy. A discovery deadline passed unnoticed, damaging a client's leverage in settlement.

Priya was devastated. She had built her reputation on diligence, but her fragile systems—dependent on individual memory and outdated tools—had betrayed her.

From Workarounds to Real Systems

When she came to Law Firm Mentor, she confessed: "I thought I had systems. But really, I just had workarounds. Now that we've grown, everything is breaking."

The first shift was mindset. Priya had to see systems not as one-time fixes, but as living frameworks that must evolve with the firm. "If it ain't broke, don't fix it" was killing her. The truth was, her systems were already broken—they just hadn't fully collapsed yet.

Together, we rebuilt her intake process. Sticky notes were banished. Calls went directly into a centralized CRM that tracked every prospect from first contact to signed retainer. Automated reminders ensured no lead slipped through. Intake staff were trained to own the process, freeing attorneys from ever touching it. Within three months, conversion rates jumped 22%.

Next, we tackled billing. Out went the Excel sheets; in came a practice management platform that integrated time tracking, invoicing, and payment. Attorneys entered time in real time, paralegals reviewed for accuracy, and invoices went out twice a month. The system flagged missing hours and ensured no billable minute was lost. Write-offs dropped by 80% in six months.

Finally, deadlines. Instead of relying on Maria's memory, we implemented a firm-wide calendaring system tied directly to case milestones. Each task was assigned, tracked, and reviewed in weekly team meetings. No more "I thought you had it" confusion. Everyone knew who was responsible, and nothing lived in one person's head.

The transformation was dramatic. Within a year, Priya's revenue climbed past $3 million—not because she added more clients, but because she stopped losing them. Profit margins grew because billable time was actually captured. Most importantly, Priya's stress *plummeted. She no longer woke up at 3 a.m. wondering if something had slipped through the cracks.*

Looking back, she admitted: "I thought systems were something you built once and forgot about. But now I see–they have to grow with the firm. If you don't evolve them, they'll strangle you."

Final Word: Protecting the Essentials

Priya's story highlights the danger of treating systems as permanent fixtures: what worked yesterday will fail tomorrow if you don't reinforce it. Systems aren't monuments carved in stone. They're bridges under constant traffic. If you don't strengthen them before they snap, chaos is inevitable.

What works with two employees will buckle under ten. What works with ten will collapse under twenty. The lesson is clear: every system has a shelf life. The system doesn't have to look broken to already be failing–it only has to be unfit for the next stage of growth.

Takeaway: Firms that thrive anticipate the breaking points before they arrive. They build review dates into every process, assume each system will eventually outlive its usefulness, and treat system-building as an ongoing discipline rather than a one-time project.

But even the best-designed system will fail if people refuse to follow it. And that's the next challenge: **rogue operators**. Every firm has them–the employees who insist their way is better, who quietly deviate from the process, who undermine consistency and drag the firm back into chaos. In the next section, we'll explore how to stop freelancing, enforce compliance, and build a culture where systems stick.

Problem 4: Rogue Operators – When Systems Exist but Nobody Follows Them

Every law firm owner has had the moment: you walk past an employee's desk and notice them doing something completely different from the process you carefully designed. Maybe the intake specialist is skipping the CRM and jotting notes on a legal pad. Maybe the paralegal is filing pleadings directly with the court instead of routing them through the calendaring system. Maybe an attorney is sending client emails without looping in the case manager, leaving everyone else in the dark.

When confronted, the excuses roll in:

- "Oh, I just find it faster this way."
- "I wasn't sure the system applied to this situation."
- "Honestly, I didn't even look at the procedure–I've been doing it this way for years."

These rogue operators aren't necessarily malicious. Most of the time, they think they're helping. But in reality, they're breaking the very systems that keep the firm from descending into chaos.

The truth is, a system ignored is no system at all. You can spend months designing airtight processes, but if your team freelances their way around them, you're right back where you started: inconsistent work, client complaints, missed deadlines, and chaos.

What makes this even more dangerous is that rogue operators often *look* productive. They're busy, they meet their individual deadlines, and they may even be praised by clients for being "responsive." But beneath the surface, they're undermining the entire firm's stability.

This is the dysfunction of noncompliance: when the owner builds systems, but the culture doesn't require them to be followed.

The Cost of Freelancing

A law firm's systems only work if people use them. That sounds obvious–until you walk the floor and see shadow processes everywhere: deadlines living in a personal planner instead of the shared calendar; drafts saved to a desktop folder called "final_final_REALfinal" instead of the document management system; client calls handled via someone's cell phone with no log in the case file. None of this looks sinister in the moment. It often even looks productive. But it's the quiet undoing of consistency, profit, and risk control.

Rogue operators don't usually think of themselves as "rogue." They think they're helping. They believe their shortcut is faster, their spreadsheet is clearer, their personal template is better. The issue isn't malice; it's misalignment. Systems exist to create one reliable way the work flows so anyone can step in, pick up context, and keep marching without error. Freelancing breaks that chain.

Why People Go Rogue (and How It Shows Up)

1. **Speed myth:** "It's faster if I just do it my way." Maybe for *that* person, *that* day. But the downstream cost is huge: the next person can't find the file, the intake is invisible to marketing, the deadline isn't on the shared tickler. Personal speed becomes organizational drag.
2. **Comfort & habit:** People cling to what they learned before. A veteran paralegal brings their old firm's checklist and quietly ignores yours. An associate tracks time in a personal spreadsheet "to reconcile later," which means hours go missing.
3. **Tool sprawl & ambiguity:** If there's no declared single source of truth, staff scatter information across email, Slack, texts, sticky notes, and side spreadsheets. "I thought it was in Slack" is how conflicts get missed and clients get ignored.
4. **Training gaps:** If onboarding is rushed or sporadic, staff never internalize *how* and *why* the system works. They default to improvisation because no one invested in mastery.
5. **Lack of enforcement:** If leaders don't audit, don't coach, and don't correct, the message is simple: systems are optional. Culture always follows what leaders tolerate.
6. **Ego or distrust:** A rainmaker who thinks the CRM is "for juniors" or a senior assistant who doesn't trust the template library exempt themselves. One exemption becomes a precedent.

The Ripple Effects (Seen and Unseen)

- **Lost revenue & conversion:** Intake that lives on a notepad can't be tracked, nurtured, or measured. Prospective clients don't get timely follow-ups. Marketing can't see conversion gaps. "Busy phones" mask "empty pipelines."
- **Deadline risk & malpractice exposure:** Calendars that aren't centralized mean dates vanish when the "keeper" is out. Even one missed response can explode into complaints, sanctions, or claims.
- **Duplicated work & rework:** Ignoring templates and checklists forces attorneys to edit basic formatting and fix avoidable errors. Ten minutes of freelancing becomes an hour of cleanup.
- **Inconsistent client experience:** One paralegal sends weekly updates; another sends none. Clients conclude the firm is disorganized, not just "individuals with styles."
- **Burnout & cynicism:** High performers resent cleaning up behind freelancers. New hires get whiplash: the handbook says one thing; the "real way" is whatever their shadow-mentor prefers. Good people leave; drifters remain.
- **Data integrity & compliance issues:** Files on desktops, personal clouds, or private devices create security risk, version confusion, and audit nightmares–especially for trust accounting or discovery productions.

The Leadership Illusion

Owners often tolerate rogues because they *look* productive. The senior paralegal who refuses the DMS "gets things done." The partner who won't use the CRM "brings in business." It feels safer to leave them alone. But this is borrowed time. The day they're sick, on vacation, or out the door, their private system walks with them–and your firm scrambles. Dependence on a person over a process isn't loyalty; it's liability.

"But we need flexibility!"

Correct—systems must flex for humans. Flexibility, however, is not freelancing. Flexibility lives *inside* structure: the *what/when/quality bar* is non-negotiable; the *how* may have lanes. For example: "All hearings must be in the shared calendar with judge, location, and docket by close of day" is the structure; whether an attorney blocks prep time at 30 or 45 minutes is a lane. Rogue behavior ignores structure entirely.

Make the System the Boss

To eliminate freelancing, you need both cultural and mechanical controls:

- **Declare a single source of truth.** "If it's not in [CRM/DMS/Calendar], it doesn't exist." Post it. Repeat it. Enforce it.
- **Master → improve (never the reverse).** Everyone must learn and use the current system first. Improvements are welcomed *after mastery*, via a clear pathway: identify friction → propose change with rationale → pilot on a small slice → measure → adopt/roll back. No unauthorized "I do it differently."
- **Onboard for comprehension, not just exposure.** Don't just show buttons—teach the *why*: risk prevention, client experience, margin impact. People follow what they understand.
- **Trust and verify (audit).** What you don't inspect, your culture will neglect. Weekly spot checks (e.g., "Are all new matters in the CRM with next action?"), monthly scorecards (compliance rates by person/team), and quarterly process reviews make the invisible visible.
- **Consequences & reinforcement.** Praise public compliance and speed-to-value; coach deviations once; escalate with written warnings if needed. The first tolerated exception becomes policy.
- **Leaders go first.** Partners and senior staff *must* model system use. A partner who refuses the CRM teaches everyone else to ignore it.

- **Design for absences.** Every critical process must be operable if any one person disappears. If one vacation threatens the calendar, you don't have a system—you have a heroic memory.
- **Emergencies without erosion.** Yes, true emergencies happen. Build an "exception lane" *inside* the system: if someone must bypass a step, they tag the matter "Exception," log the reason why, and schedule a brief post-mortem to patch the gap. That preserves velocity without normalizing freelancing.

Here's the bottom line: a system ignored is no system at all. Rogue operators convert carefully built order back into personality-driven chaos. The cure is not more pages in the SOP; it's a firmwide mindset—"we run the system, and the system runs the work"—backed by training, audits, leadership modeling, and a structured path for improvement. When compliance rises, stress falls, client experience stabilizes, and profit becomes predictable.

CASE STUDY

KAREN'S SILENT SABOTEUR

Karen owned a small but growing estate planning firm in Minneapolis, Minnesota. With five attorneys, four paralegals, and three support staff, she had worked hard to systematize her practice. Every intake call was logged into the firm's CRM. Every client file was tracked in the case management software. Every deadline was entered into a shared calendar that triggered reminders for attorneys and staff alike.

For the most part, things ran smoothly—until they didn't.

The Cracks Begin to Show

Problems began surfacing slowly. A prospective client called back, angry that no one had followed up after their consult. A filing deadline was missed, forcing Karen to scramble for a continuance. A client complained that they had emailed documents but was repeatedly asked to resend them.

At first, Karen assumed these were random mistakes. But when she started investigating, a pattern emerged. All the errors traced back to one paralegal, Jen.

Jen was a senior employee who had been with Karen from the early days. She was smart, fast, and well-liked by clients. But she had a fatal flaw: she hated the firm's systems.

Instead of logging intake into the CRM, Jen kept her own notes in a private notebook. Instead of uploading documents into the case management software, she saved them on her desktop. Instead of entering deadlines into the shared calendar, she scribbled them in her planner.

Jen wasn't lazy. She worked long hours and turned things around quickly. Clients loved her responsiveness. To Karen, Jen looked like a star. But in reality, she was a silent saboteur.

Every time Jen freelanced, she left the rest of the team in the dark. Intake prospects disappeared because they weren't tracked in the system. Documents went missing because no one else knew where to find them. Deadlines were overlooked because the calendar didn't reflect Jen's planner.

The chaos escalated until one day, disaster struck. Jen went on vacation. During her absence, an estate planning matter blew up because critical documents were sitting on her desktop instead of the shared drive. A filing deadline was missed because the date was buried in her planner, not the firm calendar. Karen had to call the client, admit the mistake, and eat thousands of dollars in write-offs.

That was the wake-up call. Karen realized that by allowing Jen to ignore the systems, she had put her entire firm at risk.

Enforcing the System

With LFM coaching, Karen implemented a zero-tolerance policy for system noncompliance. Every staff member was retrained on the why behind each process. Weekly audits checked for compliance. Scorecards tracked whether tasks were logged properly. And Karen made it clear: freelancing was not optional.

At first, Jen resisted. She argued that her way was "faster." But when presented with the missed deadlines, the lost clients, and the financial impact, even she couldn't deny the truth. Karen gave her a choice: follow the system or leave. Jen chose to stay–but this time, she complied.

Within months, the difference was dramatic. Intake conversion rates improved. Document chaos disappeared. Deadlines were never missed. The firm felt calmer, more predictable, and more scalable.

Looking back, Karen admitted: "I let Jen's freelancing slide because she looked productive. But I see now–her way wasn't faster, it was just more dangerous. Once everyone followed the system, our entire firm leveled up."

Final Word: Zero Tolerance for Noncompliance

Rogue operators are the termites of a law firm. They nibble quietly at the foundation, undermining systems until the entire structure weakens. They don't announce themselves with laziness or sabotage–they often look like your best employees. But their refusal to follow the system guarantees chaos.

The cure is culture. Systems must be non-negotiable. Everyone, from the newest receptionist to the most senior partner, must know: this is how we do things here. That doesn't mean systems can't evolve. Innovation is welcome–but only after mastery. The rule is simple: follow the system first, then suggest improvements through a structured process.

Takeaway: A system ignored is no system at all. And a firm that tolerates freelancing isn't systematized—it's fragile.

But rigidity has its own dangers. Systems that don't flex for human differences turn into straitjackets, suffocating creativity and morale. In the next section, we'll explore why **Rigid Robots**—systems without humanity—are just as dangerous as no systems at all.

Problem 5: Rigid Robots – Forgetting Systems Serve Humans, Not the Other Way Around

If chaos is one extreme, rigidity is the other.

Some law firm owners take "systems" so literally that they turn them into straitjackets. Every action is prescribed. Every step is documented. Every deviation is treated as insubordination. Staff are expected to click the same buttons, use the same words, and march in perfect lockstep, regardless of their individual strengths or working styles.

On paper, this looks efficient. The owner believes they've created "the perfect machine." In reality, it's a brittle structure that chokes creativity, frustrates staff, and alienates high performers. Instead of empowering people, the system disempowers them. Instead of making work easier, it makes work feel robotic.

This happens when owners forget the purpose of systems. Systems don't exist to control humans. They exist to serve humans. The goal of a system is to guarantee consistency in outcomes—not conformity in every motion.

Consider drafting timelines. A well-designed system ensures briefs are filed on time. But one attorney may outline first while another starts by free-writing and shaping later. If the system mandates one exact drafting method, it crushes efficiency for half the team. The output is the same—but the rigidity creates unnecessary friction.

Rigid systems repel talent. Great employees want structure, but they also want room to breathe. They want to bring their skills, quirks, and creativity into the process. If a system can't flex to accommodate different working styles, it will either burn them out–or drive them out.

The art of systems is balance: enough structure to guarantee excellence, enough flexibility to let people thrive.

When Systems Become Straitjackets

Systems are meant to create freedom. They free the owner from micromanaging, they free staff from confusion, and they free the client from inconsistent service. But when systems are taken too far–designed as rigid, one-size-fits-all scripts instead of adaptable frameworks–they stop being liberating and start being suffocating.

Law firm owners often swing into rigidity after experiencing the pain of chaos. They watch deadlines slip, see clients complain, or discover malpractice risk hiding in the shadows of sloppy processes. Their natural reaction? Clamp down. "If everyone would just follow the steps exactly as I've written them, everything would run smoothly."

At first, this feels safe. Every motion has a checklist. Every word of a client email is templated. Every draft looks exactly the same. But over time, the system that was supposed to protect the firm ends up alienating the very people who run it.

The Human Cost of Rigidity

1. **Creativity dies.** Attorneys and paralegals are professionals, not assembly-line workers. When every task is scripted to the last keystroke, they stop thinking critically. They stop bringing new ideas. They simply check boxes and disengage.
2. **Morale plummets.** High performers crave autonomy. They want to exercise judgment, not just obey. When systems leave no room for professional discretion, talented employees either burn out or leave. What remains are "clock-punchers" who do only what's written and nothing more.

3. **Efficiency paradox.** Ironically, rigid systems often slow things down. For example, requiring every attorney to draft motions in the exact same sequence–outline first, then research, then draft–ignores that some attorneys think best by writing first and shaping later. The end product is the same, but the rigid method wastes time and drains energy.
4. **Resistance grows.** Staff forced into robotic processes eventually rebel. They cut corners, ignore steps, or create shadow systems just to make their jobs bearable. The very rigidity designed to enforce compliance ends up breeding noncompliance.
5. **Clients feel it.** Scripts and templates can be helpful, but when overused, they feel inauthentic. A client receiving a templated "Dear Valued Client" email knows they're being processed, not served. Systems that strip away humanity damage relationships.

The False Comfort of "Control"

Why do owners fall into rigidity? Because it feels like control. After years of chaos, there's relief in knowing that "everyone is following the checklist." The owner can convince themselves that mistakes are impossible because every variable has been locked down.

But this is an illusion. Systems can enforce minimum standards, but they cannot substitute for human judgment. A paralegal who notices a missing exhibit but is afraid to deviate from the checklist won't save you from malpractice. An attorney who sees a creative legal strategy but isn't "allowed" to propose it won't win you the case. In the quest to eliminate risk, rigid systems often amplify it.

Structure vs. Straitjacket

The healthiest firms recognize the difference between **structure** and **straitjacket.**

- **Structure** says: "Here's what must happen, by when, and to what standard."

- **Straitjacket** says: "Here's exactly how every single step must look, no matter who you are."

Structure guarantees consistency in outcome. Straitjackets demand conformity in process. One empowers; the other suffocates.

For example:

- **Healthy system:** All discovery responses must be drafted within 21 days, proofread by a second set of eyes, and uploaded to the DMS before filing.
- **Rigid system:** Every attorney must use a 12-step drafting checklist in a fixed order, regardless of their working style, and must send drafts to a supervisor for approval–even if they've drafted the same pleadings flawlessly for years.

The former sets standards and deadlines while allowing flexibility in execution. The latter micromanages capable professionals into disengagement.

When Systems Become the Boss

The most dangerous sign of rigidity is when people start saying, "I can't do that because the system won't let me." Instead of the system serving the work, the system becomes the boss. Innovation stalls. Improvement dies. The firm is no longer client-focused–it's system-focused.

At its extreme, rigidity turns a law firm into a factory that grinds down people, burns through talent, and leaves the owner bewildered: *Why is everyone so unhappy? I gave them systems–shouldn't that make things easier?*

The answer is no. Systems alone don't create thriving firms. Systems plus humanity do.

CASE STUDY

ABDUL'S OVER-ENGINEERED FIRM

Abdul prided himself on being meticulous. A business litigator in Seattle, he had grown his boutique practice from a solo office above a coffee shop into a firm with six attorneys, four paralegals, and five support staff. Early in his career, chaos nearly sank him–missed deadlines, clients slipping through the cracks, staff who didn't know what was expected. So when he discovered the power of systems, he latched on hard.

When Control Became a Cage

Abdul devoured every book on Six Sigma, Lean, and process design. He built SOPs for everything: how to answer the phone, how to greet a client, how to draft a motion. Every process had a flowchart. Every role had a checklist. His office walls were lined with binders full of procedures. If it could be documented, Abdul documented it.

At first, the impact was positive. Mistakes went down, efficiency went up, and Abdul felt like he finally had control. Clients received consistent updates, invoices went out on time, and deadlines stopped slipping. "We're running like a machine," Abdul told his peers proudly.

But slowly, cracks appeared.

His attorneys began to complain about the endless checklists. A senior litigator, who had 20 years of experience drafting motions, bristled at being required to follow a 15-step outline for every pleading. "I've been winning cases longer than this firm has existed," he grumbled. "Do you really think I need to check a box for 'Confirm font size is 12-point Times New Roman'?"

Paralegals grew frustrated too. They weren't allowed to deviate from form templates, even when they spotted opportunities to streamline or improve. One remarked privately, "I feel like a robot. I could make this better, but the system won't let me."

Support staff, once enthusiastic, began treating their jobs like assembly-line work. "The book says I do it this way, so I do it this way," one receptionist shrugged when asked why intake follow-ups were slipping. She was no longer engaged–just going through the motions.

Turnover spiked. Two associates left within a year, lured away by firms that promised more autonomy. The paralegal Abdul considered his right hand resigned, citing burnout. Exit interviews all said the same thing: "I felt like I had no room to think. Everything was about the system, not the work."

Abdul was blindsided. He had worked so hard to eliminate chaos. He couldn't understand why his team wasn't grateful.

The breaking point came during a trial prep. One associate discovered a brilliant argument buried in case law but hesitated to raise it because it wasn't part of the "standard trial prep checklist." By the time it was brought up–almost as an afterthought–the window to fully develop it had closed. Abdul lost the case. Furious, he demanded to know why the associate hadn't spoken up. The answer stung: "Because every time I deviate from the system, I get chewed out. I didn't want to rock the boat."

That was the gut punch Abdul needed. His systems hadn't just prevented mistakes–they had prevented initiative. His quest for control had crushed the very creativity that wins cases.

Rebuilding Systems that Empower

With LFM coaching, Abdul began to rethink his approach. He learned the difference between **structure** *and* **straitjacket**. *Through work with his coach, he realized his systems were designed for robots, not professionals.*

So he rebuilt. The new intake system required that every call be logged into the CRM and followed up within 24 hours. But how the intake specialist handled the conversation was left to training, not a word-for-word script. Discovery checklists set timelines and deliverables but allowed attorneys to choose their drafting style. Templates became guides, not cages.

He also created a formal "innovation lane." If a staff member spotted a better way, they submitted a proposal, piloted it on a limited basis, and presented results. This encouraged improvement without undermining consistency.

The cultural shift was dramatic. Attorneys felt trusted again. Paralegals reengaged, excited to refine workflows. Support staff took ownership of client experience instead of hiding behind SOPs. Turnover slowed, morale rose, and clients noticed the difference.

Looking back, Abdul admitted: "I thought systems were about control. But real systems are about freedom–freedom from mistakes, freedom from chaos, and freedom to let people do their best work. I don't want robots. I want professionals who thrive inside structure. Once I stopped treating the system as the boss, my firm finally balanced consistency with creativity."

Final Word: Make Improvement Part of the Process

Abdul's story is a reminder that systems are not meant to replace humans. They are meant to support *humans. A system should guarantee the outcome–timely filings, accurate billing, consistent client updates–without strangling the creativity, judgment, and professional pride of the people who run it.*

When systems become straitjackets, they backfire. Talent leaves, morale plummets, and even victories slip away because no one feels empowered to think outside the checklist. But when systems strike the right balance–structure for consistency, flexibility for individuality–they create the foundation of a thriving culture. Staff feel safe, clients feel cared for, and the owner can trust that excellence will continue even when they're not in the room.

Takeaway: The art of systematizing is this: make the system the servant, not the master. Let it do the heavy lifting of consistency while leaving space for human judgment and innovation.

SYSTEMS AS THE SPINE OF PROFIT

Systems are the difference between a law firm that survives and a law firm that scales. Without them, you're trapped in chaos–chasing fires, losing money, and bleeding talent. With them, you create structure, consistency, and profit.

Think back over the ground we've covered:

- Prioritization systems stop urgency from devouring the essentials.
- Role alignment systems plug the profit leaks that happen when the wrong people do the wrong work.
- Evolution systems prevent yesterday's solutions from becoming today's bottlenecks.
- Compliance systems eliminate freelancing and force consistency across the board.
- Flexibility systems ensure your people thrive instead of suffocate.

Each solution by itself solves a piece of the puzzle. Together, they form the spine of a business that is scalable, profitable, and predictable. A firm where malpractice risk plummets, client satisfaction soars, and your staff operate like a coordinated team instead of a herd of freelancers.

And here's the best part: once systems are in place, profit isn't an accident–it's inevitable. Systems guarantee that your firm's work is delivered efficiently, ethically, and at maximum margin. They free you from the hamster wheel, protect your reputation, and multiply your money.

Because more systems don't just create more consistency. They create more freedom. They give you back your time. They give you back your life. And with that time, you finally get to focus on the highest and best use of *you*—leading, strategizing, and growing.

That's the heartbeat of Law Firm Mentor. Systems are not optional. They are the art and the heart of crushing chaos. And when you crush chaos, you don't just create peace of mind—**you create freedom and you make more money.**

With that, we close the discussion on systems. You've now seen how prioritization, role alignment, system evolution, compliance, and flexibility all interlock to crush chaos. But systems alone aren't enough. In the next chapter, we'll explore how leadership—the vision, courage, and personal growth of the owner—becomes the ultimate lever for scaling a firm.

The imperative is simple: **CRUSH CHAOS IN BUSINESS AND MAKE MORE MONEY!**

The Chaos Check-In

The problems that arise from a lack of systems are paired with the Chaos Check-In found in **Appendix A**. The check-in will help guide you in identifying where and how chaos is driving your current outcomes, with brief guidance on how to interpret your results. Before moving on, you may find it helpful to assess how unchecked chaos may be showing up in your firm. In addition, expanded, interactive versions of all our decision-support tools are available online, accessible via links and QR codes included in the Appendix.

PART V

THE RESULTS

CHAPTER 13

LESSONS FROM THE CHAOS JOURNEY
OPPORTUNITY ARISES

The journey through chaos has been long, exhausting, and at times deeply uncomfortable. But here's the payoff: every ounce of struggle you've endured–every fire you've put out, every sleepless night wondering if you'll make payroll, every moment of doubt–has given you the opportunity to grow. Chaos is not just noise. It's a signal. It's the compass that points to where your firm needs strengthening. And when you strengthen the weak point, you don't just solve a problem–you unlock opportunity.

This section is the roadmap. A summary of every major lesson in this book distilled into practical, actionable steps. Think of it as your **Crushing Chaos checklist**. It's the high-level action map that will guide you out of confusion and into clarity, out of reactivity and into intentional growth.

We'll cover six key pillars:

1. **Marketing**
2. **Sales**
3. **Finance**
4. **People**
5. **Leadership**
6. **Systems**

Each pillar comes with its problems, its opportunities, and its action items. Together, they form the architecture of a firm that is profitable, sustainable, and, most importantly, a business that serves *you* rather than the other way around.

1. Marketing: From Fear to Visibility

Marketing is where chaos often begins. Lawyers are trained to argue cases, not to promote themselves. The result? A tangle of fears: fear of being seen, fear of judgment, fear of underachieving, fear of over-achieving, fear of failure. These fears choke visibility and keep firms small.

But visibility is non-negotiable. If people can't find you, they can't hire you. And in today's market, where clients are Googling, scrolling, and comparing constantly, the firms that stay invisible get left behind.

Key Lessons

- ***Fear is the enemy of visibility.*** Lawyers hold themselves back from showing up on video, asking for reviews, or networking with confidence.
- ***Marketing is a system, not a gamble.*** Firms that thrive don't rely on hope–they rely on referrals, Google Business reviews, SEO, and Pay-Per-Click (PPC) digital marketing strategies, and consistent content.
- ***Marketing must evolve.*** The tools of yesterday (yellow pages, word of mouth) are not enough in today's digital-first world.

Action Items

- ***Build a referral system*** that doesn't leave leads to chance. Who are your top 10 referral sources? What's your process to engage them monthly?

- ***Ask for reviews*** systematically. Make it part of your closing file procedure. A case isn't complete until the review request is sent.
- ***Leverage AI tools*** for marketing content creation, but don't abdicate your voice. AI can draft, but you must refine.
- ***Invest in SEO/PPC*** with intention. Measure ROI. Don't just throw money at ads–track calls, conversions, and signed retainers.
- ***Commit to video marketing.*** Whether short-form reels or long-form YouTube, clients want to see and trust you before they ever meet you.

Opportunity: Marketing done right doesn't just bring leads. It brings the right leads–the clients who already trust you before they ever walk in the door.

2. Sales: From Auditioning to Authority

Chaos doesn't stop once the phone rings. Sales chaos shows up when attorneys "audition" for clients, dumping credentials and free advice in a desperate attempt to impress. It shows up when consultations are inconsistent, follow-up is spotty, and there's no structured process to close with integrity.

Key Lessons

- ***You are not auditioning.*** The client is. They need to prove they're the right fit for you, not the other way around.
- ***Consults need structure.*** Without a sales script or framework, lawyers ramble, underprice, or give away too much.
- ***Follow-up is non-negotiable.*** The majority of clients don't sign at the first consult. Systems must nurture them after the meeting.
- ***Integrity closes.*** The best sales aren't pushy. They're confident, clear, and based on value, not desperation.

Action Items

- ***Create a consultation script*** that frames the meeting: here's how we'll talk, here's what you'll learn, here's what happens if you want to move forward.
- ***Price consistently.*** No discounts based on mood or pressure. Your value is fixed; your confidence must be too.
- ***Build a follow-up system*** (emails, calls, texts) to stay in touch with prospects for at least 30 days post-consult.
- ***Train your team:*** everyone in the sales process must understand how to qualify, nurture, and close prospects.
- ***Measure sales performance.*** Track conversion rates: calls to consults, consults to signed retainers.

Opportunity: Sales done right transforms consults into clients–not by begging, but by standing in your authority.

3. Finance: From Mystery to Mastery

Financial chaos is subtle but deadly. Many law firm owners have no idea how money moves in and out of their business. They mistake revenue for profit, overspend on "shiny objects," and bury their heads in the sand when debt piles up. Without financial clarity, even growing firms collapse.

Key Lessons

- ***Clarity is power.*** You must know your numbers: revenue, expenses, cash flow, profit margin. One number clarity beats spreadsheet overwhelm.
- ***Forecasting is protection.*** Planning for payroll, taxes, and investment prevents panic.
- ***Debt can be a tool, but only with discipline.*** Undisciplined borrowing is chaos disguised as growth.
- ***Every dollar has a job.*** Budgeting isn't restriction–it's alignment.

Action Items

- ***Create a One-Number dashboard.*** At a glance, you should know: did we make money this month or lose it?
- ***Build a rolling forecast.*** Look 90 days ahead at payroll, rent, taxes, and expected revenue.
- ***Audit expenses quarterly.*** Cancel subscriptions and tools no one uses. Reallocate dollars to ROI-producing activities.
- ***Plan for taxes.*** Treat the IRS as a non-negotiable creditor. Set aside money automatically every month.
- ***Align compensation systems with profitability***, not just revenue. Incentives should grow the pie, not cut deeper slices.

Opportunity: Financial mastery isn't about making more—it's about keeping more. Profit creates stability, freedom, and the ability to invest in real growth.

4. People: From Headaches to High Performance

If money is the engine, people are the drivers. But unmanaged people create chaos. Owners hire the wrong fit, fail to optimize performance, struggle with retention, and abdicate responsibility when they promote managers. Culture collapses without vision.

Key Lessons

- ***Hiring is about fit, not just skill.*** A toxic superstar will ruin you faster than an average performer who lives your values.
- ***Optimizing performance requires systems.*** KPIs, scorecards, coaching—otherwise, you're stuck micromanaging.
- ***Retention is both in and out of your control.*** You can't stop someone from chasing prestige, but you can control whether you create a place worth staying.
- ***Managers need management.*** Abdication is not delegation. You must lead your leaders.

- ***Culture is the glue.*** Vision, values, and language must cascade from the owner down.

Action Items

- ***Build a hiring funnel*** that screens for values as well as skills. Interview for alignment, not just credentials.
- ***Use weekly scorecards*** and KPIs to measure performance objectively.
- ***Create a retention system*** with career pathing, feedback loops, and recognition rituals.
- ***Train managers.*** Hold them accountable for leading people, not just doing tasks.
- ***Broadcast your vision.*** Repeat it until your staff can recite it. A silent vision is no vision.

Opportunity: With the right people, aligned and accountable, your firm doesn't just grow. It thrives–and you stop being the only one who cares.

5. Leadership: From Lone Wolf to Leveraged CEO

Leadership is the ultimate chaos killer. Without it, even the best systems collapse. Leadership chaos shows up as owners carrying everything themselves, confusing popularity with authority, leading reactively, inspiring without execution, or failing to grow personally.

Key Lessons

- ***You can't carry it all.*** Lone wolf leaders burn out and stall growth.
- ***Authority beats popularity.*** Being liked isn't leadership–setting standards is.
- ***Emotional maturity matters.*** Stop blaming employees for not caring as much as you. They won't–and they shouldn't.

- ***Vision requires execution.*** Inspiration without systems is betrayal.
- ***Growth is personal.*** Your firm can't outgrow you. If you stagnate, your business will too.

Action Items

- ***Step back from the courtroom.*** Free your calendar to lead from the helicopter view.
- ***Embrace authority:*** difficult conversations, accountability, high standards.
- ***Stop projecting your needs*** onto staff. They aren't there to fill emotional voids—they're there to do their jobs.
- ***Operationalize vision:*** set benchmarks, track progress, reinforce constantly.
- ***Invest in yourself.*** Coaching, masterminds, therapy—whatever it takes. Remember: *Never Stop Growing.*

Opportunity: Leadership multiplies. When you grow, your people grow, your firm grows, and your impact multiplies.

6. Systems: From Fragility to Freedom

Systems are the art and heart of crushing chaos. Without them, firms devolve into firefighting. With them, consistency and predictability reign. But systems can fail when they prioritize urgency over importance, allow profit leaks, remain fragile, aren't followed, or become rigid.

Key Lessons

- ***Prioritize essentials***. Urgency is seductive, but essentials prevent malpractice.
- ***Role alignment preserves profit.*** The wrong person doing the wrong work bleeds money.

- ***Systems evolve.*** What works at five staff breaks at fifteen.
- ***Compliance is culture.*** A system ignored is no system at all.
- ***Flexibility is key.*** Systems must serve humans, not suffocate them.

Action Items

- ***Build a triage system*** to protect deadlines, filings, and essentials.
- ***Audit tasks:*** is each role operating at its highest and best use? If not, realign.
- ***Schedule system reviews*** quarterly. Assume every system has an expiration date.
- ***Enforce compliance.*** Audit, coach, and hold staff accountable for following systems.
- ***Allow flexibility within structure:*** define the "what" and "when," but give space for the "how."

Opportunity: Systems create freedom. They give you consistency, profit, and the most valuable asset of all–time.

THE BIG LESSON

Each pillar is essential on its own. But the real power comes when they work together: marketing fills your pipeline, sales converts leads with integrity, finance ensures profit, people carry the load, leadership drives the vision, and systems make it all repeatable.

This is the journey of chaos. Each problem you faced was an invitation–not to suffer, but to grow. Every crack in your firm was a signal pointing to the next opportunity. And when you answer that call, you don't just crush chaos. You build the law firm–and the life–you've always wanted.

Because at the end of the day, this isn't just about running a firm. It's about reclaiming your time, multiplying your money, and proving to yourself that you can lead a business as brilliantly as you practice law.

The opportunity is here. The tools are in your hands. Now, the work is to act.

Chaos Conundrum: Exhausting Yet Necessary

By now you may be feeling two things at once: empowered and exhausted. Empowered because you see the road map—the problems, the solutions, the case studies that prove it can be done. Exhausted because every solution seems to require work, energy, and commitment. And you'd be right.

The conundrum of chaos is that it never truly disappears. You can crush it in one area, only to see it resurface somewhere else. You can solve the intake problem, then face a sales problem. You can fix sales, then face a finance problem. You can tighten finance, then discover your leadership is the bottleneck. The process feels relentless, like a treadmill that never stops.

The Myth of Arrival

Too many lawyers chase the fantasy of "arrival"—the day when everything runs perfectly, the team hums like a machine, the money flows without stress, and the owner finally gets to coast. But let me tell you the truth: there is no finish line. Chaos conundrum means that just when you solve one problem, another emerges.

Why? Because growth creates complexity. Every new client, every new employee, every new practice area introduces moving parts. More moving parts means more friction. More friction means more chaos. The very success you crave generates the challenges you fear.

So if you're waiting for the day when chaos disappears, you'll wait forever. Instead, the goal is to build the strength, resilience, and perspective to handle chaos differently. You don't eliminate it—you *master* it.

The Exhaustion Factor

Let's be honest: crushing chaos is exhausting. It requires confronting your fears, your habits, and your blind spots. It requires retraining staff, rewriting systems, rethinking leadership. It requires starting over more times than you care to count.

- You'll spend hours building a system, only to watch it break when you hire three more people.
- You'll invest in training a rockstar associate, only to watch them leave for "more prestige."
- You'll pour energy into culture, only to watch a single toxic hire undo months of progress.

Each time, you'll feel the sting of exhaustion. You'll wonder if it's worth it. You'll fantasize about shrinking back to a smaller, simpler practice where you control everything and no one disappoints you. That impulse is normal.

But shrinking back is sabotage.

Why the Exhaustion is Necessary

Here's the paradox: the exhaustion is not a sign you're failing–it's a sign you're growing. Muscles don't build without stress. Firms don't evolve without friction. Leaders don't transform without discomfort.

The exhaustion forces you to grow in ways you never intended:

- It pushes you to confront your own avoidance habits.
- It forces you to admit when you are the bottleneck.
- It demands you develop new skills–delegation, conflict resolution, financial discipline–that law school never taught you.
- It compels you to separate identity from profession: to stop being just a lawyer and start being a leader.

Without the exhaustion, you'd never evolve. You'd stay stuck in the cycle of doing everything yourself, rationalizing mediocrity, and resenting your own business. Chaos stretches you precisely because it has to.

The Sabotage Trap

Every law firm owner must face this truth: your business cannot sustainably outgrow you. For a time, it might. You might hire brilliant people, stack revenue, and ride a wave of growth. But if *you* don't grow in tandem, you will subconsciously sabotage your own firm.

- You'll fire strong leaders because they intimidate you.
- You'll avoid strategic risks because your fear of uncertainty outweighs your hunger for growth.
- You'll create bottlenecks by hoarding decisions, because being "needed" feels safer than being a CEO.
- You'll retreat into lawyering instead of leading, because litigation feels familiar while leadership feels terrifying.

It won't be conscious. You'll justify it with clever stories: "I don't trust anyone else to handle this." "We just need to slow down for a while." "It's better to be small and profitable than big and stressed." But beneath the surface, you're shrinking your firm to match your comfort zone.

That's why personal growth is non-negotiable. If you don't evolve, your business will regress to the level of your fears.

Trial, Error, and Iteration

Crushing chaos is not about getting it right the first time. It's about committing to iteration. You'll try a new marketing campaign and it will flop. You'll roll out a sales script that feels clunky. You'll launch a financial dashboard that confuses your staff. None of it will be perfect out of the gate.

But iteration is where the gold is. Each failed attempt teaches you what doesn't work. Each small win shows you what does. Over time, your systems sharpen, your people align, and your leadership matures.

The mistake most firm owners make is mistaking iteration for failure. They abandon the experiment too soon. They think: *If it didn't work perfectly the first time, it must not work at all.* That mindset guarantees stagnation. The firms that win are the ones that commit to constant iteration, trusting that forward motion—even messy forward motion—beats standing still.

Personal Growth as the Real Work

If there's one lesson I want to imprint, it's this: your firm's growth is capped by your personal growth.

Lawyers love skills. We chase CLEs, certifications, new software platforms, and marketing hacks. We think if we just learn one more tactic, everything will click. But the growth that truly matters isn't tactical. It's personal.

- **Emotional regulation.** Can you stay calm when staff frustrate you? Or do you explode?
- **Resilience.** Do you keep going after failure? Or do you retreat?
- **Vision.** Can you articulate where you're going, even when the outcome isn't guaranteed?
- **Courage.** Do you make the hard calls—firing the toxic associate, raising your rates, stepping out of the courtroom—even when it scares you?

That's the real work. The hardest systems to build are not in your case management software—they're in your own mind.

The Necessary Choice

So here is the chaos conundrum: crushing chaos is exhausting, but it's also necessary. The exhaustion is not evidence that you're failing. It's evidence that you're building capacity. Every time you choose to confront chaos instead of retreating, you expand your ability to lead.

And every expansion creates opportunity: more revenue, more freedom, more impact.

The choice is yours. You can shrink to fit your comfort zone. Or you can stretch to fit your potential.

One path leads to a small, stagnant practice where chaos rules you. The other leads to a scalable, thriving business where you rule chaos.

The exhaustion will tempt you to quit. But if you keep going, you'll discover what every great leader already knows: chaos isn't the enemy. It's the crucible.

It's the fire that burns away your excuses. It's the storm that tests your systems. It's the teacher that reveals who you must become.

And that's why the work never ends. Because as long as you're growing, chaos will keep presenting new challenges. Not to punish you, but to shape you.

So when the journey feels heavy, when the exhaustion feels unbearable, remember this: it's not supposed to be easy. It's supposed to grow you.

And your only job is to keep going.

Never Stop Growing.

Eternal Growth: Crushing Chaos for Endless Possibilities

We've traveled far together. You've seen the chaos of marketing fears and sales mistakes. You've confronted financial blind spots and people problems. You've wrestled with leadership bottlenecks and the rigidity of systems. You've studied case after case of law firm owners just like you who faced their chaos, crushed it, and came out stronger.

And now we stand at the final step: the recognition that this journey never really ends.

Chaos as a Mirror

Chaos is not just a business problem. It's a mirror. Every breakdown in your firm reflects a growth opportunity in you.

- If marketing feels terrifying, it's showing you where fear of judgment or rejection is still alive.
- If sales feels awkward, it's showing you where your confidence in your value is shaky.
- If finance feels murky, it's showing you where avoidance or denial holds sway.
- If people feel like a nightmare, it's showing you where your boundaries, communication, or leadership need strengthening.
- If systems feel suffocating, it's showing you where control or perfectionism is winning over trust.

Chaos doesn't lie. It reveals. Every crack in your firm is an arrow pointing to the next step in your personal evolution.

And that's why chaos is eternal. No matter how many systems you build, how many staff you hire, or how much money you make, new challenges will always arise. The law changes. The market shifts. People come and go. Technology evolves. The ground beneath you is never still.

But here's the gift: every wave of chaos is also a wave of possibility. If you choose to face it, you become more.

Business as a Spiritual Path

That might sound lofty, but it's true: building a law firm is one of the greatest spiritual practices you will ever undertake. Not because of the cases you win, but because of the person you must become to lead it.

Your business asks you to confront fear, ego, scarcity, and control. It demands you learn patience, courage, compassion, and resilience. It forces you to see where you hide, where you resist, where you sabotage. And it rewards you when you step into integrity, vision, and growth.

Every invoice, every hire, every client conversation is an invitation to grow–not just as an attorney, but as a human.

This is why so many lawyers feel conflicted. They want the business to succeed but don't want to confront what success requires of them. They crave the freedom of leadership but cling to the comfort of lawyering. They dream of wealth but resist the responsibility of stewardship.

The truth is simple: your business will only grow to the extent that you do. If you stop growing, your firm will stall—or worse, regress.

The Gift of Systems and Structure

Some resist this idea, thinking personal growth is intangible. But look back at the practical work we've covered: building referral pipelines, designing sales scripts, forecasting cash flow, creating KPIs, enforcing compliance. Those are all systems. And systems are not sterile. They are spiritual tools in disguise.

Why? Because they force you to practice discipline, consistency, humility, and trust. They require you to let go of ego ("I'm the only one who can do this") and embrace empowerment ("The system lets others succeed without me").

Every spreadsheet, every checklist, every audit is a small act of surrender. You stop clutching everything in your own hands and trust the structure. That trust frees you—and it frees your team.

Systems don't just create order. They create space. They give you back time. And with that time, you can choose what kind of leader, parent, partner, or person you want to be.

Money, Time, and Meaning

In the end, that's what this is really about: money, time, and meaning.

- **Money** because profit is the scoreboard of sustainability. Without it, your firm dies, no matter how noble your intentions. With it, you can fund growth, reward staff, invest in technology, and build wealth for your family.
- **Time** because freedom is the true prize. Systems and people create space for you to step out of the weeds and into the life

you've always wanted: more vacations, more dinners with family, more mornings where you wake up without dread.
- **Meaning** because impact is why you started this in the first place. You didn't become a lawyer just to shuffle paper. You wanted to fight for people, change lives, and build a legacy. Crushing chaos lets you focus on what matters most: your purpose.

The Endless Possibility

What does eternal growth look like? It looks like never being satisfied with "good enough." It looks like finding joy in iteration. It looks like knowing that every time you hit a ceiling, you're about to meet a new version of yourself.

For some, it means scaling to a $10 million firm. For others, it means running a $2 million practice with freedom and peace. For still others, it means selling the firm one day and building something new. And for many of us, it means mentoring the next generation.

There is no one definition of success. The only constant is that you will continue to evolve.

Eternal growth means understanding that chaos is not your enemy—it's your ally. Every frustration is feedback. Every breakdown is an opportunity. Every ounce of stress is an invitation to become the person your future requires.

Crushing Chaos as Identity

By now, you should see that "Crushing Chaos" is more than a framework. It's an identity. It's the declaration that you will not be ruled by disorder, fear, or mediocrity. It's the choice to rise every time chaos tries to pull you down.

It's also a promise: to yourself, your team, your clients, and your legacy. The promise that you will do the hard work, that you will keep going, that you will refuse to shrink.

Because this is not just about building a firm. It's about building *you*.

The Final Bow

As you close this book, pause for a moment. Look at your firm. Look at your life. Notice where chaos still rules. Notice where systems are weak, where leadership is missing, where people are struggling, where money is leaking. Don't look with shame—look with curiosity.

Each weak point is not a failure. It's an invitation. An invitation to grow, to evolve, to lead.

The path of Crushing Chaos is not linear. It's cyclical. You'll revisit these lessons again and again, each time at a higher level. You'll build marketing systems, then revisit them as the market shifts. You'll train leaders, then retrain them as the team expands. You'll set visions, then reset them as your own desires change.

And that's the beauty of it. There is no end. Only evolution.

So embrace the conundrum. Embrace the exhaustion. Embrace the eternal growth.

Because in the end, the reward is not just more clients, more money, or more stability. The reward is freedom. The reward is the life you were meant to live.

Crushing chaos isn't about the business. It's about you. It's about meeting your own limits, breaking through them, and discovering that on the other side of chaos lies possibility.

And the possibilities are endless.

Crush Chaos in Business. Make More Money. And Never Stop Growing.

EPILOGUE

CRUSHING CHAOS BEYOND THE LAW

If you've made it to the end of this book, two things are likely true.

First, you're a law firm owner who's done the hard work of confronting the chaos in your business—and now, you have the tools to transform it. You've looked at your marketing with fresh eyes. You've examined your sales strategy, your finances, your systems, your team—and you've realized where things need to shift if you want to create sustainable, profitable growth.

Second, you've started to recognize that *Crushing Chaos* isn't just about business. It's about your life. It's about who you are when the laptop closes, when the court is silent, when the team is gone and it's just you, asking yourself the big question:

IS THIS THE LIFE I WANT?

For many of us, the answer is complicated. We build these incredible businesses—sometimes out of necessity, sometimes out of ego, sometimes out of ambition—and then wake up one day and realize the very thing we built to give us freedom has become a cage.

That realization was the spark for something much bigger than this book. It was the beginning of *Allison Speaks, LLC,* my platform for delivering keynotes and transformational talks to high-achieving entrepreneurs and executives who are burned out, boxed in, and ready for more—not just in business, but in life.

Through Allison Speaks, I share the same powerful origin story you read at the beginning of this book—what I call my **guardrail moment**—along with the system I developed to reclaim my time, energy, and joy: the **C.H.A.O.S. Formula™**.

- **Commitment:** To the vision, not the noise.
- **Habits:** That reinforce the identity you actually want.
- **Automation:** So you stop doing yourself what a system can do for you.
- **Ownership:** Of your decisions, your results, your leadership.
- **Scale:** Not just of income, but of impact.

This framework has become the blueprint for change for so many leaders—not just law firm owners, but powerhouse women, exhausted CEOs, and creatives who've built success but lost themselves along the way.

The truth is, law firm owners *are* high achievers. We carry the same stress, ambition, and intensity as any C-suite executive. That's why this book matters. And that's also why the conversation must continue beyond these pages.

Because the most dangerous kind of chaos is the kind you've learned to normalize.

So if something stirred in you as you read this—if some part of you knows you're ready to lead not just your firm, but your life, in a new way—then I invite you to join me at **https://AllisonSpeaks.com**. Whether you bring me into your organization to ignite your team, attend a live event, or just explore the deeper personal work that supports long-term business success, know this:

Crushing chaos isn't a one-time act. It's a way of living.

And you, my friend, are just getting started.

– **Allison C. Williams**

Founder, Law Firm Mentor

Creator of the C.H.A.O.S. Formula™

Global Speaker | Business Strategist | Chaos Crusher

APPENDIX

ABOUT THE DIAGNOSTIC TOOLS IN THIS BOOK

Crushing Chaos is built on a simple premise: most law firm leadership problems are not caused by a lack of effort, intelligence, or ambition. They are caused by misidentified constraints.

The diagnostic tools included in the Appendix are designed to help you identify which constraints are most likely operating in five core areas in your firm: marketing, sales, finance, people, and systems. Each tool corresponds to a substantive chapter in the book and is intended to be used privately, honestly, and without any pressure to have a "correct" response.

At Law Firm Mentor, we believe that effective strategies begins with accurate diagnosis. Our diagnostic tools are included not to prescribe solutions, but to clarify conditions so you can get aligned with the strategies that will help you move forward and overcome chaos in your firm!

THE MARKETING FEAR INDEX

Most law firm owners don't fail at marketing because they lack tactics. They fail because one fear—often unconscious—keeps hijacking their decisions.

The Marketing Fear Index™ helps you identify the *specific fear* running your marketing so you can stop guessing and start addressing the real issue.

How to Use This Index

Checkmark every statement that feels true—even if you don't like that it's true.

At the end, tally your checks. The section with the most checks is your **Primary Marketing Fear.**

Fear #1: Fear of Being Seen

- ☐ I hesitate to put myself front and center in marketing materials.
- ☐ Increased visibility feels risky because attention invites scrutiny.
- ☐ I'm more comfortable doing the work than talking about the work.
- ☐ I delay marketing because I don't want attention from strangers.
- ☐ I keep telling myself I'll market "more later," once things calm down.

Fear #2: Fear of Judgment

- ☐ I worry how colleagues, judges, or other lawyers will perceive my marketing.
- ☐ I worry marketing makes me look desperate, salesy, or unethical.
- ☐ I compare myself to other firms and feel like I don't measure up.

☐ I avoid posting because I'm afraid of saying the wrong thing.
☐ I revise marketing drafts repeatedly–but rarely publish them.

Fear #3: Fear of Underachieving

☐ If I try marketing seriously and it doesn't work, it will confirm my doubts.
☐ I hesitate to commit fully because failure would feel personal.
☐ I start marketing initiatives but quietly let them fade out.
☐ I keep researching because I don't feel "ready" yet.
☐ I avoid tracking results because I'm afraid of what I'll see.

Fear #4: Fear of Overachieving

☐ I worry successful marketing will bring in more clients than we can handle.
☐ Growth would strain my team or expose weak systems.
☐ I hold back on marketing because the firm already feels stretched.
☐ I fear scaling will cost me control or quality.
☐ Staying where we are feels safer than pushing growth.

Fear #5: Fear of Failure / Ethical Exposure

☐ I worry marketing will attract the wrong clients.
☐ I fear visibility increases the risk of complaints or grievances.
☐ I worry simplifying my message could misrepresent my expertise.
☐ I'm overly cautious about what I can say publicly.
☐ I avoid marketing because the risk feels disproportionate to the reward.

Scoring

Count how many statements you circled in each fear category.

The category with the **highest number** is your **Primary Marketing Fear.**

If two are close, you may have a **compound fear**, which is common.

Your Result (Brief Interpretation)

- **Fear of Being Seen:** Visibility feels unsafe; you default to staying behind the scenes.
- **Fear of Judgment:** You over-index on perception and self-edit into silence.
- **Fear of Underachieving:** You avoid committing fully because failure would sting.
- **Fear of Overachieving:** You fear success will overwhelm capacity and expose cracks.
- **Fear of Failure/Ethical Exposure:** Risk awareness has drifted into paralysis.

Continue the Conversation

If you want help translating your primary fear into a visibility strategy that fits your firm, continue here:

https://crushingchaosinteract.lawfirmmentor.net/marketing-fear-index/

THE CONSULTATION CONVERSION SCORECARD

Most law firm owners believe their consultations are "fine."

Very few have ever measured them.

This scorecard is designed to help you assess—honestly—whether your consultation process positions you as an authority, or quietly trains prospects to shop you on price.

How to Use This Scorecard

For each statement below, check Yes, No, or Unsure based on what actually happens in your consultations–not what you intend to happen.

Be candid.

This scorecard only works if you tell yourself the truth.

Section 1: Positioning & Authority

☐ Yes ☐ No ☐ Unsure
I clearly set expectations for the consultation before it begins.

☐ Yes ☐ No ☐ Unsure
Prospects understand why this consultation exists and what decisions will be made during it.

☐ Yes ☐ No ☐ Unsure
I lead the consultation rather than reacting to the prospect's agenda.

☐ Yes ☐ No ☐ Unsure
I am comfortable interrupting or redirecting when a prospect goes off track.

Section 2: Structure & Control

☐ Yes ☐ No ☐ Unsure
My consultations follow a consistent structure regardless of the client.

☐ Yes ☐ No ☐ Unsure
I control the pacing of the conversation.

☐ Yes ☐ No ☐ Unsure
I do not feel pressure to answer every question immediately.

☐ Yes ☐ No ☐ Unsure
I am intentional about what I do *not* explain during the consultation.

Section 3: Value Communication

☐ Yes ☐ No ☐ Unsure
I clearly articulate the value of my services without over-explaining.

☐ Yes ☐ No ☐ Unsure
I do not discount my fees to relieve discomfort.

☐ Yes ☐ No ☐ Unsure
Prospects understand the cost before the end of the consultation.

☐ Yes ☐ No ☐ Unsure
I am comfortable letting a prospect decide without chasing them.

Section 4: Closing & Follow-Up

☐ Yes ☐ No ☐ Unsure
Every consultation ends with a clear next step.

☐ Yes ☐ No ☐ Unsure
I do not rely on "let me think about it" as an acceptable outcome.

☐ Yes ☐ No ☐ Unsure
My follow-up process is structured and consistent.

☐ Yes ☐ No ☐ Unsure
I track consultation-to-client conversion rates.

Scoring

Count how many **Yes** answers you selected.

- ☐ **0–6 Yes answers → Revenue Leaker**
- ☐ **7–12 Yes answers → Inconsistent Closer**
- ☐ **13–16 Yes answers → Authority-Based Seller**

Unsure counts as No.

Your Result ______________

Revenue Leaker

- Your consultations feel busy—but they are doing too much work for too little return.

- You are likely explaining extensively, answering questions generously, and hoping goodwill converts into commitment.
- The cost is lost time, emotional exhaustion, and inconsistent revenue.
- This is not a confidence issue.
- It is a structure issue.

Inconsistent Closer

- You close sometimes—often when the prospect is already motivated.
- Your consultations work when conditions are ideal, but break down when clients are uncertain, resistant, or price-sensitive.
- The cost is revenue unpredictability and emotional whiplash.
- The issue is not effort.
- It is repeatability.

Authority-Based Seller

- Your consultations position you as a professional, not a vendor.
- You lead the conversation, set boundaries, and allow clients to choose without pressure.
- The opportunity now is scaling this approach across your firm—without relying on you personally.

Continue the Conversation

If your consultations are not converting consistently, the problem is not effort or ethics—it is structure.

To explore what this score means for your firm, and where revenue may be leaking, continue here:

https://crushingchaosinteract.lawfirmmentor.net/consultation-conversion-scorecard/

THE FINANCIAL CLARITY TEST

Many law firm owners believe they understand their firm's finances.

Very few actually do.

This test is designed to help you determine whether you are operating your firm from **financial clarity** or **financial assumption**—and whether your decisions are grounded in mastery or anxiety.

How to Use This Test

For each statement below, check **Yes, No,** or **Unsure** based on what you *actually know* to be true—not what you hope is true or assume to be true.

Be honest.

Financial clarity begins with accuracy.

Section 1: Profit vs. Revenue

☐ Yes ☐ No ☐ Unsure
I can clearly explain the difference between firm revenue and firm profit.

☐ Yes ☐ No ☐ Unsure
I know my firm's true profit margin.

☐ Yes ☐ No ☐ Unsure
I do not rely on my bank balance to assess financial health.

☐ Yes ☐ No ☐ Unsure
I understand how owner compensation affects reported profit.

Section 2: Financial Visibility

☐ Yes ☐ No ☐ Unsure
I regularly review financial reports that I understand.

☐ Yes ☐ No ☐ Unsure
I can quickly identify my firm's largest expense categories.

☐ Yes ☐ No ☐ Unsure

I know what it costs to run the firm each month.

☐ Yes ☐ No ☐ Unsure

I can explain recent financial changes without relying on others.

Section 3: Capacity & Cost Awareness

☐ Yes ☐ No ☐ Unsure

I understand how much revenue each attorney or role is expected to generate.

☐ Yes ☐ No ☐ Unsure

I know when hiring will reduce profit before it increases it.

☐ Yes ☐ No ☐ Unsure

I understand how utilization and capacity affect profitability.

☐ Yes ☐ No ☐ Unsure

I can estimate the financial impact of adding or losing a team member.

Section 4: Decision-Making & Control

☐ Yes ☐ No ☐ Unsure

I make financial decisions based on data rather than fear.

☐ Yes ☐ No ☐ Unsure

I do not delay decisions because I am unsure of the numbers.

☐ Yes ☐ No ☐ Unsure

I feel confident discussing my firm's finances with advisors.

☐ Yes ☐ No ☐ Unsure

I trust my financial understanding enough to plan ahead.

Scoring

Count how many **Yes** answers you selected.

- ☐ **0–6 Yes answers → Financially Reactive**
- ☐ **7–12 Yes answers → Financially Aware**
- ☐ **13–16 Yes answers → Financially Commanding**

Unsure counts as No.

Your Result _______________

Financially Reactive

- You are running your firm based on cash flow, instinct, and urgency.
- Money is coming in, but clarity is missing—and that creates stress, hesitation, and overwork.
- This is not a discipline issue.
- It is a visibility issue.

Financially Aware

- You understand parts of your financial picture, but not all of it.
- You know enough to sense when something is off, but not enough to act with confidence and speed.
- The issue is not intelligence.
- It is integration.

Financially Commanding

- You understand how money actually moves through your firm.
- You can interpret the numbers, anticipate the impact of decisions, and plan growth intentionally rather than reactively.
- The opportunity now is scaling this clarity as the firm grows.

Continue the Conversation

If money still creates stress despite strong revenue, the problem is rarely effort—it is clarity.

To explore what this result means for your firm, and how to move from financial management to financial mastery, continue here:

https://crushingchaosinteract.lawfirmmentor.net/profit-and-capacity-snapshot/

THE ROLE CLARITY & OWNERSHIP CHECKLIST

Most law firm owners believe they have a "people problem."

In reality, most have a **role clarity problem.**

This check is designed to help you identify where responsibility, authority, and expectations are misaligned inside your firm—and how that misalignment may be quietly draining your time, energy, and leadership capacity.

How to Use This Checklist

For each statement below, select **Yes, No,** or **Unsure** based on what is actually happening in your firm—not what you wish were happening.

Be honest.

Clarity—not optimism—creates relief.

Section 1: Role Definition

☐ Yes ☐ No ☐ Unsure
Every team member has a clearly defined role with documented responsibilities.

☐ Yes ☐ No ☐ Unsure
People understand what they are responsible for—not just what they help with.

☐ Yes ☐ No ☐ Unsure
Roles are defined by outcomes, not personalities.

☐ Yes ☐ No ☐ Unsure
When something goes wrong, it is clear who owns the fix.

Section 2: Authority & Decision-Making

☐ Yes ☐ No ☐ Unsure
Team members know which decisions they can make without approval.

☐ Yes ☐ No ☐ Unsure
I am not routinely pulled into decisions that should be handled by others.

☐ Yes ☐ No ☐ Unsure
Authority is aligned with responsibility.

☐ Yes ☐ No ☐ Unsure
People do not defer decisions upward simply to avoid accountability.

Section 3: Accountability & Feedback

☐ Yes ☐ No ☐ Unsure
Expectations are communicated clearly and consistently.

☐ Yes ☐ No ☐ Unsure
Performance issues are addressed early—not after frustration builds.

☐ Yes ☐ No ☐ Unsure
I do not carry emotional or operational weight that belongs to others.

☐ Yes ☐ No ☐ Unsure
Accountability conversations feel structured rather than personal.

Section 4: Owner Load & Overfunctioning

☐ Yes ☐ No ☐ Unsure
I am not the default problem-solver for the firm.

☐ Yes ☐ No ☐ Unsure
My role is primarily leadership, not gap-filling.

☐ Yes ☐ No ☐ Unsure
When someone struggles, the solution does not automatically become "me."

☐ Yes ☐ No ☐ Unsure
The firm can operate smoothly without my constant intervention.

Scoring

Count how many **Yes** answers you selected.

- ☐ **0–6 Yes answers → Overloaded Owner**
- ☐ **7–12 Yes answers → Misaligned Team**
- ☐ **13–16 Yes answers → Role-Driven Firm**

Unsure counts as No.

Your Result ______________

Overloaded Owner

- You are carrying more than your role requires.
- When roles lack clarity, leadership turns into compensation–and compensation turns into exhaustion.
- This is not a work ethic issue.
- It is a design issue.

Misaligned Team

- Your team is capable, but the structure supporting them is inconsistent.
- Responsibility, authority, and expectations do not always line up, creating friction that looks like "people problems."
- The issue is not talent.
- It is alignment.

Role-Driven Firm

- Your firm operates through defined roles rather than personalities.
- Authority is clear, accountability is shared, and leadership is focused where it belongs.
- The opportunity now is reinforcing this structure as the firm grows.

Continue the Conversation

If people issues are consuming more of your time than they should, the problem is rarely effort or attitude–it is role clarity.

To explore what this result means for your firm, and how to reduce owner load without losing control, continue here:

https://crushingchaosinteract.lawfirmmentor.net/people-load-map/

THE CHAOS CHECK-IN

Most law firm owners believe chaos is simply part of the job.

It isn't.

Chaos persists when it goes **unchecked**—when decisions, processes, and responsibilities live in people's heads rather than in designed systems.

This Chaos Check-In™ is designed to help you identify whether chaos in your firm is being contained, tolerated, or unknowingly reinforced.

How to Use This Check-In

For each statement below, select **Yes, No,** or **Unsure** based on how your firm *actually operates*—not how it is supposed to operate.

Be honest.

Systems only work when reality is acknowledged.

Section 1: Decision Ownership

☐ Yes ☐ No ☐ Unsure
I know exactly who is responsible for most operational decisions in my firm.

☐ Yes ☐ No ☐ Unsure
Decisions do not stall when I am unavailable.

☐ Yes ☐ No ☐ Unsure
Team members know what they are authorized to decide independently.

☐ Yes ☐ No ☐ Unsure
Important decisions are not routinely escalated to me unnecessarily.

Section 2: Process Consistency

☐ Yes ☐ No ☐ Unsure
Core processes are performed the same way regardless of who is involved.

☐ Yes ☐ No ☐ Unsure
Work does not break down when a specific person is absent.

☐ Yes ☐ No ☐ Unsure
Processes are documented clearly enough to be followed.

☐ Yes ☐ No ☐ Unsure
New team members can execute without constant clarification.

Section 3: Chaos Triggers

☐ Yes ☐ No ☐ Unsure
I can identify the most common sources of recurring chaos in the firm.

☐ Yes ☐ No ☐ Unsure
The same problems do not resurface repeatedly without resolution.

☐ Yes ☐ No ☐ Unsure
Firefighting is the exception, not the norm.

☐ Yes ☐ No ☐ Unsure
Urgency is driven by true priority, not confusion.

Section 4: Owner Dependence

☐ Yes ☐ No ☐ Unsure
The firm can operate effectively without my constant involvement.

☐ Yes ☐ No ☐ Unsure
I am not the default solution to operational breakdowns.

☐ Yes ☐ No ☐ Unsure
My time is spent on leadership, not containment.

☐ Yes ☐ No ☐ Unsure
I trust the systems in place more than individual memory.

Scoring

Count how many **Yes** answers you selected.

- ☐ **0–5 Yes answers → Chaos-Driven Firm**
- ☐ **6–10 Yes answers → Person-Dependent Firm**
- ☐ **11–14 Yes answers → Process-Aware Firm**
- ☐ **15–16 Yes answers → System-Driven Firm**

Unsure counts as No.

Your Result ______________

Chaos-Driven Firm

- Chaos is unmanaged and reactive.
- Your firm relies on urgency, memory, and heroic effort to function.
- This is exhausting—and unsustainable.

Person-Dependent Firm

- Some structure exists, but it lives in people rather than systems.
- When key individuals are unavailable, chaos resurfaces.
- Growth will increase stress unless this changes.

Process-Aware Firm

- You understand the need for systems and have begun building them.
- The opportunity now is integration—turning isolated processes into a cohesive operating model.

System-Driven Firm

- Your firm is designed to operate predictably.
- Systems absorb complexity, protect capacity, and allow leadership to focus forward.
- The challenge now is refinement, not containment.

Continue the Conversation

If chaos still pulls you into the weeds, the problem is rarely effort—it is design.

To explore what this result means for your firm, and how to move from reactive chaos to operational control, continue here:

https://crushingchaosinteract.lawfirmmentor.net/chaos-to-control-systems-map/